Elected Women Representatives and Empowerment

About the Author

Prof. G. Palanithurai, Rajiv Gandhi Chair for Panchayati Raj Studies, Gandhigram Rural University, India, is an academic activist. He is specializing in Grassroots Democracy, Decentralized Governance and Development Management. His action research activities are supported by the Ford Foundation, Swiss Development and Cooperation, The Hunger Project, Population Foundation of India, DANIDA, Action Aid International, Ministry of Panchayati Raj, Ministry of Rural Development, Government of India, Toolkit Foundation, Netherlands, UNDP, State Planning Commission and a few other agencies in India and abroad. He has developed a leadership school in Rajiv Gandhi Chair for Panchayati Raj Studies.

He has worked for the preparation of 10th and 11th Five Year Plan for Tamil Nadu through State Planning Commission. He worked for the 1st, 2nd, and 3rd State Finance Commissions and for which he conducted a number of studies related to panchayat finance. He has published 63 books, 139 articles in referred journals, 83 monographs, 76 popular articles in his area of specialization in popular dialies. He has availed the fellowship from Shastri Indo Canadian Institute twice, World Academy of Art and Science USA, Toolkit Foundation, Netherlands, to conduct studies and write books. He has visited the US, Canada, Singapore, Sri Lanka, Senegal and Malaysia on academic assignments. He has introduced two innovative M.A. Programmes, one in Development Management and another in Governance and Development are supported by University Grants Commission, New Delhi. He has organized 2 International programmes, 15 National programmes and 61 Regional programmes with the financial support of various agencies. He made presentations in 20 International Conferences, 145 national programmes and 67 regional seminars and conferences. He prepared two District Human Development Reports for Dindigul and Nagapattinam Districts.

Elected Women Representatives and Empowerment

Edited by
G. Palanithurai

CONCEPT PUBLISHING COMPANY Pvt. Ltd.,
NEW DELHI-110059

ISBN-13: 978-81-8069-873-6

First Published 2012

Published and Printed by

Concept
Since 1974

Concept Publishing Company Pvt. Ltd.
A/15-16, Commercial Block, Mohan Garden
New Delhi-110059 (India)
T: 25351460, 25351794, *F*: 091-11-25357109
E: publishing@conceptpub.com, W: www.conceptpub.com
Editorial Office: H-13, Bali Nagar, New Delhi-110 015, India.

Cataloging in Publication Data--*Courtesy:* D.K. Agencies (P) Ltd. <docinfo@dkagencies.com>

Elected women representatives and empowerment / edited by G. Palanithurai.
p.cm.
Includes bibliographical references (p.) and index.
ISBN 9788180698736

1. Women—Political activity—India—Congresses. 2. Representative government and representation—India—Congresses. 3. Women in development—India Congresses. 4. Panchayat—India—Congresses. I. Palanithurai, G. (Ganapathy)

DDC 305.420954 23

TO DIVINE MOTHER

GANDHIGRAM RURAL INSTITUTE - DEEMED UNIVERSITY

Dr. S.M. Ramasamy
Vice-Chancellor

Gandhigram - 624 30
Dindigul District
Tamil Nadu, India

Foreword

Though I am a Scientist belonging altogether to a different arena of specialization, I have been curiously and astonishingly watching the activities of Academia of the Department of Political Science and Development Administration of Gandhigram Rural Institute—Deemed University for the past over one and half years. It's innovative academic programmes attracting large number of students from different parts of the country; the large number of sponsored and action research projects from the World Bank, the UNDP, the UNICEF, the FORD Foundation, the Rajiv Gandhi Foundation, Action Aid International and from various departments of Government of India and Government of Tamil Nadu and the scintillating outreach activities have brought laurels to the department and to the university in the form of prestigious Rajiv Gandhi Chair for Pachayati Raj Studies, Special Assistance Programme from University Grants Commission, etc.

Besides the untiring academic activities, the Department regularly conducts conferences, seminars and brain storms and documents the deliberations meticulously benefiting all concerned with Development Administration. The present book "Elected Women Representatives and Empowerment" is one such useful addition in the hierarchy of their excellent documents, distilling the seminal discussions made over a conference entitled "Critical Mass to Critical Action". The book has brought out thought provoking packages of information on a variety of issues on the need for representation for women in local bodies, the issues confronting such elected women representatives in effectively performing their roles, categories of women in local governance and their implications, responsiveness and accountability of women representatives, the obstacles by community structures and practices in the functioning of elected women representatives, the need for affirmative action in reservation for women in local bodies and capacity building, etc. contributed by a large number of scholarly researchers from different parts of the country.

Dr. G. Palanithurai, the Editor of this book and the Coordinator of UGC-SAP of the Department of Political Science and Development Administration needs to be congratulated for all his efforts. He also deserves special appreciation for bringing the department to National attraction and international visibility by cohesively binding the team of faculty in the department.

I am confident that this book will be an useful addition in the area of development administration.

SM. RAMASAMY
Vice-Chancellor

Preface

The reservation of seats for women in the local bodies has created a hope among the feminists and suspicion among the ardent supporters of patriarchy. Since 1993 questions have been asked as do the women possess requisite qualification, skills, knowledge capacity, capability and support to manage the new institutions at the grassroots? After the women come to power through the electoral process yet another set of questions has been raised as to what extent the elected women representatives have performed their role and responsibilities? How they are performing their roles? How they face challenges and barriers? and how they are different from men leaders in performing their duties and responsibilities? No doubt the above questions have to be answered by investigating the problem. Yet, the above questions are to be seen in proper perspective. The above questions themselves will obviously indicate the conditions in which the elected women representatives are performing their roles and responsibilities.

For any research question one has to look for relevant theory for proper guidance. Since not less than one-third of total seats are reserved for women, one can assume that "Critical mass" has been formed while looking at it theoretically. But the moot question is whether the critical mass is able to perform the expected critical action. Indian society poses heavy challenges to governance establishment as it is deeply afflicted with and affected by a few factors, namely patriarchy, hierarchical caste system, feudal mindset and extreme economic inequality. The life and livelihood systems are in very poor condition to sixty per cent of the people who live in the rural areas. Majority in the rural areas are living in sub-human living conditions. which need strong intervention for improvement by the participation of the stakeholders themselves. The above critical issues have to be tackled by the elected women representatives. The elected women representatives have to face volley of problems to attack the critical issues. The issues of gender and other marginalized groups have not even been discussed in any public forum at the grassroots. But now they are to be tackled. To perform the above task the elected women representatives have to equip themselves and find out support structure and facilities. How they equip themselves and how they tackle the issues? have to be assessed. To perform the above task, a National Conference was organised on a theme entitled "Critical Mass to Critical Action" in the month of March 2010 by inviting academics, activists, researchers and the elected women representatives as part of the special Assistance Programme activities. The participants of the National Conference have made presentations touching upon various aspects of representations of elected women representatives, the conditions in which the elected women representatives are functioning, methodologies adopted by the elected women representatives to overcome the barriers and perform their duties and so on. The relevant presentations have been compiled and edited to reach out to larger audience and stakeholders.

I thank profusely the scholars those who have contributed articles for this compendium. Further I thank the elected women representatives who have participated in the conference and actively contributed in the deliberations by sharing their experiences. Equally I have to thank the activists who are involved in capacity building exercise for the elected women representatives for their effective interaction in the conference. Our Faculty members, researchers and project staff who have strengthened me by means of their active involvement in all my academic, research and outreach initiatives all they deserve my appreciation. Our University authorities are always proactive and facilitative for innovative programme. Hence, I express my sense of gratitude to them also. I also thank my family unit which never attempted to disturb my academic schedule which is always 24 × 7. I never give my time to my family. Yet they are tolerating me. For their generocity I thank my wife, daughter and son. Finally, I have to thank my publisher Concept Publishing Company (Pvt) Ltd., which has emerged as company specializing in decentralized governance by publishing more number of books and reports. I profusely thank Mr. Ashok Kumar Mittal for his innovative ventures and remain in quality publications.

Gandhigram
10.11.2010

G. PALANITHURAI

Contents

Foreword by ***Dr. S.M. Ramasamy*** vii
Preface ix
List of Tables xiii
List of Figures xiv
Contributors xv
Introduction xvii

1. Critical Mass Struggle for Critical Action: A Case Analysis from Tamil Nadu Experience 1
G. Palanithurai

2. Impact of Gendered Political Institutions on Human Development 24
G. Uma and *J. Vanishree*

3. Engaging with Democracy: Women in Panchayats 40
Alak Nanda

4. EWRs' Representation, Responsiveness and Accountability in Grassroots Governance 59
K.S. Nakkeeran

5. Gendered Citizenship for Deepening Local Democracy: A Study of Ten Villages in Maharashtra 79
Manjula Bharathy

6. Women's Reservation Bill: A Triumph or a Mirage 99
K. Deepamala

7. Empowerment of Women: A Realistic Approach 111
G. Pankajam

8. Political Representation: The Promise for Women 117
Suganda Ramamoorthi

9. Capacity Building of Elected Women Representatives 127
V.R. Vanajaa

10. Women's Empowerment through Gender Budgeting 139
R.V. Pole

11. Empowering Women: Some Aspects of the Karnataka Experience 153
K. Subha and *B.S. Bhargava*

12. Empowerment of Women Elected Members of Kerala: What Next? 167
M. Retna Raj

13. Impact of Reservation and Participation in Terms of Empowerment of Women and Dalits in Panchayati Raj Institutions in India 180
Nupur Tiwari

14. A Critique on the Political Reservation and its Utilization by the Elected Women Representatives 194
K. Sathiabama

Bibliography 212
Index 222

List of Tables

2.1	Representation of Women in Politics	28
4.1	Categorization of Members' Representation in Gram Sabha	64
4.2	Rating of Participation of Different Sections of the Community	65
4.3	Mode of Representation of Ward Members to the Panchayat Presidents	66
4.4	EWRs' Representation to Higher Authorities	66
4.5	EWRs' Representation to Government Officials	67
4.6	Responsiveness of the EWRs	68
4.7	Accountability of EWRs	71
8.1	Level of Education	120
8.2	Source of Motivation	122
8.3	Purpose of Contesting the Election	123
8.4	Persons Accompanying for Meetings	123
9.1	Coverage	128
9.2	Outcome: President	129
9.3	Ward Member	130
9.4	Gram Sabha comparison for three years (2006 to 2009)	133
10.1	Human Development Index	145
10.2	Public Distribution System	146
11.1	EWR Panchayati Raj	158
12.1	Number of Women Elected Members in PRIs of Kerala	174
12.2	Women Elected Members of Kerala and India: Analysis based on selected indicators	174

List of Figures

4.1	A Conceptual Framework of Representation, Responsiveness and Accountability in Local Governance	76
14.1	Possibilities and Obstacles of Elected Women Representatives	201
14.2	Facilitating factors responsible for the performance of Elected Women Representatives	208

Contributors

Alak Nanda, Programme Associate (Education), Sir Dorabji Tata Trust and Allied Trusts, Mumbai.

B.S. Bhargava, Regional Co-ordinator and Senior Fellow, Institute of Social and Economic Change, Bangalore.

Deepa Mala, Research Scholar, Department of Political Science and Development Administration, Gandhigram Rural Institute—Deemed University, Gandhigram.

G. Palanithurai, Professor in Rajiv Gandhi Chair, Department of Political Science and Development Administration, Gandhigram Rural Institute—Deemed University, Gandhigram.

G. Pankajam, Director of Community College, Gandhigram.

G. Uma, Assistant Professor, School of Gender and Development Studies, Indira Gandhi National Open University, New Delhi.

J. Vanishree, Assistant Professor, School of Gender and Development Studies, Indira Gandhi National Open University, New Delhi.

K. Sathiabama, Research Scholar, Department of Political Science and Development Administration, Gandhigram Rural Institute—Deemed University, Gandhigram.

K. Subha, Regional Co-ordinator and Senior Fellow, Institute of Social and Economic Change, Bangalore.

K.S. Nakkeeran, Associate Professor, Department of Political Science and Development Administration, Gandhigram Rural Institute—Deemed University, Gandhigram.

M. Retna Raj, Assistant Professor, Kerala Institute of Local Administration, Thrissur.

Manjula Bharaty, Associate Professor, Tata Institute of Social Science, Mumbai.

Nupur Tiwari, Faculty, Centre for Federal Studies, Hamdard University, Delhi.

R.V. Pole, Faculty, State Institute of Rural Development, YASHADA, Pune.

Suganda Ramamoorthi, Director, Centre for Women Studies, Lady Doak College, Madurai.

V.R. Vanajaa, Programme Director, DAC Trust, Theni.

Introduction

India is undergoing an unprecedented change and transformation in economy, polity and society due to the two major historic forces, namely globalization of economy and decentralization of powers. Both are strong global phenomena. In India, the Nation State has accepted the new global paradigm for transforming economy, polity and society. Both are in operation and started yielding results which become the subjects of public discourse in India and the world. Globalization has been loudly opposed and protested by majority in the world. Almost it is a mass movement. One could see the massive protest all-over the world. It is not a hegemony of the West over the East and North over the South. It is a deliberate design, paradigm and preparation of a group of companies through the Nation States. Nation States are only instruments and they are not the authors of the new dispensations. But globalization is being pushed and actively supported and carried out the activities fastly by a segment of the society very effectively. But decentralization is not moving forward as globalization despite the support of the people. In decentralization discourse, one important aspect which draws the attention of the whole world, i.e. reservation of seats for women in governance at grassroots. Constitution of India stipulates that not less than one-third of the seats have to be reserved for women in local bodies. Theoretically speaking it is a 'critical mass'. The critical mass is expected to work on critical issues.

In order to bring inclusiveness to our governance and the process of development, reservation of seats for women has been made. But it does not give any guarantee that their performance will be as expected as the newly included segments in governance will have a volley of disabilities. Now the question is how the disabilities are being tackled and the basic duties and responsibilities are discharged as critical mass is formed to perform the critical functions.

The present volume brings to light the details of the process of electing the women representatives to the grassroots institutions and enables them to perform their roles and responsibilities.

"Critical Mass Struggle for Critical Action: A Case Analysis from Tamil Nadu" by G. Palanithurai is a comprehensive article which tries to analyse the critical functions of the elected women representatives in rural local bodies in Tamil Nadu in the backdrop of the theory on 'critical mass'. He has succinctly explained the whole process of empowering elected women representatives at the grassroots and their activities in the rural local bodies in empowering the other marginalized sections of the society. How they are coming out from their houses to public space, how they are equipping themselves through capacity building exercises of various institutions, how they form their own support structure and through the support structure how they solve their own institutional problems for effective service delivery have been captured and analysed in this article? The whole analysis is done in the backdrop of the theory on critical mass.

G. Uma and J. Vanishree in their article entitled "Impact of Gendered Political Institutions on Human Development" have analysed the perspectives and performance of the elected women representatives in their respective domain in the backdrop of the critical mass theory. This article distinctly brought out the perspectives and priorities of the elected women representatives in their functioning and performance in the rural local body institutions through the case studies. The authors have brought to light the international and global overview of the initiatives of the women movement in the world to increase the strength of the women in public space and how the global initiatives helped the Local Bodies to get quota for women. Thus they have linked the global initiatives with local achievements. The authors have dwelt at length the theoretical nuances of the critical action theory and its operational dimensions. They have synoptically analysed the performance of the elected women representatives on the critical issues. They highlighted the essence of the role of elected women representatives in development. It provides scope for further probing the theory building.

Alak Nanda in his article "Engaging with Democracy: Women in Panchayats" explained the logic of reservation, and its expected implications based on the secondary sources. The author of this article critically examined the whole institutional mechanism for governance at the grassroots and the reservation of seats for women in local governance. Along with the above he has touched upon the categories of women coming to local governance and their implications in the society. To highlight his argument he has also cited several case studies from the field. He listed out the obstacles in the process of discharging their duties and responsibilities in transforming governance, politics and women. Finally, he indicated what is to be done? In the sameway he has listed out the steps to be taken to support elected women representatives to perform the expected roles and responsibilities.

K.S. Nakkeeran in his article "EWRs' Representation, Responsiveness and Accountability in Grassroots Governance" by using the theory on representation analysed the representation, responsiveness and accountability of the elected women representatives of rural local bodies in Tamil Nadu. It is an empirical study conducted in a district to link the participatory democracy with representative democracy. K.S. Nakkeeran has used the theory which is meant for representative democracy for participatory democracy by keeping an assumption that the participatory democracy has got the representative elements. He highlighted the responsiveness and accountability of the elected women representatives of the rural local bodies. In addition the representation of the elected women representatives is also being analysed. He highlighted the responsiveness and accountability of the elected women representatives.

In her article "Gendered Citizenships for Deepening Local Democracy: A Study on Ten Villages in Maharashtra", Manjula Bharathy moved deeper into the process of deepening of democracy in the rural areas in an engendered way. Community structures and practices are always against the practices of the provisions of the Constitution. When the constitutional provisions go to the communities at the grassroots that too in the rural areas, it is natural that they have to interact with community practices. In that process transforming the community practices by absorbing the provisions of the constitutions one will witness a dynamic transformation process. This transformation process is not smooth. It has to cross volley of problem and obstacles. But in this article the author has analysed the role of elected women representatives in altering the existing perception and practices of governance at the grassroots. She has conducted the study in ten villages of Maharashtra. She has brought to light the whole process of transformation of the dynamics of village politics.

Deepamala K. in her article "Women's Reservation Bill—A Triumph or a Mirage" brought an argument realistically and logically the imperativeness of bringing reservation for women in authoritative bodies. In the backdrop of the experience in other countries, she brought to light the need for such affirmative action. Since the policy making and law making roles are with the State and Union Governments, reservation of seats for women in all the bodies are very essential in order to alter the process of governance and development. She kept her arguments in the backdrop of the theory on citizenship.

In her article "Empowerment of Women—A Realistic Approach" G. Pankajam while explaining the process of development, she unequivocally argued for women taking power into their hands to alter the space from political to development. She highlighted the indicators of women empowerment and indicated the steps to be taken to empower women. Having said the potentials of the local governance for women empowerment she lamented on the action plan for concrete empowerment of women and elected women representatives.

Suganda Ramamoorthi's article "Political Representation: The Promise for Women" analyses the process of political socialization and political recruitment of the elected women representatives through an empirical study conducted in Madurai district. She has indicated the barriers and obstacles faced by the elected women representatives.

"Capacity Building of Elected Women Representatives" by V.R. Vanajaa is a report of the experience of an organization in Theni District, Tamil Nadu. What are the activities carried out, how they are carried out, with what objectives the training programmes have been conducted, what are the outcomes of the capacity building exercises, what are the constraints they have faced in the whole process of capacity building, how the panchayat leaders performed, have been captured in this small report? The report gives the details of the conditions of the elected women representatives and the steps to be taken to empower the elected women representatives and to empower the marginalized women. Though it is a synoptic view, it has got such substance for action.

R.V. Pole's article "Women's Empowerment through Gender Budgeting" investigates into how effective has gender budgeting been as a tool for women's empowerment, in its present form in the Indian context. He highlighted the importance and relevance of gender budgeting and women component plan. He explained the steps taken at various levels to highlight the importance of gender budgeting.

"Empowering Women: Some Aspects of the Karnataka Experience" by K. Subha and B.S. Bhargava explained the process of building the capacity of the elected leaders to empower women. While explaining the process of capacity building of the elected women representatives, the authors have brought out the schemes and programmes launched by the government of Karnataka on women empowerment. The authors have looked the exercise in the backdrop of the women's movement in Karnataka.

G. Retna Raj's article "Empowerment of Women Elected Members of Kerala: What Next?" gives an account of the status and position of elected women representatives and the potentials and opportunities for women empowerment in local governance and the implications. He lamented on the major achievements done in Kerala with the involvement of the local bodies and mere specifically with the active participation of the elected women representatives. How to maintain them and what is the way forward are being discussed in this article.

Nupur Tiwari in her article on "Impact of Reservation and Participation in Terms of Empowerment of Women and Dalits in Panchayati Raj Institutions in India" brought to notice the reservations made for women in local governance in the Constitution and the expectations from the elected women representatives. She relied on the survey conducted by the Ministry of Panchayati Raj, Government of India for her arguments and analysis. She has used data to assess the impact of the elected women representatives.

Sathiabama in her article "A Critique on the Political Reservation and its Utilization by the Elected Women Representatives" based on the secondary sources highlighted the potentials and possibilities for elected women leaders to achieve massive transformation in the rural society and she also analysed the possible obstacles and barriers in the process of handling power. She has suggested steps to be taken to overcome the obstacles and barriers.

1

Critical Mass Struggle for Critical Action: A Case Analysis from Tamil Nadu Experience

G. Palanithurai

Introduction

Reservation of seats for women in Local Bodies after the enactment of the 73rd and the 74th Amendments to the Constitution of India has raised the scope to raise a series of questions and doubts on the perception, capacity, capability, skill, commitment and performance of the elected women representatives. It is not very easy to reply to all the above questions. Slowly literatures are coming to the public fora from various research and academic institutions with different sets of results. For the effective functioning of local bodies, there are certain essential conditions that have to prevail in the society as environment, namely: (a) large scale presence of middle class, (b) high literacy rate, (c) introduction of land reform, (d) devolving needed powers, functions, finance and functionaries to local bodies (e) availability of strong, capable and committed leaders, and (f) presence of large scale civil society. But, for the effective functioning of elected women representatives, what the essential requirements are a fundamental question. Arguments are projected that the elected women representatives require capacity, negotiating skill, communication ability, leadership skill and support structure. The elected women representatives are drawn from different segments with different kinds of barriers, obstacles, and disabilities. To overcome all the barriers, obstacles and disabilities, they have to struggle on different fronts. After equipping themselves, they have to struggle for attacking the issues of women, which is considered the critical action.

Theoretical Framework

It is unequivocally explained, based on experience, that the women leaders can change the culture, behavioural pattern and performance of the institution only when their presence is large in size. So the number determines the strength of the group. If the required number of elected women representatives are in the institution, a critical mass will be formed and the critical mass will bring about a number of changes in the style of functioning of the institutions, in tackling the issues and in the methodology of tackling issues.[1] Thus Critical Mass Theory, used in Physics, has been used in social science research mostly in the Western context. This new phenomenon of inducting women representatives into policy making and legislative bodies has made researchers use different theoretical frameworks to analyse the problems, issues and actions of the women representatives. In this context, the critical mass theory is being used by many researchers to highlight the value of the critical mass and its implications for the society.[2] It is pertinent to mention that many of the frameworks developed in the Western context may not be useful in the South Asian context as South Asian women's problems are different when they are compared with their Western counterparts.[3] Yet the critical mass theory is highly useful in both contexts. In India, 33.3 per cent of reservation of seats for women in local bodies has made the researchers look at the women representatives' action in the perspective of the critical mass theory.[4]

No doubt in India a critical mass has been formed in local bodies as women constitute one-third of the strength at the entry level. But, while looking at the impact of the critical mass on critical action, one finds deeper impacts despite that critical mass having different disabilities in the Indian context.[5] In this context an action research has been carried out with the support of the Ford Foundation in organizing the elected women representatives of Tamil Nadu as a Federation at the State level to sort out their problems on their own. The problems of the elected women representatives have to be addressed only by themselves. The representatives have to interface with higher level officials on their own. Their issues will be highlighted through the media for larger dissemination for which they have to interact with the media. It was a six years' experience. Several conferences and workshops have been organized by the elected women representatives. Their problems have been discussed with the State Ministers, Secretaries to the Government, Directors of Panchayati Raj and District Collectors. There have been several achievements registered by this Federation.[6] Ultimately, after seeing the implications, the Ministry of Panchayati Raj, Government of India, has created an opportunity to form such a federation in other states. All the success stories and struggles have been documented and published periodically.[7]

After six years of Federation experience, the office bearers of the Federation of Elected Women Representatives (EWRs) at district level and state level assembled in Gandhigram Rural University and held a two-day deliberation and chalked out a future course of action for themselves. Following is the report[8] of their experience in the process of governance and administering development:

> The elected women representatives have a Federation in Tamil Nadu and it is functioning for the past six years. Sixty-four elected women representatives from twenty-nine districts—district office bearers who are in the Federation for the past six years—met in Gandhigram Rural University and discussed some of their experiences to draw a road map for their Federation jointly and individually for themselves. Their successes, struggles and needs were discussed thoroughly and openly. Deep rooted issues, memorable solid achievements, historic struggles were highlighted in their deliberations. They are covered in this brief write up.

Observation

"We have experienced power for eight years to carry out activities for the benefit of the people as seats have been reserved for women in local bodies for two consecutive terms and now the principle of rotation has to be operated and, as a result, the women who have come to local bodies in the past two terms from the same constituency will have either to contest in a general constituency or withdraw from the public space or take another lower or higher level position in the same Panchayat system", observed by Ms. Susila, one of the office bearers who assembled in Gandhigram on 11th and 12th of August, 2005. The discussion was around the space which they were occupying currently.

Struggle to Come Out from Their Houses

Reservation of seats for women in local bodies pulled and pushed them from the house to the public space. Working as MLA or MP or in any other office by women would not bring this much of pressure on the women as the elected women representatives at the lowest level who confront a multitude of obstacles and problems. Till date many of the elected women representatives are struggling to come out from their houses to the office when they have to discharge responsibilities. They claim that coming out from their houses to the office itself is victory as many of them are not able to come out from their house from the day of election. Such kind of repressive husbands co-opted their wives to retain power with them for which they have used the women. The elected women representatives' Association is working for the release of the house-arrested elected women representatives through government orders. The dominant discourse in many of the places is that as soon as the seats were reserved for women, the men who had prepared themselves to contest in the elections adopted a strategy of preparing a woman candidate from the respective families or social groups and saw the women elected to the positions. Behind all women, men were working with high enthusiasm before the election in the belief that if they were elected, the positions would be handled by the men of the respective families. After the election, the scenario changed and many players started acting in the local bodies to build up the capacity and skill of the leaders, passing orders prohibiting men to attend official meetings on behalf of the women leaders. Yet a segment of bureaucracy is not sensitive to the issues of women and, hence; the officials preferred to discuss official matters with the males of the elected women representatives based on the argument that the uneducated family women do not know anything about the administrative system. Under this pretext they ignore the elected women representatives and sometimes they are even being marginalized.

Capacity Building

Many of the EWRs do not attend training programmes not because they are not interested but because they are not allowed by their male family members to attend the training. They lay down a condition to the EWRs that they will also attend the training programme along with the EWRs. When this demand is unmet, the EWRs are not permitted to attend the training. Training is of two types. One is official and government oriented. The other is semi-official and real leadership preparation. In all government training programmes, EWRs are threatened that unless they obey the officials, they cannot run the Panchayats. They are asked to carry out the Panchayat administration as per the direction of the officials. In a sense it is a preparation of slaves to the government officials. In the other type negotiating skill is built up in the leader. A detailed analysis of devolution and where the Panchayats are now, what is to be done in the Panchayat for the people and what should be done to strengthen the Panchayat are being discussed in a participatory way.

In a residential training a book consisting of the original Act, Government Orders, details of rural development schemes, and rules are being given and training is given to EWRs on how to use all those documents for Panchayat administration. The training is not one time affair. It is a continuous process. The role of the training institution is not only to offer training but also to guide the Panchayat Presidents while they are on the job. It is almost a support structure. The EWRs attend the programmes without fail in Gandhigram as it is a support structure and it helps EWRs when they are in trouble. Whenever EWRs face problem, they use the three phone numbers 0451-2451063, 0451-2451775, 044-22235659. When EWRs are harassed by officials, even letters are being drafted in Gandhigram and sent to the concerned officials.[9]

Struggle to Succeed

A sizeable section of the women leaders have been drawn from their houses and have been made to attend meetings and interact with officials and made to realize their worth and they have started functioning as leaders in managing the Panchayats. Their vision has been broadened and their understanding of the society has been widened. When they started functioning intensively, they faced a volley of problems and yet the joy they felt was immeasurable. They felt that the stigma of incompetence had gone. The continuous crisis management in the Panchayat and the crowd management in the Gram Sabha have made them courageous. But the process is painful. Just like a student they learn everyday about society, the Panchayat and Government. Further achievements made by them in the Panchayat make them develop confidence in themselves and the system.

The achievements made by EWRs are captured through the media.[10] Their struggles are also captured and they are being published, telecast and broadcast because of the efforts of the Hunger Project. When the media brought to light the achievements, the other Panchayat Presidents developed aspirations to follow the models. The continuous sensitization programme conducted for the media helped a lot to capture such success and struggles.

Learning from Struggle

The elected women representatives, by their performance, by their struggle, and by their achievements, got recognition in the society and this recognition made the other womenfolk develop an aspiration to become Panchayat Presidents. In the past eight years, the elected women representatives have learnt the art of mobilising the people for conducting the Gram Sabha meeting, and developing partnership with officials and other social capitals to perform their role and discharge their responsibilities. Further the elected women representatives have become conscious of women issues because of continuous capacity building exercise and periodical interaction with activists. Working on the issues of women needs a specific strategy and before that people have to be conscientised. Unless people are conscientised on the issues of women, the problems of women cannot be addressed. It is also realised by the elected women representatives that the problems in society and specifically the problems of women, children, Dalits and other marginalized groups can be attacked through collectives. Thus they have realised the potential of collective action. They have a deeper understanding of the issues of the marginalized. This is because of the continuous training. The thought process and mindset of the women leaders in the beginning were in no way different from those of men leaders. But, in the course of training and regular interaction with gender specialists, the attitude, perception, view and understanding of the women leaders on the issues of women have changed.

Women to Women

Yet another serious issue is conscientising women on their own problems. They need four literacies, namely word literacy, money literacy, body literacy and civil literacy. It is a tough job to be done. Since the presence of Self-Help Groups women is visible and has become a force to reckon with, they can be used for this purpose. To some extent they are now made literate. It has been realised by the elected women representatives that, with the alliance of SHG members, women leaders in the Panchayats can perform several functions in the domain of children and women. Women leaders have come to the stage of developing a vision for their Panchayats, for the children of their village. They have realised the importance of social development. Now it is easy for the government to push through its social development agenda through the elected women representatives. To that level, elected women representatives are sensitized and oriented. Environmental protection, health governance, governance of education, vulnerability reduction and internal resource mobilization are the major subjects on which the women leaders are trained. At the Panchayat level, they are able to manage the issues effectively. But these models have to be spread to other areas. The models are limited in number. Elected women representatives have come to the level of working on millennium development goals. There are leaders who have developed leadership to attract political parties. Now political parties have started luring the elected women representatives who command a greater deal of respect among the people by their excellent performance.

The elected women leaders who have legitimately occupied their space and manage the institutions are concerned about the confinement of the other elected women leaders by their male family members. The EWRs, through their Associations and Federations, have persuaded the officials not to allow the males in any of the official meetings in place of EWRs. In many places even higher officials allow the males to carry out activities on behalf of the EWRs in the name of achieving targets. Unless this malaise is checked, the formation of a critical mass will be weakened.

EWR and CPR

Common properties are the lifeline of the poor and also another source of income to the Panchayats. Removing the encroachments is not an easy task and yet elected women representatives have taken steps to remove the encroachments. In this process they have to undergo ordeals. Urapakkam Gram Panchayat President, Ms. Menaka lost her life when she took steps to remove encroachments in her Panchayat area. Vanduvanchery Gram Panchayat President, Ms. Rani Muniyakannu moved the court to protect the silicon soil. Appipalayam

Gram Panchayat President, Ms. Easwari fought against industrial pollution in her Panchayat area. Now the elected women representatives have learnt the art of struggling for justice. A large number of elected women representatives have taken innovative steps to augment resources from the assets and natural resources of the Panchayats. Many Panchayats have regained their common properties. Series of steps have been taken to improve the conditions of the commons. The elected women representatives have changed the conflict between Panchayats and SHGs and now both are playing complementary roles to each other for the benefit of the people in the rural areas. Elected women representatives have realised the importance of governance and poverty reduction and development at the grassroots. They have internalized the practice of supervision to be done by the Panchayats on the service delivery institutions. They have given utmost importance to health governance, environment governance and educational governance.[11]

Obstacles

It is true that the so-called beneficiaries of the government (really they are not eligible to become beneficiaries but they got their names included by wielding political power) never allow the Gram Sabha to speak the truth. For this they have a strategy of disturbing the Gram Sabha meeting by using unparliamentary words and indulging in character assassination. In the absence of a strong support base many women leaders are in a disturbed mental state.

Officials always exhibit their non-cooperative attitude towards the elected women representatives and, moreover, they want to dominate the women leaders. Women leaders, whenever they go to an office, go with the statistics and the relevant government orders to convince the officials. On many occasions, the officials are exposed as the elected women representatives bring up real issues and speak with authority whereas the officials do not have authentic documents. This negotiating capacity has been injected into the blood of the EWRs in Gandhigram through training programmes. The Act, Government Orders, Rules, Scheme details are provided in the form of an anthology to everyone of the trainees and they are being oriented on how to use data and how to use the book. Every Panchayat leader should negotiate with officials with self-respect and self-dignity and this has been taught to them by the Gandhigram training team. The officials prefer only the males of the elected women representatives as it is easy for the officials to negotiate with the husbands and other family members. The corrupt system wants to co-opt the women also. But they do not succeed.

The administrative structure is so complicated in our society. Government officials find it very difficult to bring convergence or synergy among the officials working in different departments. Likewise, the departments act on the basis of directions from their officials in the line departments and not on the basis of the orders of the government. A government order passed by the Rural Development Department is not respected by the Health Department. All departments are sectorally divided and they do not have a perspective of serving the people but they have a perspective of keeping the department activities intact and in achieving their target and satisfying their higher officials.

There is a fitting case in Pudukkottai District. When K. Rayawaram Gram Panchayat President, Ms. Rani Sathappan approached the District Collector for financial sanction to desilt the tank managed by the PWD, the sensitive Collector passed orders immediately and sanctioned money. But, to carry out the work, the President had to get a no objection certificate from the Public Works Department (PWD). To get such a letter she has to visit the office fifteen times. On the fifteenth day the officials took only two minutes to prepare such a letter and she got it. From this, one can imagine how government offices respond to Panchayat leaders' demands.

As the Panchayat leaders live near to the people, they are always responsive and accountable and they perform their duties perfectly but officials do not have that mentality and people do not have any hold over the officials. Excepting politicians, nobody can control the officials. It is an irony that the leaders who are responsible and responsive do not have the power but the officials who do not respond to the people have power. Panchayat leaders submit petitions to government offices for which there is no respect. The leaders who have enough influence are respected in the offices and others are fighting against the bureaucracy. There is yet another serious issue, namely managerial perspective, which is so essential for the administration of the Panchayats. Neither the State Government nor the Panchayat leaders have a managerial perspective to look at the functioning of Panchayats. It is unfortunate that many of the Panchayats, from the perspective of management, are unviable. Such

Panchayats have to be merged with a neighbouring Panchayat to make it administratively and managerially viable. As a result Panchayat leaders find it difficult to run the administration and the people are suffering.

Our system is always favourable only to the rich not to the poor. There is a case where the Panchayat is asked to carry out a work and claim the amount later for which the Panchayat President has to invest money from her own purse and then only get the money back from the Departments. Where will a poor woman representative go for money? So she has to rely on moneylenders. Since the system is complicated and corrupt this kind of practice will lead to further corruption. For the elected women representatives, capacity building is the only salvation for their performance. Periodical interface with other leaders and officials will help them a lot. Refresher courses have to be conducted. Visiting other states and interacting with leaders of other states will help them a lot. Here also one has to recognize the role of Gandhigram Rural Institute. Gandhigram Rural Institute arranges for EWRs to visit other Panchayats within the district, within the State and also to visit other States. It is a powerful learning instrument. Elected women representatives have visited Kerala, West Bengal, Karnataka and New Delhi.

There are different strategies adopted by organisations working for women empowerment and devolution of powers and by women leaders to achieve what they ought to achieve in the space created for the elected women representatives. The strategy adopted by Gandhigram Rural Institute is to appeal to many of the elected women representatives as the strategy envisages a smooth transition for EWRs from their houses to the public space without making much noise. It always advocates building alliance with all stakeholders in the process. The assertion of the EWRs is not through oral dialogue but through performance, building capacity, skill and capability and alliance and performing their roles and responsibilities.

In the political and administrative system, one has to understand the level of corruption. Otherwise it is very difficult to manage the Panchayat. Many of them understood the corrupt practices and they moved into the track. But women leaders did not understand the whole process. The reason why officials do not like to interact with women representative is that they are not in a position to understand the nuances of corruption. They not even understood the language of corruption and its dialects. As a result many of them are struggling.

In many places, male family members of elected women representatives moved into the corrupt track by co-opting themselves with the officials and as a result there was no problem for those women leaders. In the world of reform through technology, the administrative procedures have to be made simple. Now an ordinary person cannot understand the administrative procedures and, as a result, Panchayat leaders are threatened. The women leaders time and again discuss how effectively women leaders can emerge as role models for others. In this context one has to recognize the struggle of the EWRs. On many occasions Panchayats are badly projected by the media. Of course, the media can highlight negative issues of Panchayats. But there are remarkable achievements made by women leaders and they are also to be captured by the media. But it is not happening. Of course, the scenario is changing as Gandhigram Rural Institute is taking earnest efforts to sensitise the media through its media workshops wherein outstanding women representatives are invited to share their experiences with the media. But this kind of effort has to be taken massively throughout the nation.

It is a pity that training programmes are not seriously thought of and conducted by the government. The majority of the women leaders are not trained fully. Elected women representatives who are in the women Federation are well trained as they are trained by The Hunger Project in Gandhigram. The experts who take classes for the women leaders are retired Additional Directors of Rural Development, Government of Tamil Nadu. They are thorough with the Act, Rules, Procedures, Government Orders and Schemes. They have commitment also. Whenever the women leaders have any doubt, they can contact the resource persons over phone. They give directions and advice. Gandhigram Rural Institute acts as a supporting resource centre providing the wherewithal to stand on their own legs. But it is not the case for all. Of course, the government also conducts training programmes. Resource persons are Extension Officers and Block Development Officers and they teach the subject "Follow the officials; otherwise you will be booked under Section 205". They teach what not to do in the Panchayat instead what to do in the Panchayat.

Section 205 is a provision in the Tamil Nadu Panchayat Act, 1994 which gives arbitrary power to the District Collector to remove the elected Gram Panchayat leader. This has been used by all officials in this state to threaten the elected representatives. By using this provision government officials have made them act as they like. If we take a list of the elected representatives who have been sacked by using Section 205, most of them are either women or Dalits. Weak women leaders are being easily handled by the officials through the Panchayat clerk. There are wise women leaders who carefully manage to elect another woman as Vice-President and both of them select a woman as clerk. Others, without knowing this strategy, have men Vice-Presidents who tend to dominate. In that context, the elected women representatives' Federation has demanded the state government to reserve the Vice-President's post along with President's post for women. Whenever the Panchayat leaders do not cooperate with the officials in their misdeeds, the officials threaten the Panchayat leaders by asking them to bring four years' accounts for verification to the Block Development Office. The women leaders who are strong, knowledgeable with needed support are able to stand up to this and they won't budge. Others succumb to the pressure given by the officials.

There are Panchayat Presidents who have done commendable work in the Panchayats but are not recommended for awards and incentives which are being given by the government. But, instead, ruling party oriented Panchayat Presidents have been selected for awards and incentives. This kind of practice developed by the officials is demoralizing others.

A good number of Panchayats draw the attention of the media and outsiders by their commendable performance. They are appreciated by the higher officials. But the same higher officials never help those Panchayat leaders who are in deep trouble because of the lower level officials. It is obvious from the experience of the Panchayat leaders that the lower level officials are not under the control of the higher officials. Unless the officials at the lower level are properly oriented and controlled by the higher officials, the lower level officials will continue to disturb the Panchayats and destabilize them.

There are women representatives who are in need of counselling as they are undergoing torture in the family due to the harassment of their husbands. There are umpteen number of cases and they have several stories to tell. These women leaders are neither in a position to reveal the problems openly nor in a position of to solve them amicably within the family. Women leaders have been asked to sign documents as per the directions of their husbands and all their deeds are totally corrupt deeds for which the elected women leaders are facing charges. They in fact bow their heads in front of others and officials. There are several reports of wife beating by husbands because the women leaders refuse to accept the directions of their husbands. Compared to SHGs, local body institutions are not getting due attention from the state government. In our state there is no Secretary for Panchayats, there is no Director of Panchayats. As a result all officials at all levels pay attention to reviewing the progress of schemes and programmes but no one cares for the progress of Panchayats. They find fault with Panchayats if they do not carry out their schemes and programmes. They do not have a perspective to look at the Panchayats as institutions of governance. If Panchayats are able to perform certain things it is because of the officials not because of the leaders. Officials look at Panchayats with contempt as competitors or rivals.

For Panchayat activities, the Panchayat leaders cannot get the needed support from the sectoral departments. Panchayats demand certain things based on the demands of the people but the officials do not care about these demands. On many occasions, the officials in their own way develop pet projects. While implementing these projects, they give money only to a few Panchayats whose Presidents are "yes" men or "yes" women to the officials. This kind of patronage demoralizes the other Panchayat Presidents. It is the experience of the leaders that the officials want only "yes" from the Panchayat leaders. They do not want leaders; they want only subordinates. At every level officials feel that they are the superiors. This culture has to be changed. The women leaders are fighting against this culture. Yet it is painful. Corrupt PRI leaders have a perfect alliance with the corrupt officials and nobody bothers about it. Poor women leaders and Dalit leaders are the victims of the procedures as they refuse to form an alliance with the corrupt officials.

MLAs and MPs are having constituency development fund and they spend it without having any consultation with the Gram Panchayat leaders. People project their demands in the Gram Sabha and they are consolidated by the Presidents and they are presented to MLAs and MPs. But they allocate the money to some other works which are not the felt needs of the people. They are the priority work of the party men and the same party men get that benefits and not the villagers. When such a kind of privilege is given to MLAs and MPs what is wrong in demanding such funds for Panchayat Presidents as Panchayat Area Development Fund.

Everyone knows money is being wasted by the MPs and MLAs. It is a simple calculation, that an MP will get Rs. 10 crore during the five-year period. If he or she gets 10 per cent of the total amount from the contractors through whom all activities are carried out by the MP and the MLA, one can manage Rs. one crore for the next election. Likewise one MLA can manage 50 lakh rupees. It is a known fact that MPLAD fund and MLA Constituency fund are meant for development but they are wasting people's money. Even for small facilities Panchayats are starving for money but MLAs and MPs are spending their money on sand, brick and mortar. It is sad to note that these MPs and MLAs are deciding the fate of Panchayats.

MLAs and MPs are looking at Panchayats as parallel bodies to them. A good Panchayat leader by his/her performance gets the whole-hearted support of the people and the local Panchayat leader becomes powerful. Some of the wise Panchayat leaders corner the MPs and MLAs with the support of the community. The elected women representatives adopted a strategy by which a resolution was passed in the Gram Sabha by which, for a specific work, they seek funds from their MLA and MP. For the MPs and MLAs, there is no other option except accepting it as it is the decision of the Gram Sabha. If the demands are not met, they cannot go to the village again for votes. A simple devise is enough to make everyone accountable.

Whenever training is being discussed they target only the elected local body leaders but conveniently they leave out officials from top to bottom and MLAs and MPs are also excluded. For the smooth functioning of local bodies, the cooperation of the officials and the support of MLAs and MPs are essential. But these officials and leaders are not sensitive either to decentralized governance or to the crisis of social development. It is necessary to train the officials and MLAs and MPs. MPs and MLAs are having their own domain of activities. But it is unfortunate that they are also competing with the local body leaders in carrying out the activities. Proper training is needed for all, not only for Panchayat leaders. Political parties are also doing lip service to Panchayats. They are doing a number of *dharnas* and struggles but they are not taking the devolution of powers to local bodies as a serious issue. Their stand on devolution has to be cleared.

It is unequivocally stressed that the elected women representatives should have negotiating skills to negotiate with officials and other representatives to get things done for the people. While analysing many of the successful cases in Panchayats by the women leaders it is demonstrated clearly that wherever the elected women leaders are having negotiating skills, they have succeeded in their attempts. Yet another skill is needed for the elected women representatives, i.e. crowd management. In the Indian context crowd management is essential as it is demonstrated that the public have developed a strategy for getting things done: they pull the crowd and by showing the crowd they get things done. In Panchayats on many occasions managing the Gram Sabha is a tough job for the elected women leaders. Whoever has got the art of managing the crowd has succeeded and others have drowned in it. Hence Panchayat leaders need such a kind of orientation. In the Panchayats, along with the President, the Vice-President's position should also be reserved for women. In most places, the Vice-Presidents (men) have tried their best to sideline the Panchayat Presidents with the help of the clerk and Ward Members. Only strong women Presidents can withstand the pressure from the men Vice-Presidents. If the elected woman representative is a Dalit woman, and the Vice-President is a caste Hindu, the Panchayat administration will be in the hands of the Vice-President. It will be a struggle for the elected woman representative to redeem the Panchayat from the clutches of the Vice-President.

There is yet another issue preventing the elected women representatives from occupying the position for which she was elected. Officials encourage the males of the elected women representatives' family to attend the official meetings, carry out Panchayat activities, claim the cheques etc. The elected women representatives are not oriented in the corrupt practices of the administration and hence they want to cultivate only through the males of the family. This practice has to be curbed. The concept of community well-being is not working in the minds of the people. It is always individual benefits that work in the minds of the people. In this context, it is very difficult to take community oriented decisions. In many Panchayats the elected women representatives have taken tough decisions earning the displeasure of many families and finally, after seeing the implications of such decisions, people have started supporting the Panchayat President. Till the people see the outcome of such tough decisions, the Panchayat Presidents are being disturbed.

There is yet another issue which is significant in the process of decentralization of powers. It is micro level planning. Micro level planning is important since it will alter the existing paradigm of development activities. The supply driven activities can be changed to demand driven activities only through planning at the micro level. People will look at their life, conditions and resources only through this process. The community will take over ownership of development only through a plan. But it is not happening in all the Panchayats. In the absence of the people, officials' plan is being implemented. Many Panchayats headed by women did planning successfully and now they are carrying out the planned activities. Even in implementing the plan, they have to struggle a lot. Wherever honest officials are in position, EWRs are getting the needed support to implement the plans. In other places, officials look for money.

Many of the elected women representatives, especially from the Dalit community, have carried out substantial programmes in their villages for development. They have been facing a volley of problems and this challenging position has made the Dalit women think whether the needed ambience is created for the Dalit women to contest in the elections. The difficult life does not encourage Dalit women to contest again nor attract another woman. Many of them are losing their faith, as they are not able to function independently. The Dalit women leaders who are co-opted have no problem. But they cannot address the problems of the marginalized or the Dalits.

It is also observed in their interaction that in the existing corrupt system of administration women are finding it very difficult to manage the Panchayats. There are several categories of leaders among women. One group are solid achievers. They have demonstrated their capability by which they manage the Panchayat, the people and the officials. They are forerunners. They are pathfinders. There is yet another group of leaders, struggling in the Panchayat with a little capacity and commitment to achieve. One would find more of challenges in their life. The third category are always in the hands of the men folk. Both the Panchayat President and her family male jointly run the administration. The fourth category of elected women representatives have been asked to remain in the house and the entire Panchayat work is carried out by a male of their family. The first two groups joined together to bring the other segments out of the clutches of men. They found it very difficult. That is why the elected women representatives made a plea that the males should not be encouraged to attend the official work and meetings. Women feel that they can contest only in the seats reserved for women. It is necessary to dispel this belief. Seats are limited only for men not for women. They can go beyond 33.3 per cent of seats. For men it is only 67.7 per cent; for women it is 100 per cent.

In a caste ridden and patriarchal society, women on their own provide transparent administration which in fact strengthens their leadership and they are strong in their dealings. They are the pioneers and pathfinders among the elected women representatives. They were trained by a team of experts in Gandhigram Rural Institute and other training institutions. Yet the problems faced by the elected women representatives are innumerable. How to overcome the obstacles and problems is a major question. In many consultative and training workshops they have been in search of an organizational mechanism by which the EWRs will gain collective bargaining power to deal with problems.

Working on Innovative Projects

It is interesting to note that many innovative concepts are being tested in the Panchayats where women are leaders. For instance the concept of biovillage was effectively implemented in many Panchayats headed by women as women leaders have already demonstrated their potential in making the village green by planting avenue trees in the streets, planting wood giving trees in the Panchayat lands, and planting fruit bearing trees in poramboke lands. Many of the vital policies and programmes of the State and Central Governments are being reviewed by the elected women representatives. The Government of Tamil Nadu issued a 15-point programme to make Tamil Nadu the number one state in the country and this was reviewed and they made recommendations also. Mostly the programme touched upon social development issues and natural resource management issues. It was reviewed by the elected women representatives, who suggested ways and means to improve the same and they have also pledged their support to this new programme.

There is yet another issue which is being discussed in many fora to have a separate allocation for women development. There should be a separate plan for women development. The women leaders have quoted the extensive practice of such a plan in Kerala. Yet the state government does not move forward to accept it. Relentlessly they are pursuing the matter with a sense of hope. By following the footprints of the women leaders, Dalit leaders have demanded the same for Dalits. Thus women leaders are trendsetters. There is real participation of people in public activity in the Panchayats headed by women. They allow all individuals who want to speak and the leaders patiently listen to the people. A large number of SHG women are brought to the Gram Sabha for discussion and deliberation. SHG members take keen interest in attending the Gram Sabha meeting as they are allowed to speak freely whereas in other Panchayats they cannot expect this much of freedom as the Gram Sabha has been made leader centric.

There is yet another interesting observation that many of the vital development issues which had not been discussed seriously in any of the public fora are being forwarded to the Gram Sabha by the government for discussion. The women leaders who are already sensitized and trained on social development issues seriously take up and discuss them with the people in the Gram Sabha meeting. In reality progress is made in many villages on social development and in many it does not take place because of the lack of conscientisation process on the part of the leaders and the people. The budget and resource flow to Panchayats is still a myth to many. Internal resource mobilization is being done very actively as the Panchayat leaders are aware of the nuances of resource mobilization. But resource mobilization from external sources, though mandated, is scarce. They are not sure whether Panchayats can get such resources. No perspective budget analysis is being done. But the elected women Panchayat leaders are trying their best to understand the Panchayat finance. It is necessary that a budget analysis has to be made for Panchayats and it is to be explained to the Panchayat Presidents.

On many occasions, it is the elected women representatives who have realised the potential of the media and taken steps to use the media to project the issues which are being faced by them and the achievements made by them. A cursory analysis will reveal that a large number of articles have been written on the achievements of women representatives. This media tie up has been created by the women representatives. It is noticed everywhere that in all training programmes, the elected women representatives are attentive and sincere in attending the capacity building exercise. Often they used to lament that they refer to Government Orders and Notifications whenever they meet officials, but officials are not that much familiar with them. Capacity building exercise is viewed seriously by the women leaders.

Federation

This is the narration of a woman Gram Panchayat Leader from Virudhunagar District. Initially both men and women joined together and formed a Federation. When they organised a meeting with the District Collector, all went into the room of the Collector. All men leaders sat in the first three rows and the last row was given to the women leaders. There was a discussion between the leaders and the District Collector. But the whole discussion was between the men leaders and the District Collector. The women leaders raised their voice, but they were asked to be silent as discussion was in progress. Finally, the men leaders said that the discussion was over, all could move out of the hall. The women leaders asked them what happened to the demands given by them. The men leaders said that those can be discussed outside the Collector's chamber. When all came out of the room, the women leaders asked them about their demands. The men leaders said that the Collector would consider them in due course. On that day the women leaders felt that the women had to adopt a different strategy and they formed a separate association. They got a separate audience with Collector and sorted out their problems. When they narrated the experience, the idea came to form a Federation. Thus the Federation of elected women representatives (exclusively women Presidents of Gram Panchayats) was born in Tamil Nadu, facilitated by the Gandhigram Rural Institute. In course of time there were a number of Federations at different levels.

Gandhigram took the initiative to form this Federation as it organised series of capacity building exercises to train the Gram Panchayat Women Presidents with the active support of the Hunger Project. They were not only trained to manage the Panchayats and to administer development but also to provide leadership to the people. In our country in fifty years of democratic governance we have seen many rulers in the name of democracy but we have not seen a leader to lead the society after Mahatma Gandhi. So, in all training programmes how to be with the people as a leader and lead them not rule them was emphasised. Thus the relationship started from training and it continued in forming associations and federations for women leaders. The EWR federations periodically organise regional meetings and consolidate the problems faced by the EWRs and conduct periodical interface with officials. Annually they conduct a Mela in which major issues of the leaders are highlighted for policy advocacy and they meet higher officials, political party leaders. During the time of general elections, they review the election manifesto of the political parties and check whether the issues of local bodies and issues of women are included.

Over a period of six years they have become visible and in fact they have become role models for others. Following this EWR Federation, Block Level Federation for Block Panchayat leaders and District Level Federation for District Panchayat leaders have been formed. Even among the Block level leaders, women leaders have formed their own Federation. SC and ST leaders have formed their own Federation. Among Gram Panchayat leaders, Dalit women leaders have formed their own Federation. They negotiate with officials to settle their problems. Of all the Federations, the Gram Panchayat Women Leaders Federation is strong, vibrant and vocal and it sustains its activities. Various issues have been highlighted over a period of time. Eighty meetings have been organised in different places in Tamil Nadu and each time they have focused on one or two issues which are affecting them and the people, especially women, children and Dalits.

Elected women representatives should strengthen their Federation at the district level. Its structure should be flexible. In every district the Federation should have an office. Once in two months the office bearers should meet and discuss their issues.

One major achievement is that the rotation of reservation has been set for each ten years which is being quoted by many in our country. This is the only state where reservation of seats for women has been made for every ten years. Yet another major breakthrough for the federation is getting an exclusive Government Order to make the Collector convene a meeting of officials to redress the grievances of EWRs whenever they request. By using this Government Order women leaders in seven districts have made the Collector convene the meeting of the officials and got their grievances redressed. The Federation leaders have gone to meet the Prime Minister of India and handed over petitions to him asking for direct financing of local bodies from the Central Government.

At this juncture the Federation office bearers of all the districts met at Gandhigram and invited the Rural Development Director, Government of Tamil Nadu, to their meeting. From morning till evening they raised a volley of questions before the officials and they were responded to by the Director of Rural Development.

Following the interface, they discussed the future course of action for their Federation. Their discussion was centred round their future course of action in their Panchayats. Many of them were in power consecutively for two terms. Now they have decided to contest in the open constituency along with men. It is to be seen only during the elections. They have further decided to stay in the public's space in any of the positions in local bodies whether it is in Gram Panchayats or in Block Panchayats. The acquired skills, capacity and capability could be effectively used by occupying any of the positions in the local bodies.

By creating a support structure of their own, the EWRs have highlighted the problems of the women leaders in administration. The problems are multidimensional in nature and character. Further by conducting a series of interfaces with other state Panchayats and Panchayats within the state and with officials they have equipped themselves in attacking social development issues. The leaders have been conscientised on the issues of women, children and livelihood. An army of elected women representatives has come to the public space and decided to stay on. How to stay on in the public space is the question. Almost all have decided to stay in the public space in different forms. In the next elections, women can contest in general constituencies. They can contest for different tiers, either Block Panchayats or District Panchayats. A set of leaders said that they can contest for Ward Members' posts of Gram Panchayats. Being a Gram Sabha member, the experience gained by the Panchayat Presidents could be utilized. There are Panchayat leaders who want to stake a claim to MLA constituencies. They are interested in seeking tickets to contest in the MLA constituencies. The Federation of elected women representatives could be strengthened by associating themselves with such activities.

Conclusion

The critical mass (33.3 per cent of women elected representatives) have come to perform the critical functions (attacking the issues of hunger, poverty, gender and untouchability) despite facing a multitude of problems in the process of their governance and managing the institutions. They have their own record of achievements and story of struggles. But they have determined to move further to occupy the public space. The journey has started and the support structure has been created to push forward the onward march. Their imprints in governance, management of institutions, negotiating with different partners and stakeholders, attacking issues and managing the crowd are unique and different from those of men and members of other higher level institutions. Their expressions, perceptions, opinions and observations provide an array of policy implications.

Capacity building for elected women representatives has to be conducted within a month after they assume office. The training should be intensive and residential. It should not be conducted in the Block Development Office. It should be given only in training institutions. Training should be made mandatory and on any account their males should not be allowed to attend the training. In the training programme, Tamil Nadu Panchayati Raj Act, 1994 updated version, Rules, Government Orders and details of Schemes of Rural Development should be given to all Panchayat leaders as a tool kit for Panchayat Management. The training package should include gender and social development components. In each and every training programme, a well-experienced Panchayat President should be made as a resource person to share her experience with other participants. The same training should be given to officials also at the same time. Periodical refresher courses say, once a year, can be organised. Once a month, the District Collector must convene a meeting of officials to redress the problems faced by the women leaders in Panchayat administration. Males of the elected women representatives' families should not be allowed to occupy the chair and to participate in the official meetings. This has to be followed rigorously and religiously. They should not be permitted to sign any document on behalf of the elected women representatives. Periodically an interface has to be arranged for women leaders with other Panchayats, preferably in other states. This opportunity has to be given to the maximum number of people. The women leaders Federation is a registered body and hence it has to be recognized by the government. A support structure has to be created for women and Dalit leaders.

NOTES

1. Dahlerup Drude, "From a Small to a Large Minority: Women in Scandinavian Politics", *Scandinavian Political Studies*, 1988, 11:4, 275-298, Jill. M. Bystdzienski, *Women Transforming Politics: World-*

wide Strategies for Empowerment, Indiapolis: Indiana University Press, 1992; Linda Mac Dougal, *West Minister Women*, London: Vintage, 1998.

2. Vanishree, J., "Women in Power: Critical Mass to Critical Action", *Women's Link*, Vol. 12: No. 3, July-September, 2006.
3. Sridharan Damyanty and Rodic Vesna (ed.), *Breaking the Political Glass Ceiling: Women and Local Governance in South Asia*, New Delhi: Friedrich Ebert Stiffung, 2004.
4. Even 10 per cent form critical mass. But in India one-third position has been reserved for women.
5. Palanithurai, G., "The Empowerment Process: Women Representatives in Grassroots Institutions in Tamil Nadu", *Indian Social Science Review*, Vol. 6, No. 1 (January-June, 2004).
6. _____, "Report of the Project on Associating Elected Women Representatives in Local Governance", Gandhigram: Rajiv Gandhi Chair for Panchayati Raj Studies, 2005.
7. _____, "Women in Governance for Development at Grassroots", *The Indian Journal of Public Administration*, Vol. 10, No. 1 (January-March, 2004).
8. _____, "Are they Withdrawing from Public Space", Gandhigram: Rajiv Gandhi Chair for Panchayati Raj Studies, 2005.
9. _____, "Capacity Building for Local Body Leaders", New Delhi: Concept Publishing Company, 2003.
10. The Hunger Project, *Thus Spoke the Press: Select Articles on Elected Women Leaders in Village Panchayats*, New Delhi: The Hunger Project, 2006.
11. Palanithurai, G., "Leadership Matters in Grassroots Governance", New Delhi: Concept Publishing Company, 2006.

2

Impact of Gendered Political Institutions on Human Development

G. Uma and *J. Vanishree*

Introduction

Grassroots institutions are the real instruments of democracy to make the people directly participate in the governance and decide on the issues which are affecting the life of the people. Towards this steps were taken to the decentralization of power in India. After the introduction of 73rd Amendment to the Constitution of India provided opportunities for multifarious social groups who has been hitherto marginalized. The marginalized cannot come to the mainstream like the dominant social groups in the decision making process in the governing institution at the grassroots. To make marginalized to bring into mainstream politics 73rd Constitutional Amendment is an instrument. This process was started in India after the failure of Community Development Programme. At the international level, the process was started by international agencies. Since the late eighteenth century social scientist have developed a variety of theories to explain differences persisting among human beings. Feminist anthropologists have argued that the organization of social and production relations such as social stratification, the monogamous family, ownership of property and forms of work and production have greatly influenced the differences in gender relations around the world. At the international level, the United Nations have contributed the major share to bring to universal notice the status and the condition of women and incorporated women issues in all development agenda. Eleanor Roosevelt raised the issue of women's rights in the United Nations General Assembly in the year 1948. Apart from United Nations in the twentieth century there are a number of strategies and ideologies adopted to network, empower and associate women. Reservation or Quota is one such strategy to increase women's participation in politics. The underrepresentation of women in formal politics is widely regarded as a problem and there are a number of agencies like the United Nations, the European Union, the Inter Parliamentary Union and the International Institute for Democracy and Electoral Assistance, which have recommended and run projects on women and decision making.

The Role Played by International Institutions

The contribution of international women movements, human rights movements and movement against colonialism and the women participated in the nationalist struggle paved the way for the United Nations to declare 1975 as the International Women's Year. Subsequently, the United Nations organized four international conferences for women. In the year 1970, United Nations reviewed the results of the first development decade of the 1960. Based on the review various approaches to women development were formed. The review concluded that both men and women must be lifted from poverty and both Men and Women must benefit from development efforts. The first International Conference in Mexico City was organized to mark the celebration of International Women's Year in the year 1975. The United Nations Voluntary Fund for Women (later called the United Nations Development Fund for Women) and the International Training and Research Centre for Women were soon established within the United Nations system. In the meantime, feminist in the United States lobbied to integrate women issues into the policy of the government especially USAID policy. Their constant efforts resulted in bringing in a new amendment called the Percy Amendment in the year 1973. This paved the way for integrating gender sensitive social impact studies in all development projects. The feminist also started using the term Women In Development (WID) which comes under liberal feminism. In the mid-1980s, development experts started concentrating on basic human needs. In the meantime, Structural Adjustment Programme (SAP) was designed to reduce government expenditure and increase the market force. According to liberal feminist economists, prosperity will automatically bring about the development of women. Many development theories agreed that the structural adjustment programme would benefit men and women in the long run. But in the short run vulnerable people especially women and children would be affected. In the meantime, some feminists and development theorists maintained that both the Women In Development (WID) and the Women And Development (WAD) approaches did not address gender inequalities so they propounded the gender and development approach referred to as the empowerment approach or gender aware planning.

Gender And Development Approach (GAD) emerged from the grassroots organizational experiences and writings of Third World feminists and has been most clearly articulated by the group called the Development Alternatives with Women for a New era (DAWN). The process of developing this new paradigm began in the early 1980s. DAWN was launched publically at the 1985 Nairobi International NGO forum. DAWN called for an approach to women's development that recognizes the importance of global and gender inequities.[1] GAD approach emerged from the experiences and analysis of Western socialist feminist interested in development issues.[2] In the year 1985, the Third United Nations Conference was held in Nairobi. The Decade of Women 1975-1985 provided an opportunity for women from economic south to grow more visible. Nairobi provided a platform to show the leadership of the women movement from the economic south. Third World women had come into their own in the international community and with the great sense of their own identity now ready to redefine the notion of global sisterhood into global solidarity among women. While the north-south divide did not disappear there was new confidence among women from the south that facilitated the creation of a partnership between them in the struggle for the better world.[3] The final report of the Forum, for the record Forum 85, summarized the meaning of the event to women as follows: "Today women see themselves as the force for change, not just for women but for the whole of the society. Women seek the power and the strength to work equally with men to change the social, political and economic structure in the direction of integral and equitable development."

Since the participants expressed little hope for the ability or willingness of present governments to help realize women's alternative visions, they repeatedly stressed the need for women to organize independently for political action to assume responsibility to challenge existing policies and programmes and to work to bring about an integral development. Central to feminist alternative vision is a people centred international order. It is concerned about the poorest and most oppressed. Stress is also placed on the importance of understanding class, race, ethnicity, gender and age. All these are essential factors in the analysis and design of strategies not only in relation to society as a whole, but among women themselves.[4]

One of the recommendations from the Nairobi Conference was that the United Nations should hold another World Conference on Women in ten years, to take stock of the implementation of the platform of action formulated in Nairobi. This Conference took place in Beijing in 1995. One of the significant goals set out by the Fourth World Conference on Women, in Beijing in the year 1995, was adequate representation of women in all decision making bodies (Beijing Platform Action, 1995). It suggested that in any representative body there should be a logical balance of men and women to voice the concerns of the society *en masse*. Good governance means being participatory, accountable and transparent, which reasonably calls for a gender balance in political decision making. It is believed that women's rights and values of governance can enhance and enrich the overall decision making process. It is also generally assumed that women at the local level are more sensitive to community issues.[5]

The Beijing Platform for Action also recommended:

- Setting a timetable to end all manner of legal discrimination against women along the lines of United Nations Convention on Elimination of All Forms of Discrimination Against Women (CEDAW), as well as establishing a framework to promote legal equality initiating specific measures targeted at acquiring a short-term threshold of 30 per cent for women in national decision making positions, with a long-term aim of 50 per cent.
- Mobilizing national and international efforts to facilitate for everyone and for women in particular, greater access to economic and political opportunities.

Women in Politics

In 1997, in Cairo, the Inter Parliamentary Union Council adopted the universal declaration on democracy and urged Governments and Parliaments throughout the world to be guided by the context. The total Members of Parliament in the world is 44,204. Out of this only 7,160 are women (16.3%). The percentage of women in Parliament (Lower House and Upper House) in the following countries are:

Table 2.1: Representation of Women in Politics

Sl. No.	*Countries*	*Percentage*
1.	Nordic Countries	40
2.	America	20
3.	Europe-OSCE excluding Nordic Countries	16.8
4.	Sub-Saharan Africa	16.6
5.	Asia	15.9
6.	Pacific	13.9
7.	Arab States	6.8

Source: www.ipu.org

The underrepresentation of women in high offices in politics and government is well documented. There have been some women heads of State or Government (24 Presidents and 30 Prime Ministers from 1954 to 1999), and the number of women Ministers across the world doubled between 1987 and 1996. This represented an increase from 3.4 per cent to 6.8 per cent but this is not an impressive figure. Moreover, 48 (out of 187) countries had no woman in Ministerial position at all. In fact, in the Asia-Pacific region and Eastern Europe, the proportion of women Ministers has been under 5 per cent. There is also an unmistakable pattern in the nature of portfolios held by women. In 1999, the most substantial concentration of Women Ministers worldwide was in Ministries of Social Affairs, Health, Women Affairs, Family, Children, Youth, Culture and Heritage, Education, Environmental and Labour. Very few Ministers held portfolios related to Defence, Finance and Trade and only one country had a woman Minister of Home Affairs.[6]

As for the representation of women in national legislatures, only 8 countries have achieved the so-called critical Mass of 30 per cent (Sweden, Denmark, Finland, Norway, Iceland, Netherlands, Germany and South Africa). An assessment of the "Beijing effect" in Parliament suggest that the percentage of women parliamentarians worldwide increased from 11.3 per cent in 1995 to 12.9 per cent in 1999, a rather meagre increase of +1.6 per cent. In the same period, the percentage of female presiding officers of the House of Parliament registered a marginal decline.

In the countries of Eastern Europe, the percentage of women in National Parliaments has actually declined in the last decade, partly as a backlash to the perception that participation under Communist regimes was forced. In terms of regional representation, however, it is notable that female representation is lowest in the Arab countries, followed by the countries of South Asia (with the notable exception of Bangladesh) where representation is even lower than in East Asia and Sub-Saharan Africa.

In 1995, the United Nations Development Programme posed two cautionary arguments. First, the very definition of governance needs to be engendered before we embark upon the project of engendering governance itself. Secondly, the project of engendering governance should be received in terms of more exacting than simply placing women at the higher echelons of governance—of the state, the private sector and NGOs.[7]

For women who have minimal exposure to the public realm, politics and processes of the state may be equated almost exclusively with electoral politics and voting. Others who have greater mobility and cause to challenge the state and its policies, whether by accident or design, including politically active students and workers, may see politics as an expression of the competitive tendency and contests for power that permeate all levels of governments.[8]

Notions of governance may include ideas about—

1. the legitimacy of government, which is linked with participatory process and the consent of those who are governed;
2. the accountability of government officials for their actions and the existence of mechanisms by which individuals and institutions can be held accountable;
3. the competence of a government to formulate appropriate policies, make timely decisions, implement them effectively and deliver services; and
4. the respect of human rights and the rule of law to guarantee individual and group rights and security in order to provide a framework for political, economic and social activity.[9]

A negative conception of rights (in terms of liberty or freedom) alone is an inadequate instrument, because the principle of freedom from the state has often (from the liberal political philosopher John Locke to the contemporary libertarian philosopher Robert Nozick) been invoked to assert the indefensibility of state interference in the private sphere. From the feminist point of view, negative rights are suspect because social practices are often oppressive and partriarchal, and the absence of state interference may give licence to such forces. A positive conception of rights, on the other hand, has the merit of providing not just a formal structure of rights, but also enabling conditions that make their fulfilment possible. A gendered view of governance must be a rights based view in this latter sense, because it has to engage with and address long histories of exclusion, marginalization and invisibility. Women's claim to voice, and to recognition of their contribution to the productive life of society, have therefore to be couched in the language of rights.[10]

The main policy response to the underrepresentation of women in the formal structures of politics has been the attempt to enhance representation through quotas, whether in political parties or in legislatures. The case for quotas is often justified by an appeal to argument that the politics of ideas (political choice between the policies and programmes of political parties rather than on the basics of group concerns and interests) does not include adequate policy concerns for groups which are marginalized or excluded. This suggests the importance of a politics of presence in which women, ethnic minorities and other similarly excluded groups are guaranteed fair representation.[11]

The Need for Reservation

The issue of quotas is contentions for at least two sets of reasons. The first relates to the lack of genuine commitment in the political parties to increasing women's representation. There are ways in which political parties may effectively circumvent the quota by, for instance, putting up candidates in constituencies where the party is weak and unlikely to win anyway, or treating the quota as a ceiling rather than a minimum to be improved upon, or nominating women candidates who will be pliable because they are dependent on the male party leadership. Of course, there are exceptions like the African National Congress (ANC) in South Africa which adopted a self-administered quota of 30 per cent even if many of the women candidates were clustered at the bottom 15 per cent of the list. Other parties in that country followed the African National Congress's (ANC) example, with the result that women comprise 27 per cent of the National Legislature.[12]

One of the significant goals set by the Fourth World Conference on Women in Beijing in the year 1995 was adequate representation of women in all decision making bodies (Beijing Platform Action, 1995). It suggested that in any representative body there should be a logical balance of men and women to voice their concern of the society *en masse*. Good governance means being participatory, accountable and transparent, which reasonably calls for a gender balance in political decision making. It is believed that women's rights and values of governance can enhance and enrich the overall decision making process. It is also generally assumed that women at the local level are more sensitive to community issues than women at higher levels.

More than 103 countries have taken measures to increase women's participation in formal politics. In India, this process started in the 1930s. Women's organisations like the All India Women's Council, the National Council for Women in India and the Women's India Association demanded women's political participation. So the issue of reservation for women has been on the political agenda since pre-independence days. But in the spate of issues before the rationalist movement this issue receded to the background. Women's organisations have since long advocated the need to promote and harness the political resources of women in nation building. The question of women's political participation and reservations has also evolved over the last 60 years and a considerable degree of debate, discussions and social searching has ensued. In the post-independence era, the issue came back in focus through the Kalelkar Commission for Backward Classes (1950), but the debate was not pursued and no further action was taken. In 1975, the Committee on the Status of Women in India recommended electoral reservation for women. This was also endorsed in 1988 in the policy document. With a national perspective plan for women under the leadership of the late Rajiv Gandhi, the government in power initiated a Panchayati Raj bill, but it was passed only in the Lok Sabha.

In India a critical mass of women has been formed at the local level through radical constitutional amendments. It is a top down approach. Apart from the above legislation, the Indian Government is trying to bring in legislation to provide reservation of seats for Women in the Parliament and in State Assemblies. Most of the political parties oppose the reservation of seats for Women in Parliament and State Assemblies.

At the same time most of the women have come to power at the grassroots with gender related handicaps. Some of the handicaps are:

1. Increasing workload.
2. Customs, norm and cultural barriers.
3. Illiteracy.
4. Traditional domination of male members.
5. Negative attitude of the officials.
6. Marginalization of Dalit leaders.
7. Domination of party politics.
8. Lack of Gender Sensitization.
9. Domination of Males.
10. Interference of Family members.
11. Restriction of movements.
12. Made not to raise the development issues.
13. Information blockade.
14. Nomination and selection.

Critical Mass and Critical Action Theory

According to Critical Mass Theory, critical mass of women platform the critical action and the assumption is that the women leaders have to concentrate on social development issues. The concept of the critical mass was first introduced by Rosabeth Moss Kanter. He studied the concept by applying it to fortune 500 companies for the exploration of token behaviour. According to Kanter, there are four sets of proposition when he explored token behaviour in the year 1976 in the fortune 500 companies. According to him, the Uniformed Groups show the character of a single person and also shows one significant social type. With regard to Skewed Groups, one group predominates over others in the ratio up to 85 : 15. Unlike other groups, Tilted Groups begin to move towards less extreme distributions and less exaggerated effects. In this situation, with a ratio of perhaps 65:35, dominant are just a majority and tokens a minority. Balanced at a typological ratio of about 60:50 to 50:50, the group becomes balanced.[13]

Many scholars and activists raise the concept of the 'Critical Mass' to explain the importance of providing quota to the women in the legislative. They also stressed the significance of the concept of critical mass because if women become in significant number in the legislative body, they will bring considerable changes in the overall business of the legislative. The reason that, as the number of women grow, women will not only be able to work more effectively together for womenfriendly policy change but also influence their male colleagues to a greater extent to accept and approve bills promoting gender equality.[14]

Many authors have applied the critical mass theory to study the impact of the increasing number of women in Parliament. Unlike Kanter, Drude Dahlerup made a strong claim about critical acts also. Apart from Kanter and Dahlerup, Sandra Grey tested the impact of increased number of women politicians on policy processes and outcomes in New Zealand over a 25 years period. A content analysis was carried out on selected Hamard Parliamentary Debates from 1975 to 1999. During this time, the proportion of women institutions in the New Zealand House of Representatives rose from 4 per cent to 29 per cent. Grey tested the concept of critical mass by scrutinising 25 years of Parliamentary Debates. She correlated the rising numbers of women in the House of Representatives and changes in political culture, the political agenda, and public policy decisions. Based on the scrutiny, it was found that in 1975 more female MPs promoted discussion on women issues than their male counterparts. Initiating discussions on child care and parental leave was also done by women MPs from 1994 to 1999. This clearly shows that once women reached the critical mass, gender gaps in the Parliamentary discussion will decrease. Not only gender issues, personal attacks among women MPs decreased when compared to their male counterparts. Another area found in the study was interruptions. During the year 1975 to 1999, Male MPs in the New Zealand Parliament were interrupted often than their female counterparts while discussing the issue of child care and parental leave. Women MPs were also susceptible to general harassing remarks than their male counterparts. This was found when Grey scrutinized New Zealand Parliamentary Debates on child care and parental leave. Female MPs were the subjects of 14 of the 17 harassing remarks found in debates on child care and parental leave. Only two of the harnessing comments were made by women politicians; the rest came from male colleagues. A point here is that

14.4 per cent of the seats in the New Zealand House of Representatives were held by women politicians.[15] Grey concludes that the critical mass is a concept and it can explain the reasons for the minorities, including women, struggling to influence the various spheres of political aspects. We have also a variety of critical masses like Parliamentarians, Academicians, etc., depending upon the goal which the group wants to achieve. Studler and Ian McAllister in their paper "Does a Critical Mass Exist? A Comparative Analysis of Women's Legislative Representation (1949-1997)" with a previous study, tests the critical mass theory with the following factors. First, they state that institutional roles should be favourable towards women. For example, the Indian Government has brought in a constitutional amendment favouring women. This amendment to the Constitution of India in 1993 provided one-third reservation of all seats as members and chairpersons for women in rural local government. They also stated that where there is less competition, the chance for women to be elected is more. Norris (1993), Mabland and Shudlar (1996) and Reynolds (1999), hold a different view. If there is more competition in the party system combined with lower percentages of votes for the largest party, the parties search new voters. This will increase the chances for women to be elected.

The second set of variables for testing the theory is an "Egalitarian Political System". To measure the egalitarian political system, they tested the period of time since women were enfranchised and the time when the first woman became the head of the Legislature.

The third variable is the efforts of political parties to promote women candidature. The last variable is dependent upon social and economic development. This can be found through Human Development indicators like gender empowerment measure, achievement in education, number of women entering labour market, etc. Based on the above indicators, a study was conducted in 17 countries. The results showed that the electoral process, egalitarian political culture, women legislatures contribution are the contributing factors to change the political system towards women. The assumption is that women will retain or reveal a greater gender consciousness and change the institutions in which they serve. But such an expectation conflicts with the generally accepted socialisation process in Legislature. The longer people serve, the more they become enamoured of the existing procedures and the less willing they are to change them. As long as the party is the dominant force in legislative behaviour, it will be difficult to generate women's unity. Any changes in behaviour that occur are likely to be incremental, brought about through wider patterns of mass socialisation for both women and men.

The study conducted by Tremblay and Pelletier in the Canadian Legislative concludes that an increase in feminist attitudes is more important than simply adding to the number of women in the Legislature. Gendered political institutions are unlikely to change significantly without a broader social transformation. What is required is not a critical mass of women, but a critical mass of feminists. According to the study conducted by Drude Dahlerup, there are six changes expected when women achieve the critical mass:

1. Changes in the political discourse.
2. Changes in the social climate of political life.
3. Changes in policy.
4. Changes in culture.
5. Changes in behaviour.
6. Changes in political attitudes, policy priorities, legislative styles and decision making roles.

In the Western countries, all the abovesaid factors are analysed in the light of Parliamentary Institutions. In the Indian context, the critical mass was formed at the grassroots level through two radical amendments to the Constitution of India. The Indian state has taken affirmative action by introducing minimum quotas for women in rural and urban local bodies. This legitimised women to increase participation in the governance process. However, most of the women came to power with gender-related handicaps. These include, increasing workload at both places (family as well as official work), custom norm, cultural barriers, illiteracy, traditional panchayat domination, domination of male members in the Panchayat, negative attitude of officials, marginalisation, domination of party, lack of gender sensitivity, lack of exposure to governance, interference of family members, and information blockade. Due to the abovesaid factors, women's leadership comes under severe criticism.

But women came to power at the grassroots brought a considerable changes with respect to human development. The human development paradigm argues that when choices are provided to the people they will bring change not only in their well-being but also in the well-being of other people's life as well. The basic purpose of development is to enlarge people's choices in principle these choices can be infinite and can change over time. Greater access to knowledge, better nutrition and health services, more secure livelihoods, security against crime and physical violence, satisfying leisure hours, political and cultural freedoms and the sense of participation in community activities. The objective of development is to create an enabling environment for people to enjoy long health and creative lives. The human development paradigm covers all aspects of development whether economic growth or international trade, budget deficit or fiscal policy, savings, investment or technology, basic social services or safety nets for the poor. The human development paradigm fairly broad agreement, i.e. development must put people as the centre of its concern. The purpose of development is to enlarge all human choices and not just income. The human development paradigm is concerned both with building human capabilities and using those human capabilities more fully. Human development has four essential pillars—equality, sustainability, productivity and empowerment. The human development paradigm defines the ends of development and analyses sensible options for achieving them.[16] The critical mass of women at the grassroots level brought the critical changes and focused on people centred development as per human development perspective. This was reflected in their activities. The following case studies were analysed based on the human development perspective.

Women in Action

The 73rd Amendment Act provided a space for the critical mass to perform critical action. By using this space the critical actors not only deepen the democracy at the grassroots level by concentrating on people centric issues they have realized its full potential and engender the governance. They have collaborated with civil society organizations, women's movement, political societies towards mainstreaming and democratizing political system. They also brought human development centric approach to their governance. This was proved through the following case studies.

Chinnammal, the President of Urathupatti Gram Panchayat, developed a plan for her Panchayat. After the preparation of the plan, she paid attention to the implementation of the nutritious noon meal scheme in the schools. She constructed good kitchen for the preparation of food. She provided a nail cutter to the balwadi. The ration shop was constructed. She provided safe drinking water to the schools.

Veerakalaiarasi, President of Veppankulam Gram Panchayat of Sivagangai District, formed nine committees. She helped ultra poor to get ration cards and ensured that needed provisions were supplied by the ration shops to them. Further she corrected the BPL list of beneficiaries. The planning exercise made the people think together and act together. The planning exercise made the people think that the Panchayat is an affair of the people and not an affair of the Panchayat President.

Bhavani Elango, the President of Merpanaikadu Gram Panchayat was totally opposed by a section of the menfolk. She was kidnapped by the opposition group. She decided to move closely with the women. She formed 23 Self-Help Groups and the SHGs helped the Panchayat to desilt a tank which provided drinking water to the entire area. Valuing work done by the women in the tank as worth Rs. 60,000, the officials who witnessed the contribution of the women helped the Panchayat by laying a pipeline for the entire area for the supply of drinking water.

Sukanya, President, Vellimallipattinam Gram Panchayat from Coimbatore District created awareness among the self-help group members who took the initiative to take care of their children in terms of health, cleanliness and education. Now one can see in her Panchayat the way the balwadi is maintained and the school is maintained. Even Dalit children are clean and neat and they are regular in attending school and they use the toilets.

Eswari, the President of Appipalayam Gram Panchayat, Karur District said that environmental issues have become acute and as a result the people have lost their source of drinking water. Some people in the name of development have spoiled the natural resources. In the Karur area people have sold their lands to industries which manufacture dyes. The waste coming out of the factories has completely spoiled the drinking water source. What can the Panchayat do in this regard? As a Panchayat President she started her agitation against all these industries. Everyone is aware of what type of trouble the industrialists can give. Officials normally support the powerful. The officials, as per the instruction of the industrialists, took action against the President under Section 205. She brought it to the notice of the Government. The Government instructed the officials to take steps to provide protection to her. Yet they have not done anything. But the people have extended support to the Panchayat to fight against such atrocities.

Siddeshwari, the President of Koonavelampatti Gram Panchayat in Namakkal District concentrated on the improvement of educational institution in Koonavelampatti Panchayat. There is one primary and secondary school. She constructed proper noon-meal centre building near the schools and she ensured that the food is provided under the supervision of the teachers. Toilet for the students is available in the nearby sanitary complex but due to lack of water collection it has not been opened. She realized the plight of the girl students. With the help of Parent Teachers Association (PTA) she constructed separate toilet for girl students. Parent Teachers Association meetings held regularly and the required needs are immediately fulfilled. At the request of SHGs the PTA recommended the extension of teaching hours for the students and one woman teacher was appointed by the PTA. And the newly appointed Head Master of the school actively participates in the Panchayat activities voluntarily. The President motivates the students by distributing prizes during competition. The President's constant rapport with the Canara Bank made them to adopt her Panchayat for development activities.

Conclusion

These women have reinstated that when women come to power they redefine the governance process by concentrating on not only developing infrastructural facilities they will also concentrate on human development aspects. Women's power and initiative can uplift the lives of all human beings—women, men and children.[17] Therefore, women's power plays a crucial role in the well-being of all individuals irrespective of their sex and age. This can be noted that women is no longer a passive beneficiary of the government programmes in turn indeed they are active agents who bring upliftment for the society and its transformation. Increasing the number of women's positions in politics opens doors for women in terms of presence and visibility. The critical mass of women has the potential to transform gender relations and issues affecting marginalised. By proving this reservation for women in Parliament and Assemblies can bring considerable changes in the development of social issues.

NOTES

1. Parpart, Jane, *et al.*, www.idrc.ca/en.en/ev-27444-20\-\-Do-Topic.htm\
2. *Ibid.*

3. Antrobus, Peggy J., *Global Women's Movement, Origin, Issues and Strategies*, Bangalore: Books for Change, 2004.
4. *Ibid.*
5. Sharnin, Ishrat, Kumari Ranjani, *Gender and Local Governance: A New Discourse in Development*, SANEI, 2001.
6. www.ipu.org
7. UNDP, *Essays on Gender and Governance*, New Delhi: Human Development Resource Centre, UNDP, 2003.
8. Tambiah, Yasmin (ed.), *Women in Governance in South Asia: Reimagining the State*, Colombo: International Centre for Ethnic Studies, 2002.
9. *Ibid.*
10. UNDP, *Essays on Gender and Governance*, New Delhi: Human Development Resource Centre, UNDP, 2003.
11. Philips, Anne, *The Politics of Presence*, Oxford: Clarendon Press, 1995.
12. UNDP, *Essays on Gender and Governance*, New Delhi: Human Development Resource Centre, UNDP, 2003.
13. Childs, Sarah, and Krook Mona Lena, "The Substantive Representation of Women: Rethinking the Critical Mass 'Debate'," paper presented at the annual meeting of the American Political Science Association (Washington: American Political Science Association, 1-4 September, 2005).
14. Grey, Sandra, "Women and Parliamemary Politics: Does Size Matter? Critical Mass and Women MPs in the New Zealand House of Representatives", paper for the 51st Political Studies Association Conference (Manchester, United Kingdom: 10-12 April, 2001).
15. Childs and Krook, "The Substantive Represemation of Women: Rethinking the Critical Mass 'Debate'."
16. Mahabub-ul-Haq, "The Human Development Paradigm", in Fukuda Parr and Shivakumar (eds.), *Readings in Human Development*, New Delhi: Oxford University Press, 2004.
17. Sen, Amartya, *The Argumentative Indian: Writings on Indian History, Culture and Identity*, London: Allen Lane an imprint of Penguin Books, 2005.

3

Engaging with Democracy: Women in Panchayats

Alak Nanda

> *Feminism has major implications for the way we should think of Democracy, but we cannot presume in advance that these will transform the very foundations of the debate.*
>
> —Anne Phillips, 'Engendering Democracy'

The core of politics is the exercise of power. The sphere of politics extends beyond the formal institutions of government to include nearly every human grouping, where individuals conflict over collective goals and find means to arrive at consensus for progress. In this context, the right to vote for women seems to be a basic and only basic achievement. The fight for rights—social, economic and political—must not be only symbolic but real. The centuries-old domination and discrimination against women necessitates that affirmative action is necessary for bringing women in the realm of politics and making their presence substantial and meaningful.

Understanding universal suffrage as political rights to women is a naive assumption. Voting is a necessary but not a sufficient condition for gender parity. To expect that after being allowed the freedom to vote, women can effortlessly claim the freedom to participate and the freedom of contesting elections is not just naive but political convenient. There is unanimity that women have been handicapped because they have been bereft of power. The solution, therefore, is that they should be endowed with power, i.e. they should be 'empowered'.

In the early 90s, India took a small but substantive decision to include 33 per cent reservation for women in the revived Panchayati Raj Institutions system (PRI). The women whom PRI has brought into politics are now governing, be it in one village, or larger area such as 100 villages or a district. Over the last decade, a number of studies have covered the phenomenon of women's entry into formal strictures of governance: its impact on governance policies, society, and on women themselves.

With the help of a few such studies this chapter aims to look at women's empowerment through the PRI system with some critical questions. Has the reservation policy actually brought women into politics or has it been misused to bring in the '*Biwi-beti* brigade[1] ?' Are women able to raise issues they want? Can they take traditionally unacceptable decisions if they want? Do women conduct themselves and think differently than male politicians? Are their areas of concern different? Do women representatives have a different approach towards governance? Do women stand up for other women? Are women's representatives taking up issues and concerns specified to women? These are some of the questions looked at in this chapter.

The chapter has been divided into four major sections. The first section gives a background understanding of Panchayati Raj Institutions (PRI) system in India and the question of reservation for women. The second section deals with the ways in which women's presence in PRIs is transforming views on politics, affecting governance and transforming women themselves. The last two parts are try to place the discussion in a critical perspective and make some recommendations, which seem pertinent.

1. Understanding PRI and Reservations

1.1 Impetus for PRIs

The word *Panchayat* is a traditional one referring to a council of five elders in the village who mediated conflict and spoke on behalf of all the residents of a village in pre-modern India. Carrying the legacy of Lord Ripon's Resolution of 1882 and the almost consistent commitment of the nationalist government, the panchayat system was being practiced in varying forms in 20 states in 1948.[2] However, it was one of the major issues hotly debated in the Constituent Assembly. It was advocated passionately by Gandhian members of the Assembly who believed in gram-swarajya as the key to national development, and fiercely contested by Dr. Ambedkar as dens of ignorance, narrow-mindedness and communalism. Nehru shared this view.[3] As a result, the provision for the setting up of village panchayats was included in the non-justifiable Directive Principles of State Policy [Part 4, Article 40]. There was no pressure on any state to set up such a system, or alter any existing system.

The Union in those early days took up what was called the Community Development Programme with an emphasis on village leadership and community participation. This top-down effort at socio-economic development of villages soon declined in importance and effectiveness, with the gradual dominance of the Union. The Balwantrai Mehta Committee in the late 1960s came up with the idea of panchayats as links between local leadership and the government. Later, in another context, the Ashok Mehta Committee in the late 1970s made recommendations for the setting up of local governments. Criticizing the apathy of the political elite and the unhelpful attitude of the bureaucracy, the Committee called for a substantial devolution of powers to PRIs. These reports had on important impact many years down the line. It is from the Union's experience of development programmes that the idea/need for local governments came to be pushed.

Given the overall centralization trends in the Indian polity the states too developed authoritarian systems of governance. Strong hierarchical systems developed. The bureaucracy grew in influence. It became a top down system. This is the context in which women were brought into politics and had to find their way out to make same meaning of reservation.

1.2 Genesis of the Constitutional Mandate

The women's movement in India has debated the logic of reservation for women in political institutions and government at different points of time for more than 70 years. Women leaders rejected the idea of reservation for women as a retrograde step in 1929.[4] Acceptance of the principle of gender equality in the Fundamental Rights resolution in 1931 and in the Constitution of independent India seemed to have settled the issue at that time. In 1939-40, the women's subcommittee of the National Planning Committee rejected the idea of reservation categorically. (Report of the Subcommittee, 1941). In the early 1970s, the Committee on the Status of Women in India (CSWI) once again debated the reservation issue. It pointed out that rights guaranteed by the Constitution have helped to build an illusion of equality and power which is frequently used as an argument to resist special protective and accelerating measures to enable women to achieve their just and equal position in society. However, the idea of reservations even as a 'transitional measure was rejected by a majority of the members of the CSWI.'[5]

The legislative action which enacted the reservation of seats for women did not result from any significant campaign by the women's movement, nor from an unusually gender sensitive leadership of a political party. There may have been some pressure from the women's wing of the Janata Dal party[6], in which there was history of demanding more place for women in the allocation of constituencies for the Central Parliament. However, this line was subsumed under the rhetoric of a 'people-led' progressive politics.

Today, not only the women's movement (despite some dissenting voices) but also elected women representatives themselves are demanding reservations. But women's movement in the early 1990s was primarily mobilizing around issues of dowry, rape/sexual harassment and prohibition. They were not challenging the gender ratios of formal political institutions and certainly not demanding a special entry. Finally, the fact that reservations were applied to Panchayti Raj Institutions makes their appearance even more striking. In the vast majority of rural areas, women rarely exercise power in the formal political sphere, and were not even being more equally treated in other spheres. How can this be explained? Shilpa Jain has raised the doubt[7] that the majority of the national political parties supported quotas for women because they did not expect women's participation to be empowering. Instead perhaps they assumed that women would take on a passive subdued role in the formal political sector, which can be easily dominated by party pressures. Historical evidence can be taken from Partha Chatterjee who analyzes notions of women during the nationalist struggle as equalled with motion represent the values of "self-sacrifice, benevolence and devotion".[8] Central to this idea were the contrasts between spiritual and Western, Indian and modern, men and women. Women were vote to participate in the Independence movement, could not break from their ascribed feminine role. It was a presence without empowerment.

However, this does not eliminate the possibility that women's entry and participation in local government was believed will be conducive for the effectiveness of PRIs. Various study committee had suggested cooption or nomination of women members to facilitate the operation of centrally sponsored women's programmes. Reservation of 1/3rd no. of seats was probably understood only a step ahead of nomination. Women's entry in large numbers into local government arose from a mixture of political opportunity and an ethical sensibility that regarded the implication of gender as integral rather than peripheral to the creation of a more just society. More important to note, it arose from the actions of both women and men.

1.3 The Panchayati Raj Institutions System

A bill (64th Constitutional Amendment) for introducing the PRI systems all-over India, which talked of 30 per cent reservation for women was introduced in Parliament in May 1989, but defeated on the ground that it was imposing a uniform pattern on the entire country. The 73rd and 74th Constitutional Amendments were passed in April 1993 and ratified by the states by April 1993. The Amendments envisage a significant structural change by decentralizing power and redressing the gender imbalance in the institutions of self-govemance. The question has been not whether the basic principle of equality was violated but whether such interventions will bring about a redistribution of power and resources and whether it will lead to women's empowerment.

The PRI system operates on a three-tier level in most states at the village, intermediate and district levels. The State Legislatures pass laws to define the powers, authority and responsibilities of the PRIs These may include preparation of plans for Development implementation of government schemes, levy certain taxes, and take measure for all-round development of the village block or district.

1.4 The 73rd Amendment to the Constitution of India

This Amendment, dated 24h April, 1993, directed all State Legislatures to amend their respective panchayat legislation to conform to the Constitutional Amendment within a year. The states were expected to complete division on new Panchayats by April 1995. Those who delayed ran the risk of losing Central Government assistance as announced by the Prime Pinister.

The features of the Act in brief are:

1. There will be a three-tier system at the village intermediate and district levels.
2. The gram sabhas which will be a body comprising all the adult members registered as voters in the panchayat area will be the foundation of the Panchayati Raj.
3. Panchayats shall have a uniform five-year term and elections to constitute new bodies shall be completed before expiry of the term. In the event of dissolution, election will be compulsorily held within six months.
4. In all Panchayats seats shall be reserved for Scheduled Castes (SCs) and Scheduled Tribes (STs) in proportion to their population and one-third of the total number of seats will be reserved for women.
5. One-third of the offices of Chairperson of Panchayats at all levels shall also be reserved for women. Office of the chairperson of the Panchayats shall be reserved in favour of SC and STs in proportion to their population in the state.

2. Women's Experience with PRIs

The 73rd Amendment Act has brought almost a million women into politics. Once a part of faceless number's statistics under 33.3 per cent reservation women are increasingly emerging as leaders and fighters. They have to face each new day as a challenge, and educative experience, an assertion that they too can be a part of this male bastion. This subject has been extensively studies by many, in particular, the Institute of Social Science, the National Institute of Rural Development and the Institute of Social Studied Trust. Various Non-governmental and women's organizations have also presented focused case studies as well as research papers.

There are only a few states that have experience over several electoral cycles with Panchayati Raj. In many states, institutional loopholes and general apathy has led to intermittent elections, having an effect on overall PRI structures besides on women's participation. West Bengal, Karnataka, Andhra Pradesh, Gujarat and Maharashtra have a well-oiled system, operational even before the amendment. Kerala, Rajasthan, Himachal Pradesh, have shown exceptionally good results either due to effective political leadership at state level or the influence and pervasiveness of NGOs.

2.1 Who are these Women?

The women who have entered politics through PRI are from local areas, representing various backgrounds; rich and poor, dominant and oppressed social classes, educated and illiterate, working and non-working. Devaki Jain, in her study, notes that age wise, they are mostly middle-aged women (25-50 years old) compared to elected men, who are usually of an older age group. Women of a younger age (less than 28) were usually seen to be daughters or daughters-in-law of existing political leaders of the village.[9] More preferred are women who are not burdened by reproductive/care or family responsibilities.

A heartening fact is that the suddenness of the amendment brought in many politically inexperienced as well as experienced women into politics. While a large number were in fact elected because of the status enjoyed by their husbands, fathers or sons and act as proxies for men's views, a fair amount of women gained entry into politics for the first time without any connections. Nevertheless, the encouragement and support of the family has been described as crucial in almost all cases. However, after being elected, training and orientation programmes by Governmental and Non-Governmental Institutions have influenced their political participation.

Initially most of the women elected were illiterate or semi-literate. This was unavoidable given the percentages of women's literacy in rural India. However, amendments in some states on literacy as a qualifying condition have affected women's participation. The pattern of caste representation has been emphatically altered, considering reservations for women in general, SCs, STs and women from the SC and ST category.

While the true nature of this caste shift and its translation into a shift in power-base is a sphere of acrimonious debates, PRIs have undoubtedly played an important role in bringing power to those women who would not have been allowed this without the amendment. However, caste and class concerns have, in more cases than not, been on the forefront in shaping the agenda of women representatives.

A large number of lower caste or class women are earning members, while majority of upper caste and class women declare themselves to be homemakers. This, we know, is a broad category which includes heavy work, besides income-generating activity.

2.2 Transforming Politics

Women have gained a sense of empowerment by asserting control over resources, officials and most of all, by challenging men. Sibamma, a 50-year-old Scheduled Caste member of the Brahamasandra Gram Panchayat says[10]:

> The men have always ridiculed us, and perceived us as incapable of the management of public affairs. We now make up one-third of the councils. This adds to our sense of strength. We must be 50 per cent or more. We must overpower them with our numbers.

While many cases of women being elected due to the power and influence of their male relatives have been seen the entry of such women cannot be dismissed. As one women elected through PRI noted[11]:

> It is true we came through our men the first time and are often proxies for them but we know what it is about and will come on our own next time.

Women's entry into Panchayati Raj Institutions in such large numbers, often more than the required 33.3 per cent, and their success in campaigning, including the defeat of male candidates has shattered the myth that women are not interested in politics, that they have no time to go to meetings or to undertake all the other work that is required in political party processes.

Women's empowerment challenges traditional ideas of male authority and supremacy. It is unsurprising, then, that PRI has been opposed by some men. Reservation for women as chairpersons is the biggest irritant to many male aspirants. They are ready to allow women to be members, but not as the Gram Panchayat President. Ratnaprabha Chive (Ratna) is the Sarpanch (head) of the Grera Purandar Panchayat. Ratna was beaten up as soon as she assumed offices by her rival who could not accept the fact that a female had outwitted him.[12] Yet, Ratna has effectively launched programmes for adult education, digging wells for drinking water and repairing school buildings, working in the male dominated office.

Strong women candidates are discouraged by men in order to retain their hold over the case of public spaces of local politics. Mohini, one of the most confident and competent *sathins* of the Women's Development programme in Rajasthan was widely known for her work and activities. When she filed for elections a major disinformation campaign was launched against her. Village elders from the dominant caste requested her to withdraw for the honour of the village. Unable to withstand the psychological pressure, she withdrew.[13] Similarly, women who have got recognition through community leadership or are perceived as having strong political ambitions are usually resented, while "mild, soft and accommodating" women are elected.

Women's dress, election campaigns meeting and strategies have been areas of male control and direction. Fieldworkers in a study on women and Panchayati Raj being conducted by CWDS found that a training programme conducted by an agency in a tribal area also included a dress code for women making it compulsory for women to wear sari to Panchayat meetings.[14] Women who go unescorted are castigated as bad women, character assassinations and the denigration of the women candidates is common. While many women do face opposition or passive non-cooperation from home, they convincingly point out family support or the support of male leaders or elders as crucial to their political participation.

Election Campaigns involve costs and compromises. In some areas, attempts were made to discourage women from contesting so that they would not have to face the darker aspects of election process. The strategies followed are mostly those controlled by men as free liquor to ensure votes, fear of family pressure, offer of money and use of political institution and women have to devise ways and means to bypass them (Aalochana).[15] Concerns are also expressed on the election process dividing women into rival factions. By using traditional custom/practice of nomination, women were saved from the ills of elections and corrupt partisan politics.[16]

2.3 Transforming Governance

Though not completely, increasing the representation of women has gradually led to a more gendered analysis of the issues confronting local government. The ways in which authority is exercised and the issues, which gain priority, show a marked difference. While male members have been known to give priority to development, infrastructure projects, women tend to prioritize issues of food and water security, health and education. Being different from men has also made women more effective.

We are better representatives than men, as we can be always found at home or in the nearby fields. Men wander about, they are either in the town or the beer shops.

Women are also seen as less corrupt then men, raising the efficiency of Panchayat work. Rekha Pundir, a woman trainer who knows many village Pradhans closely, says[17]

> Women don't have habits like drinking liquor or eating frequently in hotels, so the chances of squandering public funds are less. By habit they are more careful in spending money.

Beyond simply increasing the numerical presence, there is a minority of women who are in politics because of their leadership qualities or feminist consciousness. Women who were earlier part of government schemes like Mahila Samakhya Programme or self-help groups are more active in their roles as elected representatives. Visible changes in the articulation of ideas and leadership qualities exhibited by this minority were noted in the survey between 1987, the first gear and 1990 (ISS, 1994).[18]

Some of the ways in which women, through PRI are changing governance are evident in the issues they choose to tackle: water, alcohol abuse, education, health and domestic violence. For example, forty teams of women in Sonbhadra (Uttar Pradesh) area had carried out systematic *yatra*, or processions, covering ten villages each, or 400 villages in all to explain the salient features of the 73rd Amendment and the place given in it to women.[19] In the discussions that took place during these *yatras*, women voiced clear priorities. For nearly 90 per cent of the women, the top priority was water. They expressed a need for clean water for fields, for their cattle and for their families. They said life was unbearable and cultivation impossible without developing the water resources of the area. Even as they were determined to prevent the outflow of water from their areas, they were equally determined to prevent the inflow of liquor into their area.

> We have been ruined by liquor. We are being ruined day after day. The day's wages are drunk by the menfolk. There is no money for groceries. Hence no cooking.

Aalochana, a centre for documentation and research of women in Pune, found that only two to the nine members in Bittargaon could sign their names. However, in this village, which has a 16,000 population, Alochana found out that the women have "learnt to keep accounts from the local school teachers and the gram sevaks (rural workers). They have put an end to gambling and have come down heavily on liquor dens. The policy they adopted was to shut the door on every drunken husband. Any protest made by them or children is met by physical assault.

> We will not bear it. Once we acquire some position and power, we will fight it out. We know that it is not going to be easy because this battle will be carried out in each home. But the fact that the Panchayats will have a minimum number of women, we will use that strength for mobilizing women at large and keep liquor out, as a priority.

Women are also taking action against child marriage and child domestic labour, while promoting girl-child education as is evident from the stories of women from Nellore, the heart of the successful anti-arrack movement.

> We want education for our children. There are schools and teachers who draw their salaries regularly. They mark the attendance of non-existence students in their registers. But they scarcely come to the schools. With this sorry state of affairs, how can you have education for your children? We are going to tell those teachers: either teach or go.

Similar stories of women's representatives prioritizing anti-liquor efforts, education are heard in several other villages in Himachal Pradesh as well. In addition, education for girls, maternity help, women's health, sanitation toilets have received more support from women. In hilly villages, saving forests, ensuring fuel and fodder supplies also get high priority.[20]

Women representatives also accord higher importance to settling village disputes at the village level instead of allowing them to drag on for several years. They appear to favour compromise and consensus and show higher ability to achieve these in spite of numerous divisions in the village. Crimes against women get priority attention from then.

Women value proximity[21], whether it be to a drinking water source, a crèche, a health centre, a court of justice or an office of administration. Poor women have to walk to access these facilities, which is exhausting and consumes valuable time. If institutions for seeking redress are near, the chances of effective action are greater.

Women are beginning to change not only the issues and values of governance but are also adopting different methods to those of men. They do not let official protocol stand in the way. The case of one Panchayat official Suman, who mobilized other sources when denied help by officials, to get the old village tank revived, is a case in point.[22] Radha Devi, the village Pradhan of Mithiberi, Dehradun made officials search records to prove that a road had indeed been sanctioned for her village, and insisted on getting it right away rather than being postponed to next year.[23]

2.4 Transforming Women

What are the effects of this PRI participation on the women themselves? Jagrani Devi, a SC Gram Pradhan of Hamirpur Gram Panchayat in Sitapur, U.P. says that after winning the elections:

> Instead of calling me by my name, people now started addressing me as 'pradhanji'. It was as if my entire personality had changed.[24]

Self-confidence gained through belonging to local organizations has been critical to enabling women to step out of unequal relationships.[25] This sense of freedom is even more profound when the group to which women belong is the PRI. The women carry this freedom into the very activity of politics.

There have been increasing evidences of politicization of women by the electoral process. Women have not only started understanding the workings of politics, but also began to take an active part in it. Women who choose to not contest elections again do carry distinguishing marks of political socialization. There is small but steadily growing number of women who are using this political experience to graduate to higher levels of block and district

Panchayats. Understanding the importance of party politics women are definitely being involved into the political process.

Some women's involvement in PRI has helped them affirm their identity as women with particular and shared experiences. Such women seem to be drawn to an identity above caste or party. This self-perception arises from two sources: women's own sense of their shared experiences and from attitudes and imagery imposed on them by the men.[26] The men see these new political actors as women not as party colleagues. Women bring a non-competitive or cooperative ethic to party politics as they are drawn to work together across party lines and seen to have similar interests. Gender can supersede class and party lines in some cases.

One of the most important question of the political presence of women in the way it is thought it will *transform political agenda and debates*, to include women's issues. While many women politicians do not see themselves as representing women's issues and may be divided along party lines on key issues, but the ideology of sisterhood continues to exert some influence in giving political legitimacy to mobilizing around women's issues. Women's solidarity is continuously challenged by class, caste and identity politics. However discrimination against women cuts across these divisions and unites women on issues of rape, violence against woman and discriminatory laws. Women have been mobilized as groups, based on the assertion that division of roles and responsibilities leads to a different set of priorities, needs and perspectives for women.

3. Obstacles and Challenges Ahead

There remain many obstacles to the realization to the PRI's transformative potential. Skepticism about decentralization persists in many quarters. This continues to be a resistance to really devolving power and funds from centres of male power to the periphery.

Women are handicapped in a variety of ways in their effective participation in politics: illiteracy; the burden of reproductive family roles; wage-earning responsibilities; restrictions on their mobility; dependency on male relatives or village functionaries; the weight of the bureaucracy and problems in learning rules, regulations and procedures—are major road blocks.

Several paradoxes emerge from field studies. Women have been given political power but are not yet seen as political entities. The attributes considered necessary for their political effectiveness are seen as masculine (connections, clout). Women lack familiarity with male politics political models and discourse. In the sphere of the family, women are involved in a daily struggle against authority patterns and powerlessness in order to play their new social political role. The familial structures now embody dual patterns of subservience and resistance, strength and submission.

Negative popular media responses emphasizing women's representation as being largely proxy in nature also undermine the possibilities that reservation offers it was to be understood that not just political strategies but the liens of women are controlled by their husbands, in-laws and political parties.

The question of caste over gender, also cannot be ignored. Panchayats replicate the rural power structure and deeply embedded patterns of dominance and inequalities.[27] The impact on women is mediated by their class/class positions. In cases where caste and class overlap, the imperatives of limited freedom of choice are perceivable. Whereas in some cases where caste backwardness and lower class are not interlinked, especially in case of Backward Castes (BCs) and Other Backward Castes (OBCs), the complexities are increased. In a given situation, where they do not necessarily have to make a choice, do women align themselves with their caste or along gender lines? And, in a situation where they have to make a choice, experience has shown that alignment is predominantly on caste lines in both cases.

While representation of women in these governing bodies is a welcome move, it is not reasonable to expect that it will change the caste balance of power in favour of the most disadvantaged groups. It is a matter requiring a more intense and separate examination and therefore cannot be undertaken in this chapter.

It has been noted consistently that new reforms in the system have not replaced the old system. Rather the inertia and resistance of the patriarchal power structure have forced the reform to accommodate and adjust to the existing system. The candidacy and work of women is acceptable only to the extent that it does not disturb male privileges and does not challenge the power of men. Any change in the division of labour and gender roles are strongly resisted.

Proposals for training women in Panchayat work are met with the typical refrain, '*who will make the chapatis?*'[28]

There is an unwillingness to alter division of labour at home as there is an apprehension that the entry of women into the public domain would mean passing of household chores to men. Thus, the participation of women in politics is controlled and limited by some male members of the family.

4. Observations from a Critical Perspective

Need for an Amendment—The percentage of women at various levels of political activity has shifted dramatically as a result of the Constitutional Amendment. An inevitable question, which arises is, if this increase could have happened without reservations? There is evidence to suggest that women would not have entered these councils in such large numbers without the Constitutional mandate.

Presence and Visibility—There has been a significant increase in the sheer number of women who are part of the local PRI system. The implicit confidence shown in them by the Government/ Constitution has been a liberating-empowering realization for many women. The women representatives are seen as a challenge to the existing male supremacy in many cases. The nature of possible candidates as well as the nature of work done is both subject to societal pressure to stay '*within limits*' and not seriously undermine existing power structures. They are more easily accepted as Panchayat members than as the heads of Panchayats, reservation for which has been a major irritant.

Effectiveness—The involvement of women in politics is still handicapped by several factors—social, economic and political. Yet, despite the odds, women seem to be taking on new roles positively, showing that they are willing learners. While impediments to their effective functioning need to be handled, they cannot be used for criticizing the system or calling for an abandonment of the reservation policy.

Exercise of Authority—It has been seen that women do show a distinct change in governance priorities and values. While men were more concerned with concrete and cash-earning projects, women chose to highlight issues basic in nature and related to an overall environment of security.

Nature of Politics—It is generally expected that the entry of women will affect the nature of politics. While some cases of a differential approach (co-operational than competitive, less corrupt and trust-oriented) were found in scattered places, the general trend has been that of co-option of women into the political process.

Nature of Social Relations—Not many aspects of social relations are changed by women's political participation. Their entry into the public domain has given them rights to influence the development process but they have had to negotiate their positions carefully to include their other roles of caste, class and family relations. However, there is a significant rise in their social as well as socio-political awareness and soon they will be questioning the inequalities and injustices imposed on them.

Conclusion

The positive discrimination of PRI has initiated a momentum of change. It is beginning to affect the processes and priorities of local government as well as the women participating in it. But sustaining this transformative momentum is the challenge. Elected women need support, which extends beyond technical training. They need support to build solidarity amongst women through strengthening links between women organizations and elected bodies. They need information about innovative organizations and schemes to improve their own policies. There is a need to build feminist consciousness and strengthen women's sense of common identity. While many NGOs are already providing this kind of support to women representatives, a more coordinated and focused approach is necessary.

The debate on participatory democracy at the grassroots is an attempt to give a meaning and dimension to the political empowerment of women. The largest participation of women was expected not only to ensure effective operation of development programmes but also an attempt to revise the process of degradation in public life. The gains evidently make a shift in the strategy of women's movement since the 1980, while the response of political parties to women voters has changed and is reflected in their party manifestoes.

However, to make women's share in power more meaningful and substantial there is a need to go beyond the numbers game to proceed towards larger social and political goals. The PRIs should be viewed as *nurseries of political leadership,* opening up other areas for women to assert their equal rights.

NOTES

1. Sharma, Kumud: "Transformative Politics: Dimensions of Women's Participation in Panchayati Raj" from *Indian Journal of Gender Studies*, p. 28.
2. *Ibid.*, p. 29.
3. Poornima and Vinod Vyasulu: *Women in Panchayati Raj: Grassroots Democracy in India*, p. 4.
4. Sharma, Kumud: "*Transformative Politics: Dimensions of Women's Participation in Panchayati Raj*", p. 27.
5. *Ibid.*, p. 27.
6. Jain, Devaki: *Panchayati Raj: Women Changing Governance*, p. 5.
7. Jain, Shilpa: 'Redefining the Politics of Presence: Women in Panchayati Raj Institutions in Rajasthan and Kerala'.
8. Chatterjee, Partha, as quoted by Shilpa Jain, p. 5.
9. Jain, Devaki: *Panchayati Raj: Women Changing Governance.*
10. *Ibid.*, p. 6.
11. *Ibid.*, p. 4.
12. *Ibid.*, p. 7.
13. Sharma, Kumud: *Transformative Politics: Dimensions of Women's Participation in Panchayati Raj*, p. 37.
14. *Ibid.*, p. 38.
15. Aalochana Report, quoted by Kumud Sharma: *Transformative Politics: Dimensions of Women's Participation in Panchayati Raj*, p. 38.
16. *Ibid.*, p. 39.
17. Dogra, Bharat: 'Women make a remarkable Contribution', *Mainstream*, p. 21.
18. Noted by Jain Devaki: *Panchayati Raj: Women Changing Governance*, p. 8.
19. *Ibid.*, p. 7.
20. Dogra, Bharat: 'Women make a remarkable Contribution', *Mainstream*, p. 21.
21. Jain, Devaki: *Panchayati Raj: Women Changing Governance*, p. 9.
22. *Ibid.*, p. 10.
23. Dogra, Bharat: 'Women make a remarkable Contribution', *Mainstream*, p. 20.
24. *Interview with Jagraani Devi, Gram Pradhan from U.P.*, from Seminar, 514, p. 48.
25. Jain, Devaki: *Panchayati Raj: Women changing Governance*, p. 8.
26. *Ibid.*
27. Poornima and Vinod Vyasulu: *Women in Panchayati Raj: Grassroots Democracy in India*, p. 16.

28. Aalochana report, cited by Kumud Sharma: *Transformative Politics: Dimensions of Women's Participation in Panchayati Raj*, p. 39.

REFERENCES

Amitabh, Behar, Yamini Aiyar: 'Networks of Panchayat Women: Civil society space for political action' from *Economic and Political Weekly*, November 22, 2003.

Basu, D.D.: *Introduction to the Constitution of India*, New Delhi, Prentice Hall: 1994.

Bharat, Dogra: Women make a remarkable Contribution, from *Mainstream*, June 21, 2003.

Devaki, Jain: *Panchayati Raj: Women Changing Governance*, Monograph Series from UNDP/BDP/SDG—Gender and Development Programme. Accessed from http://www.undp.org/gender/resources/mono_05.htm.

Gariyali, C.K.: *Inching Forward—Political Empowerment of Women in Commonwealth Countries*, Vetri Publishers: 2000.

Kumud, Sharma: 'Transformative Politics: Dimensions of Women's Participation in Panchayati Raj' from *Indian Journal of Gender Studies*, 5: 1, Sage Publications: 1998.

Leela, Kasturi: '*Pernicious or necessary?*', Discussion on Women's Reservation Bill, from *Indian Journal of Gender Studies*, 6:1 (1999) Sage Publications.

Mrinal, Pande: *India's nurseries of politics—political rise of women in India*, UNESCO Courier, June, 2000 Accessed from http://www.findarticles.com/p/articles/mi_m1310/is_2000_June/ai_63692788

Pandey, Sumana: *Women in Politics*, Rawat Publications: 1990.

Pateman, Carole: 'Democracy, freedom and special rights', from David Boucher and Paul Kelly (ed.): *Social Justice: From Hume to Walzer*, Routledge Publications: 1998.

Phillips, Anne.: *Engendering Democracy*, Pennsylvania State University Press: 1991.

Phillips, Anne: 'Must Feminists give up on Liberal Democracy', from *Democracy and Difference*, Polity Press: 1993.

Poornima and Vinod Vyasulu: *Women in Panchayati Raj: Grassroots Democracy in India*, Paper presented in 'Meeting on Women and Political Participation: 21st Century Challenges' org. by United Nations Development Programme, 24-26 March, 1999 New Delhi. Accessed from http://magnet.undp.org/events/gender/india/VYASULU3.htm.

Sahbhagi Shikshan Kendra: 'Interview with Jagraani Devi, Gram Pradhan from U.P.', from *Seminar*, 514, June 2002.

Saksena, Kiran (ed): *Women and Politics*, Gyan Publishing House: 2000.

Shilpa, Jain: *Redefining the Politics of Presence: Women in Panchayati Raj Institutions in Rajasthan and Kerala*, Online Article Accessed from http://www.swaraj.org/shikshantar/papers_politics_presence.html.

Young, Iris Marion: 'Representation and Social Perspective' from *Inclusion and Democracy*, (chapter 4), Oxford University Press: 2000.

4

EWRs' Representation, Responsiveness and Accountability in Grassroots Governance

K.S. Nakkeeran

Introduction

The process of decentralization has gained momentum during the past fifteen years, mostly in the developing countries. This new institutional mechanism was adopted due to extreme political pressure on the central system of governance with the expectation of proper delivery of services, effective mobilization of resources and allocations, and stability in the macro economic system along with equity.

The decentralization process is expected to bring about changes in these conditions and the passing of the 73rd Constitutional Amendment Act is a landmark towards this end. The establishment of rural local governance as a self-governing institution has been effected through this Act. The highlight of this Act is the provision of reservation of seats for women by which one million women have come to power at the grassroots and became critical mass to perform a critical function. Contemporal theories and studies suggest that women are capable of bringing changes in the governance system. This study therefore aims at understanding how far this assessment holds good in the rural India. As an empirical exercise it highlights the representation, responsiveness and accountability of women in local governance.

Statement of the Problem

The 73rd Constitutional Amendment providing for not less than one-third of the reservation to women in all the rural local self-government institutions (Panchayati Raj Institutions) is considered as an attainment towards political empowerment of women.[1] The 73rd Constitutional Amendment Act aims at bringing about good governance in rural local bodies by paving the way for participatory, accountable, responsive and transparent administration. Through passing this amendment an exclusive space has been created for women at the grassroots to work with the community, which is totally engrossed in the local feudal hierarchical social system and patriarchy.[2] The aim of this Act undoubtedly is the ideal situation the country envisages to reach. But, in practice, the responsiveness and accountability have to be tested in our plural society. Hence this study attempts to evaluate representation, responsiveness and accountability of Elected Women Representatives (EWRs) in local governance adopting Pitkin's Theory of Representation.

Pitkin's Theory of Representation

Hanna Fenichel Pitkin, has proposed theory of representation. According to Pitkin, there are four kinds of representation. They are formal representation, descriptive representation, symbolic representation and substantive representation. Based on these four theories concerning the concept of representation, theories to explain the actions of elected officials have emerged. Pitkin argues that one must know the context in which the concept of representation is placed in order to determine its meaning.

Formal Representation: According to Pitkin, the first major dimension of representation is formal representation. It addresses the relation between the representative and the represented abstractly. The emphasis is on two aspects. First, whether those represented authorize the representative to act for them, second, whether the representatives are accountable to those whom they represent. Pitkin gives an example of a pure "authorization" theorist, Hobbes, for whom a contact between citizens and government leaders empowers the latter to govern as they see fit.

Descriptive Representation: For Pitkin, descriptive representation is associated with plural institutions and their operations. An institution is an organization designed to achieve a specific social end. Political representation, she says, is primarily a public, institutionalized arrangement involving many people and groups, and operating in complex ways of large scale social arrangements. A descriptive definition of political representation also looks at the social and demographic characteristics of the people inside representative institutions.

Symbolic Representation: Symbolic representation focuses attention on the psychological impact that representative institutions and their leaders have on the people. Pitkin argues that a Legislature, like a flag or a parade, is a psychologically pleasing condensation symbol. Symbolic representation, however, entails more than a passive process of psychological integration. The basis of symbolic representation is the power that a representative leader has over the people. This power derives from the people's attachment of their irrational beliefs and the deepest emotions on to public objects, such as the leaders of representative institutions. According to Pitkin, a leader uses his/her power to shape people's belief systems so that he/she gets their support by making them want what he/she wants. Through symbol manipulation, he/she creates a "larger than life" personality that draws attention. He/she invites people to attach their hopes, fears, aspirations, and allegiance on to his/her public image.

Substantive Representation: Substantive representation means that representative institutions can claim a legal or a moral right to pursue independently their trustees' interests. Political representation has a substantive dimension because it embodies "trusteeship". For Pitkin, trusteeship refers to "the substantive acting for others: but she abandons the traditional explanations of substantive representation. She finds that the analogies of an individual acting as an agent or a trustee of his/her constituents" interests are inconsistent with practice. A democratic government, to justify its substantive representativeness claim, must have "Potential responsiveness". Potential responsiveness means that the governed get their way (control the government) when they have an explicit will.

Among the above-mentioned views of representation, symbolic and substantive representations are selected for the present study. Symbolic representation provides a platform to analyze the representation of reservation groups in local governance. Substantive representation analyses the method of response of the elected representatives in the decision making process at the Panchayat level.

The other two forms of representation were not studied as they are not applicable to the local government.

Objectives

The important objectives of the study are:

1. To study the process of representation of the elected women representatives.
2. To study the responsiveness of the elected women representatives.
3. To study the accountability of the elected women representatives.

Hypotheses

The following hypotheses are examined in the present study:

1. The higher the level of representation of the people, the higher will be the representation of the EWRs to higher decision making bodies.
2. The higher the level of representation of EWRs, the higher will be the responsiveness.
3. The higher the level of representation of EWRs, the higher will be the accountability.

Sample Selection

The universe of the present study, comprising 134 women Village Panchayat Presidents of Salem District, was divided into three segments for the purpose of adopting stratified random sampling technique. These segments were: (i) General (Women), (ii) Scheduled Castes (Women), and (iii) Scheduled Tribes (Women). Out of these three segments, census method was adopted for the 2nd and 3rd segments due to their negligible sizes (31 Women Panchayat Presidents). Out of the remaining 103 General Women Panchayat Presidents, 50 per cent (52 General women) of the Panchayat Presidents were selected for the study by adopting the simple random sampling technique. So *in toto* 83 Women Panchayat Presidents were taken as sample for the study.

Tools for Data Collection

Data were collected from the selected sample women Village Panchayat Presidents of Salem District. An interview schedule was prepared to collect data from the representatives. The interview schedule covered question on (i) profile; (ii) views about representation of people; (iii) mode of representation; (iv) responsiveness; and (v) accountability.

Scoring and Analytical Technique

This study has its focus on four variables, namely: (i) representation of the people; (ii) representation of EWRs; (iii) responsiveness of EWRs; and (iv) accountability of EWRs.

In order to assess and study these qualitative aspects, indicators are fixed for each variable. For collecting sufficient data in respect of each indicator a set of questions were framed. The answers to such questions are measured buy adopting a two unit scale (0,1) to four unit scale (0, 1, 2, 3) as per the choice of the respondents. Linear regression method was used to test the hypotheses.

Delimitation

Local governance includes both urban and rural local governance. This study focuses on rural local governance, which has three tiers, viz. Village Panchayat, Block Panchayat and District Panchayat. But this study has been carried out among the EWRs of village panchayats only. This study was carried out in Salem District of Tamil Nadu. Salem District was chosen because the number of ST Presidents is more in this district, providing scope for symbolic representation.

Representation in Local Governance

Representation is taken to mean "a relation between two persons, the representative and the represented or constituent with the representative holding the authority to perform various actions that incorporate the agreement of the represented."[3]

The role of representation is multifaceted. Often, it is described as the range of expectations that people possess regarding the government and hence related to public officials and leaders. Edmund Burke considered the representative as "one who ought to respect his constituents opinions, who ought to prefer their interest above his own, but who ought not to sacrifice his unbiased opinion in deciding for the good of the whole nation."[4]

Pitkin also regards representation as "an action in the interests of the represented, in a manner responsive to them."[5] Accordingly, representatives can be considered "trustees" who can act according to their free judgment for the good of the whole nation.

Sartori discusses representation in terms of three quite different meanings: first, "the idea of mandate or instructions"; second, "the idea of representativeness", that is resemblance and similarity; third "the idea of responsibility or accountability."[6]

A person's claim to be a representative depends upon what she or he represents. Viewed from this point, one can find four different entities that are to be represented; identities, beliefs, constituencies and interests.[7] Representation is a concept of social interest largely in the context of power relations among leaders or representatives and their followers or constituents.

Corresponding to the above views, the concept of representation can be seen in three different senses. First, it can be just the articulation of the views of the constituents. Second, it can be a reflection of views of people of the Constituency but influenced by the representative's own judgment. Third, it can be entirely the judgment of the representatives without any relation to what the people of the constituency think or expect.

The role of representatives is closely associated with the idea of participation. Their interaction with constituents and the overall participatory nature of the functioning of the Panchayat need to be taken into account while assessing the levels of representation and the accountability of representatives.

Table 4.1: Categorization of Members' Representation in Gram Sabha

Details	*No. of Respondents*	
	Number	*Percentage*
Women	83	100
Representative of women groups	83	100
Ward Members	83	100
SC/ST	83	100
Other caste Hindus	83	100

Source: Computed from field data.

The Gram Sabha is a common body where every eligible voter has equal rights. It has universal membership. As such, men and women of different age groups belonging to different religions and castes as well as interest groups attend the Gram Sabha to express their grievances and demands.

The EWRs under study reported that the Gram Sabha had women group representative, Ward Members, members from different caste groups in almost all the meetings conducted in the past.

The Gram Sabha serves as a forum for representing the needs of the people to the representatives—not only individual needs but also collective needs. Collective representation raises the voice of the people. Further, they can serve as a pressure group which in turn increases the responsiveness of the representatives. Collective representation is done through groups such as women's group, and SC/ST group. Their representations serve as Symbolic representation. It gives Psychological integration to the group they belong to.

Table 4.2: Rating of Participation of Different Sections of the Community

Rating	*No. of Respondents*					
	Women		*SC/ST*		*Others*	
	Number	%	Number	%	Number	%
Very good	37	45.0	12	14.0	46	55.0
Good	40	48.0	48	58.0	18	22.0
Poor	06	7.0	15	18.0	12	14.0
Very poor	—	—	8	10.0	7	9.0
Total	83	100	83	100	83	100

Source: Computed from field data.

Table 4.2 shows the rating done by EWRs regarding the participation of different sections of the community in the Gram Sabha. About 48 per cent of the respondents rated the participation of the women as good followed by 45 per cent respondents who rated it as very good.

With regard to the representation of the SC/ST members, in the view of the Presidents, 58 per cent respondents rated their participation as 'good' followed by 14 per cent respondents as 'very good'. The participation and representation of other members, i.e. other than SC/ST and women, was rated as very good by over 55 per cent respondents followed by 22 per cent respondents who rated it as good.

Table 4.3: Mode of Representation of Ward Members to the Panchayat Presidents

Mode of Representation	*No. of Respondents*	*Percentage*
During the Panchayat meeting and in the Gram Sabha	83	100.0
Through petitions	45	54.0
Orally as and when they meet	74	89.0

Source: Computed from field data.

In the village Panchayat meetings, the ward members participate and represent the needs of the people to the Panchayat Presidents. Also the ward members make suggestions for the development of the village. Village Panchayat meetings are conducted once in fifteen days. All the representations of the ward members irrespective of the political affiliation are discussed and solutions are found by consulting the government officers. 45 (54%) Panchayat Presidents said that ward members are giving written representation. The complaints of the ward members are scrutinized and necessary steps are taken to solve the problems. 74 (89%) Panchayat Presidents said that they have received oral complaints from the ward members. The complaints are mostly on drinking water, drainage problems, street lights, motor repair etc.

Table 4.4: EWRs' Representation to Higher Authorities

S. No.	*Authorities*	*Number of Respondents*	*Percentage*
1.	P.U. Councillor	70	84.0
2.	P.U. Chairman	65	78.0
3.	D.P. Councillor	83	100.0
4.	D.P. President	83	100.0
5.	M.L.A.	75	90.0
6.	M.P.	75	90.0

Source: Computed from field data.

As seen in Table 4.4 70 (84%) EWRs said that they represented the problems of the village to the Panchayat Union Councillors. They said that they met the Panchayat Union Councillors for fulfilling the demands of the people. The village Panchayat Presidents' representations to the Panchayat Union Councillors were concerned with the use of village Development fund, and implementation of Central and State Government schemes in their villages.

This shows that the mobility of elected women representatives has increased when they represented the needs of the people to higher authorities. In rural setting, the mobility of women is restricted due to socio-cultural norms and these elected women representatives have broken the prevailing social practices in order to bring more responsible administration. This also indicates their way towards getting empowered.

Table 4.5: EWRs' Representation to Government Officials

S. No.	*Officials*	*No. of Respondents*	*Percentage*
1.	Block Development Officer	83	100.0
2.	Project Officer	83	100.0
3.	Revenue Officer	83	100.0
4.	Tahsildar	83	100.0
5.	District Collector	83	100.0
6.	Other Officials	83	100.0

Source: Computed from field data.

As shown in Table 4.5, all EWRs said that they have met the government officers and represented their demands regarding the basic needs of the villages. All the EWRs stated that they met the Block Development Officer, the Project Officer, the Tahsildar, the Revenue Officer, the Extension Officer and the District Collector seeking funding and assistance for development works to fulfil the needs of their village.

All the EWRs reported that the Village Presidents meeting is conducted twice a month. The meeting is presided over by the District Collector. The progress of development works and the funds position are appraised.

The Directorate of Rural Development has issued an order (No. 45387/2002 dated 20.5.2002) stating that the District Collector shall meet the Village Panchayat Presidents every month at least once to discuss the problems faced by them. This serves them as a forum to represent their demands and express their grievances. Moreover, the meeting of Village Panchayat Presidents is also held once in every month at the Block level. The Block Development Officer and the Extension Officers participate in the meeting. This meeting also gives an opportunity to the Panchayat Presidents to make substantive representation to the officers regarding the demands of the people.

Responsiveness of Elected Women Representatives

Responsiveness in democratic set up means acting in the interests of the people and considering their priorities and needs with the required attention. The Presidents, as elected representatives, have to act in a responsive manner to fulfil the desires/choices of the majority. When the authorities make decisions regarding the common issues on behalf of the people, the decisions should respect the will and desires of those people. This authority to decide also makes them responsible to deliver the goods. That is both making of decisions on various subjects in the interests of the people and the execution of the decisions so taken depend on the awareness and understanding of the Presidents of their duties and responsibilities as people's representatives.

The Village Panchayat Presidents are vested with the powers to fulfil the needs of the people at the Village Panchayat level. Therefore, it becomes the duty of the Village Panchayat Presidents to act in the interests of the people and to redress the grievances of the people.

Table 4.6: Responsiveness of the EWRs

S. No	*Details*	*No. of Respondents*	*Percentage*
1.	Responding to the complaints of the women/SC/ST people	83	100.0
2.	Responding to the appeal of the people in Gram Sabha	83	100.0
3.	Taking decisions in Panchayat Council Meetings	70	84.00
4.	Immediate solution to the Complaints	83	100.0
5.	Utilization of Central and State Governments	83	100.0
6.	Allocation of funds from Central and State Governments	83	100.0
7.	Fulfilling the needs of the people	83	100.0
8.	Information to the people about the decisions	83	100.0
9.	Information to the people about the welfare plans	83	100.0

Source: Computed from field data.

The 73rd Constitutional Amendment Act has given the right to SC/ST and women to participate in the meeting of the Gram Sabha. All the people, including women and SC/STs are given the right and the liberty to represent their views and suggestions in the Gram Saba.

As shown in Table 4.6, in the opinion of the EWRs, women and SC and ST people were given opportunity to make representations. The Presidents and the Ward Members concerned answered such representations with facts and figures.

The Gram Sabha is an organization which consists of all the voters of a village.[8] The 73rd Constitutional Amendment Act has given rights to men and women to participate and discuss the problems and development issues in the Gram Sabha. People make their representations in the Gram Sabha. The representatives have the duty of answering the questions and accordingly, Panchayat Presidents answer properly and actions are taken to rectify the grievances of the people and they are of the opinion that representations are being answered without any favour and bias based on party affiliation. The term "decision" means the act of determining in one's mind upon an opinion or course of action.[9] It is choosing an alternatives from among the several alternatives given in a particular situation. 70 (84%) Panchayat Presidents said that decision making power rests with the Panchayat Presidents. They have the right to take decisions at the Panchayat meeting itself in all matters assigned as subjects under the purview of the Panchayats.

Elected women representatives felt that it is not possible to take immediate decisions on all the representations due to some practical and strategic difficulties. To initiate actions on some issues they have to depend on the government for the approval and release of funds, it took time for them to do the needful on each of the representations. But, these elected women representatives ware conscious of their action and they inform the steps taken then and there to the people.

The Village Panchayats get revenue through taxes, fees and grants from the Central and State Governments.[10] All the Panchayat Presidents informed the people about the funds received from the State Government in the Gram Sabha. All the EWRs said that invariably the fund allotted by the governments for the development works has been a hot subject of discussion both in the Gram Sabha and in the Panchayat meetings.

EWRs also said that, for the implementation of development plans and programmes, approval and financial assistance from the government are important. If these two are granted at the earliest, they can carry out the works to the fullest satisfaction of the people. If the government allots the funds timely, the basic requirements like drinking water, road facility, street light, sanitary conditions can be completed at the earliest.

Accountability of Elected Women Representatives

Accountability involves a relationship between the bearer of a right of legitimate claim and the agents or agencies responsible for fulfilling that right.[11] Public accountability is considered to be an important feature of democratic government, wherein the elected representatives and the public officials are expected to remain accountable to the citizenry at large. In a democratic political system, accountability generates good governance and, at least in theory, it is considered important in getting optimal performance from elected representatives and the public departments.[12] Blair observes that democratic governance at both the national and the local levels can succeed if government employees (bureaucrats and public officials) and the elected representatives are accountable to the public. While in a governing system the elected representatives remain (or should remain) directly accountable to the people, the bureaucrats do so indirectly by being answerable to the representatives. Thus, the system becomes accountable to the people.

Lederman identified three main factors to determine the degree of accountability in a political system. These are degree of competition in the political system, the check and balance mechanism of government and the transparency of the system.[13] The checks and balances mechanism of a government, along with the separation of power into different bodies, works towards ensuring accountability, where different agencies of the government control each other in the citizen's favour.

The checks and balances mechanism during policy formulation and implementation requires that policy choices should not be restricted to governing Members, but extended to the opposition, affected parties and groups and individuals who can offer special knowledge.[14]

Accountability in Panchayats involves a relationship between the citizens and the elected representatives, which is strengthened by frequent interaction and communication between them. One of the important ways by which the representatives can be made accountable to the constituent is encouraging deliberations over the issues affecting the citizens, engaging in consultation and providing explanations on the decisions taken.[15] Public deliberations over issues of common concern involve exchange of ideas, values, proposals and reasons aimed at evaluating alternative courses of action to be undertaken by the representatives.[16] Other mechanisms to ensure accountability in democratic local governance are competition, existence of checks and balances, transparency, answering and controllability.[17]

Table 4.7: Accountability of EWRs

S. No	Details	No. of Respondents	Percentage
1.	Maintaining Records	83	100.0
2.	Financial Administration	83	100.0
3.	Transparency in Administration	68	82.0
4.	Displaying on the notice board	83	100.0
5.	Supervision of work	83	100.0
6.	Service provided to the people		
	— Drinking water	83	100.0
	— Road	68	82.0
	— Street light	67	81.0
	— Drainage	69	83.0
	— Toilet	59	71.0
7.	Successful Implementation of Government Schemes (SGRY-I,	83	100.0
	SGRY-II, Namathu Gramam) IAY)	69	83.0

Source: Computed from field data.

The Village Panchayat should maintain fund account, Village Panchayat earmarked grants account, Village Panchayat scheme fund account and Village Panchayat drinking water account. All the EWRs under study reported that their Panchayats are maintaining these records properly. These records, letters and accounts are under the safe keeping of the Panchayat Presidents.

The administration of Village Panchayat is not an easy task as the President has to maintain thirty-one records. These records will be verified by the officials at the block level and district level. These records are also subject to local fund audit. Women being naive to sternum procedures like this face lots of problems in this record. The respondents of this study reported that they put great efforts to maintain these records properly and they are always kept open for the perusal of the general public.

Finance is the main requirement for any development plan of a Village Panchayat. Village Panchayats can have the following accounts in the branches of Nationalized Banks/Post Office located within the Panchayat or in the nearby villages. Village Panchayat fund account, earmarked fund account, scheme fund accounts, earmarked drinking water account. All the Village Panchayat Presidents informed that the Panchayat got income from housing tax, professional tax, tax levied on TV and cable services, tax on cultivating land, miscellaneous taxes levied by the Panchayat.

The EWRs stated that they used the grants from the Central and the State Governments for the development of the people. The grants have been used for cleaning tanks, school buildings and toilets and maintaining colonies with SGRY-II, laying concrete roads and cement roads and cleaning public wells. Transparent administration is essential to discuss the village administrative activities openly in the presence of the elected and the people.

These women representatives have taken measures to display the activities of the Panchayat in the notice board. Full details of the village have been displayed including the infrastructure work carried out during the particular financial year. These are the ways through which the elected women representatives try to provide transparent and accountable administration at the local panchayat level.

The Panchayat President is the political executive of Village Panchayat. The Panchayat President is empowered to look after the basic needs of the Panchayat. All EWRs stated that their village Panchayats have drinking water facilities in all wards. 68 (82%) EWRs stated that they have made complete arrangements for road facility. They also have established metal road, cement road, etc. 67 (81%) EWRs reported that they have made complete arrangements for street lights in all the wards. 69 (83%) EWRs stated that they have arranged proper and enough drainage facilities. 59 (71%) EWRs reported that their Village Panchayat have enough toilet facilities. Under the health scheme, all the Wards are having both public as well as private toilets.

All EWRs said that they have established school toilets, cement road and other basic facilities under the SGRY-I scheme. They also said that under the SGRY-II scheme they have constructed common building for the society, Threshing floor, drainage facilities, toilet facilities, building for Self-Help Groups, small bridges etc. All EWRs said that the 'Namadhu Gramam' scheme is functioning in all the Panchayats. 69 (83%) EWRs said that under IAY scheme group houses are constructed for the people living below poverty line, including SC/ST peoples.

Integrated Analysis

Based on Pitkin's theoretical framework, the study is devised to correlate: (i) the representation of representatives in response to peoples' representation; (ii) the representation of representatives and their responsiveness; and (iii) the representation of representatives and their accountability. The hypotheses based on the above correlations are tested by using linear regression.

In the decentralized local power system, representation emerges from the base, that is, from the people. The people present their appeals to the President and also to the Ward Members either through petition or by direct contact. People also place their grievances or queries in the Gram Sabha. The weight of the people's appeals varies, depending upon the types of groups, such as women, SC, ST, and so on.

The success of people's representation is dependent on the representation of the Village Panchayat Presidents because they can solve the people's problems only by representing them to the higher level bodies and authorities (Panchayat Union Councillor, Panchayat Union Chairman, District Panchayat Councillor, and District Panchayat President and Government officers of various departments) by meeting them directly. The Presidents also meet the MLA and the MP whenever there is a need in connection with the development of the Village Panchayat.

The first hypothesis, stating that the higher the level of representation of the people, the higher will be the representation of EWRs to higher decision bodies is tested using linear regression analysis. The regression equation to test this hypothesis is of the form given by:

$$y = 35.83 + 0.761x$$
$$r^2 = 0.7131$$

where

y stands for the representation of the EWRs
x stands for the representation of the people.

That is, there is a positive correlation between the level of representation of the people and the level of representation of the representatives to higher decision making bodies.

The success of grassroots governance is based on the responsiveness of the representatives. The Village Panchayat President is empowered to fulfil the needs of the people at the village level and to redress the grievances of the people. Further, it is the moral responsibility of the Panchayat Presidents to answer the queries raised by the people.

The people represent their demands and needs to the Panchayat President. The Village Panchayat President, in turn, has the sole responsibility of explaining and also convincing the people about the action taken regarding their demands. In addition, any decision taken by the President should fulfil the needs and demands of the people.

The duty of the Village Panchayat President is to place the problems of the people before the higher bodies and authorities. Another responsibility of the President is seeing that funds received from Central and State Governments are utilized for fulfilling the needs of the people.

The second hypothesis, the higher the level of representation of EWRs, the higher will be the responsiveness, is examined by employing the same tool. The regression equation is:

$$y = 60.25 + 0.65x$$
$$r^2 = 0.4712$$

where

y stands for the responsiveness of the EWRs.
x stands for the representation of the EWRs.

The result shows that there is a positive correlation between the level of representation of the representatives and their responsiveness.

The accountability of the representatives is another important aspect of grassroots governance. Accountability in the Panchayat mainly stresses the mutual cooperation and the evolving relationship between the people and the elected representatives. The relationship is accentuated by frequent interaction with freedom, openness and sharing of thoughts through concrete dialogue.

One of the competent approaches to instil accountability in the constituent is providing a platform for deliberately discussing the issues that really expose and entertain the feelings and the needs of the people. This process of realizing accountability is engaging them in consultations and providing explanation, which pave way for a fruitful decision making process. Another factor ensuring accountability in democratic local governance is the maintenance of mutual trust, transparency and controllability.

The third hypothesis, the higher the level of representation of EWRs, the higher will be the accountability, is put to test by using linear regression analysis. The obtained equation is:

$$y = 24.758 + 0.825x$$
$$r^2 = 0.35$$

where

y stands for the accountability of the EWRs
x stands for the representation of the EWRs.

The result shows that there is a positive correlation between the level of representation of representatives and their accountability.

In the present study, three hypotheses are formulated and tested. The results prove that the representation of the people as a variable is found positively correlated with representation of the EWRs. In other words, representation of the people as a variable increases the level of the representation of the EWRs. This study reflects significantly the representation of the EWRs as a variable is affecting the responsiveness and accountability of the EWRs.

The quantum of variations obtained while testing the hypotheses are in the order of 71 per cent, 47 per cent and 35 per cent variations respectively. All these variations are on a positive scaling, though the decrement of variations obtained for the second and the third hypotheses suggest that improvements in these variables are desirable.

A conceptual framework is evolved based on the findings of the study and also Pitkin's Theory of Representation. Pitkin's theory is suitably adapted to local governance. Consequently, it is identified that symbolic representation and substantive representation are the only viable factors in Indian local governance. The concepts and their mutual relationships are schematically presented in Figure 4.1.

A synthesis of the influence of the representation of the people on the representation of the EWRs, which compounds responsiveness and accountability, is visualized. This conceptual framework will lead to further studies on representation, responsiveness and accountability in local governance.

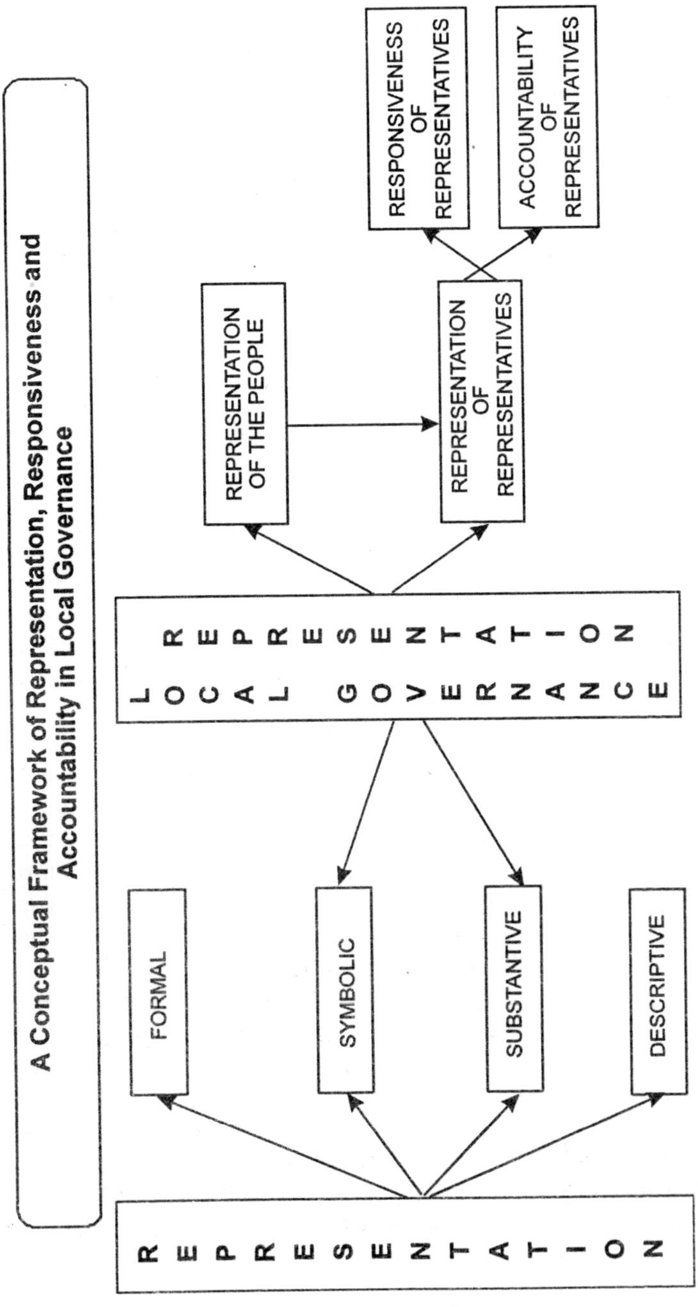

Fig. 4.1: A Conceptual Framework of Representation, Responsiveness and Accountability in Local Governance

Conclusion

The 73rd Constitutional Amendment Act has been seen as the major amendment which enabled forming of the critical mass among women in the local bodies. Several studies have shown that these women have showed their responsiveness and accountability in spite of the drawbacks and problems they face from the society. From this study it can be understood that women can bring upon Responsive and Accountable local governance through becoming critical mass in representing the problems and issues of the people. A woman in political sphere faces lot of problems from the patriarchal and hierarchical social structure, but they do not while away their responsibility. If their performance is recognized in the polity and the society and if the problems confronting them are curtailed and solved, the spirit of decentralization of power will become a reality.

NOTES

1. Suguna, B, "Strategies for Empowerment of Rural Women", *Social Welfare,* Vol. 49, August 2002, p. 6.
2. Palanithurai, G., *Women in Governance at Grassroots*, Gandhigram: Rajiv Gandhi Chair for Panchayati Raj Studies, 2004, p. 5.
3. Grazia, Ade, "Representation: Theory", in *International Encyclopedia of Social Science,* New York: Macmillan, 1968, pp. 461-465.
4. Burke, E., "Speech to the Electors of Bristol", *The Works of the Right Honourable Edmund Burke,* Vol. 2, Boston: Little Brown, 1774.
5. Pitkin, Hanna Fenichel, *The Concept of Representation*, Los Angeles: University of California Press, 1972, pp. 209-210.
6. Sartori, G., "Representational System", in *International Encyclopedia of Social Sciences, op. cit.*, pp. 465-474.
7. Squires, J, "Rethinking the Boundaries of Political Representation", in Sylvia Walby (ed.,) *New Agendas for Women,* London: Macmillan, 1999, p. 178.
8. Mehta, H.S., "The Constitutional Legal Perspective on Panchayat Raj", in R.P. Joshi (ed.,) *Constitutionalization of Panchayati Raj: A Reassessment,* New Delhi: Rawat Publications, 1998, p. 87.
9. Prasad, R.N., *Governance of India: Issues and Perspectives*, New Delhi: Concept Publishing Company, 2002, p. 112.
10. Joshi, R.P. and Narwani, G.S., *Panchayat Raj in India: Emerging Trends Across the States,* New Delhi: Rawat Publications, 2002, p. 101.

11. Gloppen, S., Ranker, L. and Tostensen, A., "Responsiveness to the Concerns of the Poor and Accountability to the Commitment to Poverty Reduction", *Working Paper* 2003; 9, Norway: Chr Michelsen Institute, 2003.
12. Moncrieffe, J.M., "Accountability: Idea, Ideals, Constraints, Democratization", *International Political Science Review*, Vol. 8 (3), 2001, pp. 26-50.
13. Lederman, D., Loayza, N. and Soares, R.R., "Accountability and Corruption: Political Institutions Matter", *World Bank Working Paper no. 2708*, Washington, DC: World Bank, 2001.
14. J.M. Moncrieffe, *op. cit.*
15. *Ibid.*
16. Hunold, C., "Corporatism, Pluralism and Democracy towards a Deliberative Theory of Bureaucratic Accountability Governance", *International Journal of Policy and Administration,* Vol. 14, pp. 151-67.
17. Lederman, D., Loayza, N. and Soares, R.R., *Op. cit.*

5

Gendered Citizenship for Deepening Local Democracy: A Study of Ten Villages in Maharashtra

Manjula Bharathy

In a landmark move in April 1993, the 73rd Amendment to the Constitution of India directed that one-third of the total number of seats in all panchayats be reserved for women. By 1995, states across the nation had implemented requisite changes and the presence of women in local government or Panchayati Raj Institutions (PRI) increased manifold. Close to a decade and half since, this chapter documents women's perspectives on the implications of such change spanning over ten villages across four regions in Maharashtra. (Vidarbha, Konkan, Western Maharashtra and Amravati).

The history of social reform for women and the women's movement in Maharashtra is closely linked with the political and social reform which began in the late 19th century. Emerging from the enlightened and 'benign' shadows of their husbands, the wives of many progressive Brahmin reformers went on to carve deep inroads into the centuries-old, rock-solid base of patriarchy in Maharashtra. While men's socio-cultural initiatives and agitations for political autonomy were in the public gaze and well documented, women's socio-cultural interventions were considered more private and 'domestic', and were, therefore, marginalized. Maharashtra's men have been visible and active in the field of nationwide social reform since the 1800s, but the state's many women reformers remain relatively unknown outside of Maharashtra and sometimes even within it.

One of the enduring contributions of women's activism and feminist theorizing is the challenging of the definitive political boundaries between public and private politics. Feminists argued that public political life was built on the absence of women from it, that the exclusion of the private sphere was essential for the primacy of the public. By expanding the definition of politics to encompass both the public and private spheres—indeed by asserting that these two are mutually constitutive—feminists have challenged the dominant understanding of the politics itself, and therefore of democratic practices and discourse. It is from this understanding of political boundaries that we need to position the politics of absence of women at the micro and macro levels.

For this, having asserted the need for representational governance is not enough. One also needs to understand the role of the representative in representing her community. The role of representatives in governance is of great significance because it is not confined to raising issues. More importantly, they engage in the politics around the issues. Representatives are not only expected to articulate issues of local concern, but are part of the formation of a political discourse. Thus, representatives play an important role in determining the nature of governance in a structure. In a governance system that is dominated by upper class and upper caste men, issues of mass concern will be interpreted through a hegemonic lens. The resulting political structure will, accordingly, be highly unequal. It is obvious that the discourse of equality in conditions of inequality only results in deepening inequality. Most of history is a thing of the past invisible to us, as written history is that of the privileged. The argument for reservation is that it is positive discrimination for historical correctives seeking to subvert regressive structures.

Women's Reservation and Politics of Presence

There are two important aspects of a woman's invisibility, and her negotiation with her invisibility. One is her invisibility to the public eye, and the second is her invisibility to herself, thus speaking volumes of the 'phenomenology of absences'. Women's reservation in the context of 'phenomenology of absences' is an issue that has since the earliest days of its conceptualization excited deeply divided opinion, as much on grounds of ethics as around form. As early as 1931, Sarojini Naidu and Muthulakshmi Reddy in a letter to the British

Prime Minister refused 'preferential treatment', stating (in an accompanying declaration), "we look upon nominations, reservation of seats, and the co-option in any sphere of activity as a pernicious and humiliating system which must run counter to any real progress" (cited in Dhanda, 2008). In more recent times, Vina Mazumdar, Member Secretary of the Committee on the Status of Women in India (CSWI) admitted that as 'daughters of independence', her generation had been skeptical of special representation but gradually 'found our understanding of nation-building changing radically'(Mazumdar, 1997).

Arguments for the reservation for women fall broadly into two categories. First, reservation for women can be seen to ensure a higher level of gender justice. Thus, for representation to be meaningful, female representation in governance should be proportional to the population of women in society. Further, if women are seen as an interest group, their interests can be represented only by ensuring that more women participate in governance. It is also argued that quotas are needed to compensate women for the social barriers historically imposed upon them within a patriarchal structure, which result in their unequal participation in comparison to men. Another line of argument for reservation is based on the assumption that since women go through different processes of socialization, their role in governance will be markedly different from that of their male counterparts.

The argument against reservation is that women representatives elected through reservation can end up only as token representatives, who are actually represented by their husbands. The question of proxy governance is a serious issue and has been observed in the course of this study. This has to be seen in the context of the hierarchical division of labour within the family and the lack of women's access to education or control over resources. However, the argument that we want to stress on is that empowerment is not a one-step event. On the contrary, it is a long process, often accompanied by violent backlash. A woman is not singularly 'empowered' when she is elected representative. That is just a step in facilitating the further assertion of her agency in a patriarchal system. Reservation can act as a potentially powerful tool of redistribution, not only of economic resources but also of political spaces that have been dominated traditionally by the upper class, upper caste men in patriarchal governance systems.

Any attempt to understand reservation for women would be incomplete without touching upon the theoretical contribution of Anne Phillips, whose work on the subject has been reflected, debated or contested in almost every paper on the subject. Phillips has a fairly straightforward case. There are particular needs, interests and concerns that arise from women's experience and this will be inadequately addressed in a politics that is dominated by men. While women may find a few powerful allies among men, they cannot really expect, as she puts it, 'the degree of vigorous advocacy that people bring to their own concerns' (Phillips, 1995). Phillips terms this a shift from a 'politics of ideas to a politics of presence'. The politics of ideas suggests 'a broadly secular understanding of politics as a matter of judgment and debate, and expects political loyalties to develop around policies rather than people'. A politics of presence on the other hand, privileges the question of 'who' rather than 'what' and demands equal representation of women, ethnic minorities, and other groups that see themselves as excluded (Phillips 1995).

The politics of presence has had predictable criticism. Louise Vincent (2004) for instance paints a cynical picture of the real use of quotas based on the South African experience. Vincent maintains that the improved presence of women in South Africa's National Legislature due to the African National Congress's quota has done little more than advance the careers of a select group of already well educated, politically highly well-connected women (Vincent, 2004). Philips acknowledges the possibility of failure to know particular women's interests, perhaps even more likely in India where a single constituency may be sharply divided along caste-class-ethnic lines. 'Changing the gender composition of elected assemblies is largely an enabling condition (a crucially important one, considering what is disabled at present), but it cannot present itself as a guarantee' (Phillips, 1995). Nevertheless, with or without 'guarantee of good intent', as Phillips puts it, discourse on quotas for women at least in India, is no longer grappling with questions of its desirability. The terrain of debate, both academic and political, is quite clearly around its possible form and details, and its likely ramifications for women as well as for governance in general.

When one tries to understand the 'politics of presence' of women at PRIs and the ways in which they negotiate with the hegemonic power centres in Maharashtra, caste structures are an explicit factor, which when coupled with gender, give a montage effect (Eisenstein,

1923) and not a cumulative one. This montage effect, which we could discern and decipher from the empirical data, tells us that 1+1 is neither equal to two nor does it have any character of one, it is different from both.[1]

Nakoshis (Unwanted) and Gender Discrimination at PRIs

There are certain core themes that recur in the otherwise diverse narratives of Elected Women Representatives (EWRs) whom we spoke to in Maharashtra. Predominant among these themes are those of caste, local administrative corruption, alcoholism/prohibition, domestic violence/repression, definition/reorganization of 'women's work', availability of and access to water, village infrastructure (toilets, roads etc.). Many or in fact most of these are (gendered) concerns they had had in their prior identities as daughters, wives, mothers, (caste) community members, citizens and so on.

Hegemonic notions of gender relations are often internalized by women, so that often even EWRs have similar notions of gender relations. Both Pratibha Tai (SC Panch, 33 years, Thatri village) and Mayawati Tai (SC Panch, 32 years, Vadval village) observed that women are blamed for all the problems related to having children, whether it is the inability to have any, or the 'misfortune' of having only girls. Mayawati Tai said that a woman who could not give birth to a son to carry on the family line was rebuked and treated badly by society. Most women reported that a woman who had not borne kids is neither allowed to hold the '*aarti*' at any function, nor is she allowed to participate in the baby showers celebrated during the seventh month of pregnancy. Beholding such a woman first thing in the morning was considered a bad omen.

The historicity of gender discrimination starts right from naming a child. Acts of precedence and popular mythical stories validate such notions of discrimination. It is disturbing to see how the ideology of gender is getting translated into day-to-day events and practices. For instance, in some cases, the discrimination begins in infancy, with the issue of the baby's primary identity, or its name. Jyoti Tai reported that the first two girls are given normal 'girl' names, but in some places, the third girl child in a family is usually given a boy's name like 'Kiran'. In other places, the third daughter is called 'Sarali', 'Sarita' or 'Sampathi'—all indicative of the hope that there will be no more girl children born to the family. If a fourth girl is born, she is named Shadu, Ambu or 'Nakoshi', the 'Unwanted'. Women bearing this name are still found in many villages. Often this name is not on the birth certificate and as the women grow up, they switch to another name. But the formative years of many girls' lives are spent being called 'Nakoshi'. 'Nakoshi' or 'Unwanted' girls are often treated badly at home and are discriminated against in matters of food and education. Preference for boys had its interesting ramifications at the Panchayat level, especially with the two-child norm.

The birth of a son is considered more important than anything else, including a Panchayat post. In Halkarni, for instance, the post of the Sarpanch was reserved for an OBC candidate in the 2000 Gram Panchayat elections. Shankar Vishnu Sutar, a teacher became the Sarpanch of Halkarni as a result of this reservation. His wife was also a teacher and they had two daughters. Within three-and-a-half years of becoming the Sarpanch, his wife gave birth to their third child, a boy. He said that losing the post was less important to him than having that child. Had it been a girl, he would have had it aborted, while he waited to complete his term. But when he knew it was a boy, he was willing to forego the Panchayat post in order to have the child.

Caste as the Principal Marker of Exclusion

We found that the women in the Panchayati Raj space in the villages of Maharashtra encounter certain issues and problems. These are problems that may differ from each other in their manifestations, but grow out of the central well-springs of caste and power equations. In the different villages of the four regions of Maharashtra, we see similar struggles which emerge when power and caste identity are placed in opposition to efficiency, sincerity and proactivity.

Caste-related mindsets and pollution practices are still a significant part of life in rural Maharashtra, and this is true even in spaces like the Panchayat, as many women reported during the FGDs. Jyoti Meshram reported that at weddings, people belonging to the SC community are served at the end. Sangeeta Waghmare (SC Sarpanch, 26 years, Mendsi village) says that tea is offered to SC women in broken cups which are kept separately. Water is mainly supplied to the centrally located village homes and not to Dalit settlements located on the outskirts. Earlier, upper caste women were so intolerant that they would not suffer the touch of even the tip of a

Dalit's saree when they went to fetch water. Mayawati Tai recalled an incident when she first came to her husband's village. One day, as she was fetching water, her hand accidentally brushed the water pot belonging to the Patil's wife. The Patil's wife rushed at her angrily and broke the pot because it had been 'contaminated'. She even asked Mayawati Tai to buy her a new one. Over the years, both Mayawati and Jyoti feel that this attitude has changed.

Caste-based discrimination and segregation begins early in most villages. The concepts of pollution and purity are indoctrinated into children at school itself. This finds different expressions. Rajani Tai (SC Panch, 36 years, Undil village) reported that OBC and SC children are seated separately on different mats. SC children are not allowed to sit on the mats designated for OBC children. There is a caste hierarchy followed in answering questions—even if an SC student knows an answer, s/he gets a turn only after an OBC child has replied.

Even today, caste would seem to be powerful marker of social identity and status in most regions surveyed in Maharashtra, recurring as it is in the narratives of individual respondents as well as in focus group discussions. In the present context, the interrelationship between caste and sex-based exploitation is significant in Maharashtra. However, the struggles by Dalit women have led to their increasing participation in the Panchayati Raj Institutions. Violence that is both casteist and sexist is used against Dalit women to control their mobility and participation. And this violence has multiple manifestations. Not only is the violence direct and upfront, but often the ownership of resources and the institution of the family itself can be a means to exercise a casteist, sexist and patriarchal form of violence. Men from the household of women contesting elections are accused of not being able to control their women and are asked to wear bangles.

For instance, Geeta (SC Panch, 34 years, Katri village) who spoke to this study in a focus group discussion recalls how she was asked to keep standing by other members as her husband was a peon in the Panchayat. Another EWR, Pratibha recounts how when a statue of the Dalit icon Babasaheb Ambedkar was to be erected in the chowk opposite her house, the proposal was refuted as people from all (upper) castes would pass the chowk. When the statue was being erected, 'others' threatened a repeat of the Khailranji incident.[2] Caste also appears as the predominant concern in the narratives of at least four (of a total of nine) EWRs interviewed in Maharashtra. The strength of caste structures in these regions is perhaps evinced best from the fact that despite holding elected positions of power in local Councils (at the Gram Panchayat/higher level), these women were subjugated to open discrimination and humiliation. Mayadevi recalls facing years of discrimination as a Dalit social/political worker in the village. When she and her (upper caste) colleagues would go to people's houses to meet women (to organize Self-Help Groups or SHGs), her tea cup was always kept separately.

Challenging the Caste

This section seeks to theorise how women's inclusion into the hitherto unavailable domain of 'formal politics' intersects, and often intervenes with their existing alternate identities and concerns. How do these women in new found locations of power in the public sphere challenge and negotiate with old power structures of caste, class and gender in their local contexts? How does such affirmative action alter the existing structures of governance? How do women's experiences as elected women representatives relate to existing discourses on gender and governance?

Though narratives of all respondents of this study across caste-class-ethnic identities portray evidence of such gendered stratification, we look more closely into the narratives of caste-oppressed women to understand how access to political power (via assisted entry into Panchayat Raj Institutions in Maharashtra) has played with their gender identities, and interestingly, therefore caste status.

For instance, take the case of Ratnamala (SC Panch, 46 years, Ganeshpur village), an ordinary Dalit, who when her mother-in-law developed a heart condition, was labelled a 'Pandharyapaychi', literally 'a woman with white feet' or a witch. Ratna stood for elections and won a (reserved category) seat in the Gram Panchayat. Her narration of an incident during her tenure as an EWR helps us understand exactly how gender, when brought into play from a hitherto powerless category to an (newly) empowered category is capable of being effectively pitted against another powerful category of social repression such as caste.

Ratnamala recalls that when she was in hospital for some treatment, the Sarpanch started repairing a sewer in her ward without the consent and signature of all the members. This was against the rule and when she heard about it, she asked him to show her the signatures and the consent of all the members of the Gram Panchayat. The Sarpanch, who belonged to the Teli caste (OBC) told Ratnamala, 'People from my caste don't even urinate in the mouth of people from your community (SC). How have you gathered the courage to speak to me and look at me in the eye?' Angered, Ratnamala grabbed him by the collar, slapped him and went to the police station to file a complaint against him for abusing her on the basis of her caste. Though the sarpanch demanded that she be arrested, he was informed that he could be booked under the Prevention of Atrocity Act (a non-bailable offence). Predictably he withdrew his complaint and requested Ratnamala to withdraw hers, which she did after he had apologized to her.

Let's also revisit the case of Mayadevi, the Dalit EWR who had grappled with poverty, untouchability as well as gender discrimination since her earliest years. Her parents were landless agricultural labourers. When her father married for the second time, Maya and her mother were abandoned. She recalls that she had an upper-caste friend whose house she used to visit; she often ate there. Her friend's grandfather loved Maya like his own grandchild, and she was grief-stricken when he died. Yet at his funeral, as she moved ahead to pay her respects, people objected to her presence and refused to let her do so. A confident, extroverted child, she was married when she was barely in her early teens, as her relatives believed that she needed to be 'tamed'. (As a consequence of the 'taming', she became a mother when she was barely a child herself.) However, today as an elected woman representative of the Gram Panchayat, she has been able to alter an age old purity-pollution practice in the village. Every year a religious ceremony is performed in the temple of Nagnath and people are fed prasad. On this occasion, a common dinner is organized for all the villagers with the fund collected from the entire village. However, the Dalit families are served at the end, after everybody else. They are served by an upper-caste person, but have to bring their own plates and glasses. By the time it is their turn to eat, it would be almost midnight. Maya Tai, who had always hated the discrimination, now (as an EWR) advised the Dalit community to boycott the prasad as a symbol of protest. It worked, and today the entire village participates together in all the festivals and rituals.

Finally, let us also look again at Jyoti's narrative. Despite initial resistance, she finally managed to push back opposition and non-cooperation by other (male, upper caste) members of the Panchayat.

With great difficulty (her husband was beaten up), she managed to reach the Panchayat, and hoist the flag on Republic Day in her village.

All is not perfect for these women, or at least not yet. Ratnamala, for instance, lost the next round of elections. A day before the election, the ex-Sarpanch distributed pamphlets alleging that she was a sex worker and had slept with various men to get developmental work done in the village. Nevertheless her story—that of a Dalit and a woman, who had slapped an upper caste man, that too the Sarpanch of the village, and still completed her term unharmed, and similar ones of her colleagues have lessons for transformative possibilities.

They were women, and also Dalit, ostensibly a category of citizens doubly oppressed. Yet, it was evident that an 'empowered gender' identity worked in the case of caste oppressed women as a powerful, strategically useful tool, actually capable of being pitted against (oppressive) caste 'others', and winning. Political empowerment based on gender status, in fact, worked as a quick route to bring women in circumstances as structurally constrained as theirs not just into the restricted domain of state policy and initiative, but actually gave them space and voice to emerge as effective 'subaltern counterpublics' (Fraser, 1990) in the larger public sphere(s). That they are state representatives in the current context should not matter if we see affirmative action (in this case through forums of the state) as creating (a possible set of—there may be others) core conditions that enable the emergence and development of counterpublics, and therefore discursive contestation in times to come.

Politics of Recognition

Initially, many EWRs, who were stepping into the public space for the first time, found it difficult to cope. Eventually, as is evident from their narratives, most of these women not only coped but delivered to the imperatives of their role as political administrators with initiative and vision. These are the visible, material benefits of the women's foothold in the local political sphere. The narratives of women EWRs reveal much more, they reflect the deep sense of personal confidence, satisfaction and individual fulfilment they developed with their entry into PRI, and thereby into the public domain.

A simple but telling instance, when these newly empowered women, especially those from the oppressed castes speak at functions and programmes in the presence of Taluka officers and village people, it is a matter of great pride and joy to them and their families. Fulma, an Upa-Sarpanch and an illiterate *adivasi* from Korku village is proud that she could address as many as 250 women (not so different from her) at a 'Melava', telling them about Gram Panchayats and Gram Sabhas, and answer their questions confidently in Hindi. When asked about her future plans, she says that she wants to work at the district level in the Zilla Panchayat. Several other respondents of this study too aspired for higher 'posts' and larger spheres of influence. Jyoti plans to stand for elections at the district level. Rita wants to be an MLA. She says she is happy that 'she has gained so much respect'—not from the 'others' but from the community and from her peer group.

Do these answers perhaps have more to do with self-actualization than equalization? Narratives of women EWRs in Maharashtra do seem to indicate that (access to) these multiple public spheres are also important sites for the construction/reconstruction of individual identities of people in oppressed groups, along pathways not always predictable by the imperatives of the group itself.

Democratic Decentralization and Engendering Citizenship

Decentralization, as enacted by constitutional amendments and enforced by state governments, is minimalist in its conception and design. However, the implementation of a proper form of decentralization remains unachieved as it is inundated by various institutional as well as social and political issues. Theoretically, the normative appeal of arguments for local democracy has resided in the belief that the quality of political participation and therefore of public life itself will be substantially transformed only when people gather to debate and deliberate on issues of common concern collectively, and are provided with decision-making powers to give effect to their shared concerns (Niraja Jayal, 2006).

The aim for decentralization in India was the normative-political project of greater inclusion and representation of historically disadvantaged or marginalized groups. The setbacks for decentralization in India have been due to inherited social inequalities, an absence of the required reform in law and a clear reworking of the relationship between local elected institutions and administrative structures. The picture is indeed complex and requires an understanding of the old and new institutions, of the changing rules of engagement between citizen and state, of politics and society on the one hand and law and administrative structures on the other. These complex engagements also make the public sphere vibrant with discussion and debate.

The evolution of the public sphere with ideas like nation, nationalism and freedom marked the beginning of the demand for citizenship in India. The most widespread and accepted hegemonic notion of citizenship is in the framework of the liberal school where an individual's citizenship is centred on the concept of individual freedom. Such a conceptualization of citizenship has however been criticized by Marxist and feminist scholars from the point of view of women and marginalized social groups like lower castes and religious minorities. Gopal Guru (2009) argues that 'Dalits in India are exiled citizens', and the purity-pollution logic has extended into the formal public sphere. The privileges of a citizen are restricted to those who are bestowed with the status of being 'full members of community' (Yuval-Davis, 1997). To use Anupama Roy's (2005) terminology, women have been, both in historical and in the present-day contexts, 'inadequate citizens'. It is necessary to emphasize that we do not believe that the woman herself is the reason for her inadequacy, and this does not imply that the onus to come out of this inadequacy needs to be on the woman herself. The inadequacies in the status of a woman's citizenship arise because of the structural aspects of the social relations that she engages in during her lifetime as an individual, and over generations within contexts of caste, class, race and nationality.

Once we recognize that citizenship is beyond 'given' privileges of equality, (because in fact, communities are not equal), we will also recognize that there is a dynamic nature in the formation of citizenship. With the evolving notion of community, the individual goes through a process of acquiring citizenship. Thus, this paper looks at the idea of gendered citizenship, how these women travel from being 'inadequate citizens' to (if at all) achievable 'citizens' with the deepening of democracy. In reformulating the question of democratic citizenship, it is interesting to look at Murdock's definition of democratic citizenship, in which he defines the 'fundamental prerogative of citizenship as the right to participate fully in social life with dignity and without fear, and to help formulate the forms it might take in the future' (Murdock, 1999). The notion of the 'full participation' is coterminus with that of 'adequate citizens'. In the case of gendered citizenship, one finds that this is a problematic feature in the everyday lives of women.

These are the questions that we face in the socio-economic context of inequality where we are located at various levels: Who are the citizens? Who is excluded from being a citizen? What are the various levels or tiers of this exclusion? What sort of process does an individual go through in the course of becoming a citizen? How does the perception of herself change in the course of her becoming a citizen? Is the process of becoming a citizen a democratizing process?

In the post-1990s context, the political and socio-economic scenario of the country has undergone much change, with a transition of the nation-state that was taken for granted in the post-independence era. Lower caste, minority and gender politics have moved substantially from existing patterns with a rise of various contradictions. Feminist voices have emerged, not in academic spaces, but also in the day-to-day lives and politics of citizens. Women's movements have reflected the unfolding nature of citizenship. The conceptualization of reservation has emerged in changing contexts—that of the post-Mandal agitation on reservations for OBCs, emergence of caste parties like the Samajwadi Party (SP) and the Bahujan Samajwadi Party (BSP), widespread emergence of Naxal ideology, the demolition of the Babri Masjid and the communal violence that followed in its wake.

The tabling of the Women's Reservation Bill took place in this context in 1996. The women's issue had never been exclusive of the concerns of caste and religion, and in this era, the overlaps were even more obvious. Thus, a monolithic understanding of the term, 'patriarchy' is no longer viable, and the need of the hour is to understand the diverse patriarchal forces that come into play in making the representation of women unequal. Mary John asserts the need for 'a complex articulation of unequal patriarchies' [Mary E. John, in Dhanda (ed.), 2008 p. 54.].

Politics of Being

'He is the Subject, he is the Absolute, she is the other' wrote Simone de Beauvoir (1949, xxviii), summing up why the visibility of the self is such an important issue for women. The main thesis of *The Second Sex* revolves around the idea that woman has been held in a relationship of long-standing oppression to man through her relegation to being man's 'Other'. In agreement with Hegelian and Sartrean philosophy, Beauvoir finds that the self needs otherness in order to define itself as a subject; the category of the otherness, therefore, is necessary in the constitution of the self as a self. What Beauvoir discovers in her multifaceted investigation into woman's situation is that woman is consistently defined as the 'Other' by man who takes on the role of the Self—while woman 'is the incidental, the inessential, as opposed to the essential' (1949, xxviii). To be the Other is to be the non-subject, the non-person, the non-agent, an invisible self in a patriarchal society. In customary practice, in cultural stereotypes and in political and economic spheres, women's visibility has been systematically subordinated, diminished, belittled and deprived. Feminists account for this phenomenon by explaining that women internalize these pernicious patriarchal values and norms which then become integrated in the cognitive, emotional and psychic structure of womanhood. Once embedded in a woman's psyche, internalized oppressions condition her desires. To maximize the satisfaction of her desires, then, would be to collaborate in her own oppression. Paradoxically, the more completely she fulfils these desires, the worse off she becomes.

Women are consigned to selflessness—to invisibility, subservient passivity and self-sacrificial altruism (Burman, 1998). Most often this happens in an unconscious way as the hegemony of gender is strongly internalized by women, supporting their current *status quo* by providing visible roles to men, while women assume invisible roles in all spheres of life. The reservation of women at the PRIs and the politics of reservation assumes interesting dimensions in this intersectionality of politics of being, which is embedded in the 'phenomenology of absences' and 'politics of presence', which brings forth an 'epistemology of presence'.

The process of becoming citizens results in many changing and conflicting identities. Each changed identity is a rupture from the existing identity and these ruptures are often very violent. An EWR on her new identity of being a politically active citizen has the multiple identity of caste, class and gender historicities. The ruptures in these women's lives in these multiple roles are in contradiction, and the process of various contradictions coming together dialectically brings about continuity in the process of struggle. These struggles are important events in women's lives and they change the perspective of the women's 'being' and citizenship.

The story of Dhakuli Gundu Naik, better known as Dhakuli Maushi, an Adivasi (Naik) woman from Halkarni Village in Kolhapur district elucidates this. The process of politicization for Dhakuli Maushi happened as a reaction to alcohol abuse within her family. Dhakuli Maushi's struggle began as one against the menace of alcoholism in her village. What started as a personal struggle gained political proportions. Her struggle was seen as a micro-movement, wherein she mobilized the collective consciousness of women. This demands recognition of its merit and significance at the level of local village politics. The caste and gender equations in Dhakuli Maushi's village have changed considerably from the time she started her struggle. Women's mobility has increased considerably and they are a lot more politically conscious. Now more women participate in the Gram Sabha and other committees. At this juncture, we return to the question of empowerment of women through reservation. We want to argue that the politics of reservation is not limited to a woman's participation in the public sphere, but has a notable effect on her domestic life. Dhakuli Maushi herself has never contested the Panchayat election (citing illiteracy as the reason). However, her political participation did increase her bargaining power within her family.

It is important to note how the micro politics of oppression within families work to reinforce patriarchal state structures and how women confront these structures. Day-to-day travails in women's lives act as a motivation for change, and their positive role in governance is often seen to have increased their power of negotiation within the microcosm of their family. This is of course to be noted with a word of caution. Often the patriarchal structures within the family are far too violent for the women to feel empowered with the new role as elected women representatives. Many women feel that this is an additional burden to their already heavy burden of housework.

There is a clear interrelatedness between the economic and political spheres. There is an assertion of agency through a sense of control of their own access to economic and other resources, which in turn redraws the lines of the political spaces. We, in our study, have witnessed cases where women representatives not only managed to ensure more access to resources within the family, but also engaged other women in the struggle to claim property rights. Anuya Kulkarni from Sherpe Gram Panchayat motivated 22 women from her village to claim joint ownership of their houses with their husbands and made efforts to transfer land in women's names at the Gram Panchayat.

Another area where the woman representative's role is significant is in trying to ensure a higher level of nutrition within the family by pressurizing ration dealers to provide women with their entitlement. Women representatives seem to have a positive influence in countering the feminization of poverty. Unequal distribution of resources within and outside the family, coupled with patriarchal social norms, results in women and children being the most vulnerable to poverty and malnutrition and EWRs concern themselves with ensuring nutrition for the members of their households.

Collective Action as Political Mobilization

Collective action has a two-way effect on political mobilization. On the one hand, it helps mobilize the collective, and on the other hand, the woman representative, having realized that she has mass support, is able to deal better with patriarchal, caste and class structures. Also there remains a continuous pressure on the women to perform. Revathi Narayan argues that this is the collective's realization of their political rights in the most fundamental sense, of being able to question and demand credibility of their elected representatives.

An example of successful collective action is the one undertaken by Mayadevi Sorte, a Dalit landless labourer from Kharola village, to protest against caste discrimination in her village. Anuya Tai achieved a reasonable amount of success in providing land in the names of female agricultural labourers because she succeeded in mobilizing 2500 women in a morcha in 2000, demanding land rights for them. Similarly, one of Jyoti Meshram's (ex-Sarpanch from Kotgal village) greatest successes was in forming women's collectives and Self-Help Groups. Rita Sukhdeve had organized a collection of Rs. 10,000 in her Panchayat through the collective action of banning alcohol. Further, she organized the women and men of the village to seize and set fire to liquor from liquor shops. Collective action helped women in governance to garner support and claim legitimacy. A lot of the achievements of the women representatives have been primarily because of the collective mobilization that they ensured. Their experiences of leadership and collective action need to be channelized to form political resistance.

Conclusion

Governance is presumed to be gender neutral. But in fact, the discourses, procedures, structures and functions of governance remain heavily skewed in favour of men. This unequal sharing of power leads to an unequal sharing of resources—time, income and property—between men and women. As discussed before, women at the grassroots level politics in Maharashtra did make a dent in the hegemonic power structures of the socially stratified structures of the village, and challenged the invisibility of women in political and public spaces. But the study also argues that Panchayats replicate rural power structures. Deeply embedded patterns of dominance and inequalities in women's lives are mediated by their class and caste positions. Interestingly, EWRs had bitter experiences of being labelled 'immoral' or 'non-womanly' when they crossed the thresholds designed to curtail them. They were called 'inadequate' when they were well within the boundaries of patriarchal societies.

To quote Archana Jatkar, a Sarpanch, "I wonder why they insisted on humiliating me in spite of the fact that I was a responsible Sarpanch. Is it because I am a woman? Isn't a woman capable of this kind of work?" This double gaze is problematic when one has to engage with the governance and family structures in both public and private domains in day-to-day engagements. Despite these hurdles, one cannot ignore the positive changes in the socio-political lives of EWRs, where some of them are playing meaningful roles in the current PRIs.

A more inclusive and democratic governance structure enables history to be re-read through the lenses of the subaltern. The negotiation of everyday casteist and sexist violence enables them to question the existing history and in turn, facilitates the subalterns to write their historiographs in negotiation of the powerful voices against them. The subaltern body is a site of vulnerability and marginalization. Their struggle to rewrite history is through their claims to political spaces. The role of governance in facilitating this can be achieved through their proportional representation in governance at least partially if not totally. The experiences of the Peoples' Planning Campaign (PPC) in Kerala—the largest of its kind in the local democratic decentralization process in India—showed that one can in no way argue that the PPC completely changed the internalized structures of patriarchal subjugation and the invisibility of women. Challenges and problems highlighted by various studies (Chatukulma and John, 2000, Vijayan and Sandhya, 2004, Radha and Roy Chowdhary, 2002) need to be read along with the successes scored by at least some EWRs in Maharashtra, both as participants in local governance and as representatives articulating the interests of women. Patriarchy cannot be overturned or even significantly eroded, overnight. But the entry of women into public spaces via grassroots institutions means that they are leaving behind the private and circumscribed spaces of the home. That they are—to an extent at least—neglecting the question of '...Who will make the chapattis' (Datta, 1998) is an important indicator of change. Many EWRs shared the feeling of an enhanced sense of social and personal status within and outside the family. While the fact that the EWRs are now invited to weddings in upper caste/class families and that their men are willing to share household responsibilities, might seem trivial at the level of macro analysis, but at the micro level, it becomes a significant gain (B. Manjula, 2008). A dialectic view of truth must include the notion that there are always emerging possibilities that are not yet visible. A new trend of micro politics is emerging as part of this engendering process in rural Maharashtra. This could be the seed of a new democratic formulation.

NOTES

1. Sergei Eisenstein (1923) believed that film montage could create ideas or have an impact beyond the individual images. Two or more images edited together create a "tertium quid" (third thing) that makes the whole greater than the sum of its individual parts. Eisenstein's theory of montage involves the combining of fragmental shots of film into intellectual series and contests. How the fragments combine and are formed is the essence of his notion of montage by conflict. This theory challenges traditional narrative movies because it involves taking an idea and recombining broken fragments in an incongruent way to produce new ideas, and occasional shocks.
2. Four members of a Dalit family were lynched and the women were stripped, paraded and killed by Kunbis in Khairlanji, a small village in Bhandara district of Maharashtra for "opposing" the requisition of their field to have a road built over it.

REFERENCES

Dhanda, M (ed.). 2008. *Reservations for Women.* New Delhi: Women Unlimited.

Foucault, M. 1981. "Power/Knowledge". *Selected Interviews and Other Writings—1972-1977.* (ed.) Colin Gordon. New York: Pantheon Books.

_____, 1988. "The Ethic of Care for the Self as a Practice of Freedom", in J. Bernauer and D. Rasmussen (eds.), *The Final Foucault*, Boston, Mass: MIT Press.

_____, 1991. 'Governmentality' in Graham Burchell, Colin Gordon and Peter Miller (eds.) in *The Foucault Effect: Studies in Governmentality.* Chicago, IL: University of Chicago Press.

_____, 1993. 'About the Beginning of the Hermeneutics of the Self' (transcription of two lectures in Dartmoutn on November 17 and 24, 1980), (ed.) Mark Blasius in Political Theory. Vol. 21, No. 2. May: pp. 198-227.

Fraser, Nancy. 1990. "Rethinking the Public Sphere: A Contribution to the Critique of Actually Existing Democracy". *Social Text.* No. 25/26: pp. 56-80.

_____, 1998. 'Social Justice in the Age of Identity Politics: Redistribution, Recognition and Participation'. *The Tanner Lectures on Human Values.* (ed.) Grethe B. Peterson. Salt Lake City: University of Utah Press.

_____, 2000. "Rethinking Recognition". *New Left Review.* May-June.

Habermas, Jurgen. 1981. *The Theory of Communicative Action.* Vols. 1 and 2. London: Heinemann.

_____, 1989. *The Structural Transformation of the Public Sphere: An Inquiry into a Category of Bourgeois Society.* Cambridge MA: The M.I.T. Press.

Hindess, Barry. 1996. *Discourses of Power: From Hobbes to Foucault.* Oxford: Blackwell.

Kishwar, Madhu. 1996. "Women and Politics: Beyond Quotas", *Economic and Political Weekly*, Vol. 31, No. 43, 26 October.

Mazumdar, Vina. 1997. 'Historical Soundings'. *Seminar.* 457.

Menon, N. 1997. "Reservations and Representation", *Seminar*, Special Issue on 'Empowering Women', No. 457 (September): 41. September: 15-16.

Menon, N. 2000. "'Elusive Woman': Feminism and Women's Reservation Bill". *Economic and Political Weekly.* WS 35, 28 October: 3835-43.

Multiculturalism. (ed.). Amy Gutman. Princeton: Princeton University Press.

Philips, A. 1995. *The Politics of Presence: The Political Representation of Gender, Ethnicity and Race.* Oxford: Clarendon Press.

Schutz, Alfred. 1967. *The Phenomenology of the Social World.* Trans. Walsh G. and Lehnert F. Evanston: Northwestern University Press.

Schutz, Alfred (with Luckmann T.) 1973. *The Structures of the Life-World.* Trans. Zaner R.M. and Engelhardt T. Evanston: Northwestern University Press and London: Heinemann.

Vincent, Louise. 2004. "Quotas: Changing the Way Things Look without Changing the Way Things Are". *The Journal of Legislative Studies.* Vol. 10. No. 1. Spring: 71-96.

6

Women's Reservation Bill: A Triumph or a Mirage

K. Deepamala

Concepts and Constructions of Democracy are under contestation around the world. In reading the literature on democracy, we are confronted with a paradox. On the one hand, there is a view that democracy has spread as never before. On the other hand, from other sources one gets the sense that democracy is in crisis, faced by a series of democratic deficits which are calling its very vitality and meaning into question. Democracy-building is not only about spread in quantity and largely about creating a standardized recipe of institutional designs around the world but also about deepening its quality and meanings in ways appropriate to the settings in which it is found. The process of deepening democracy is the creation of equality of opportunity for the hitherto deprived sections of society.

Women, the Other Half

For the women, the deprived section of the society, inequality and exclusion have, on the whole, has been continuing for centuries. As per 2001 census, women constitute 48 per cent of the total population. Women as an important human resource were recognized by the Constitution of India which not only accorded equality to women but also empowered the state to adopt measures of positive discrimination in their favour. Drawing strength from the Constitution, the Government of India has been engaged in committed and continuous endeavours towards ensuring all-round well-being, development and empowerment of women. One of the six basic principles of governance laid down in the National Common Minimum Programme[1] is to empower women politically, educationally, economically and legally.

Women's rights and civic responsibilities have always been subject of serious concern. From pastoral society to contemporary well-advanced society, the role of women has changed significantly. The change in socio-economic and psycho-cultural aspect of human living has influenced the role of women. In today's world, the responsibilities of women have attained new definitions and standpoints as they now share the financial responsibilities also. Statistically the rate of literacy among women has also increased. Women have come outside the four walls of house; there has been a rise in the percentage of women joining service sector especially banking, teaching and IT. But they encounter many difficulties.

The Constitution of India pledges to secure to all the people equality of status and opportunity. Many laws are made by government to protect the decency of women but it is appalling that the reverse has happened. It is outrageous to mention that we all have proudly entered the 21st century and claim that ours is an excellent and sophisticated modern civilization. But the ground reality is that we experience the same evils as our ancestors.

Women, the Citizens of Democracy

Citizenship is about belonging to a group or community and about the rights and responsibilities associated with such membership. In addition to being about a status, that confers rights and obligations, citizenship is also a practice whereby people are able to participate in shaping their societies. It implies not only rights and responsibilities, but also interaction and influence within the community. The concept originated in Western political thought on liberalism and democracy and is based on the notion of the individual as member of a democratic nation state. It described the relationship between the individual and the state in which the individual was able to secure protections and participate in the public life and decision-making of the nation.

Citizenship rights in Western thought were traditionally conceived as civil and political rights that enabled people to engage in political debate and decision-making in the public arena. Citizenship bestowed a legal status on such rights, thus giving the individual the means of claiming them and also an avenue by which to seek redress should they be violated (Lister, 2003b).[2] Citizenship, as conferred equally on all people who succeed to "membership" of the nation, is based on a neutral, abstract person, without a gender, race, class, ethnicity or any other social relation that marks real, living people. Equality, therefore, implies that all citizens are the same with the same needs. The law, which guarantees the rights of citizens, is itself seen as neutral and applying to all citizens equally. Such concepts are referred to as "universal" citizenship.

Ideas of universal citizenship—equal rights for all members—are a feature of many understandings of citizenship. Feminists, amongst others, have pointed out that this hides the reality of unequal power on the basis of race, class, ethnicity and gender, that can render women subject to double discrimination. These inequalities lead in reality to some people being excluded from the rights and responsibilities of full citizenship on the basis of their difference.

Citizenship is a relationship with the state and/or a group, society or community. Citizenship is both a status—or an identity—and a practice or process of relating to the social world through the exercise of rights/protections and fulfilment of obligations. The concept of membership by definition means that some are included and some excluded; and for people the worldover, citizenship has been about exclusion. We only have to look at the experiences of migrants in all societies to see how certain groups are excluded from the benefits of membership of nations and communities and the effects that this can have. Such exclusion has served as the basis of citizenship struggles—for example past anti-colonial struggles to include the colonised as full and equal citizens, and more recent citizenship struggles to include the right of poor people to basic resources. Exclusion and marginalisation from full citizenship are not only about being an outsider in a geographical sense. Groups such as women, ethnic minorities and the poor can fall outside full citizenship. Experiences of citizenship are therefore also dependent on societal position and roles—roles that are dictated by social relations of unequal power formed on the basis of race, ethnicity, caste, class and gender. The roles and relationships within societies dictate who is "inside" and who is "outside" and which activities are valued. They lead to different types and levels of exclusion from the advantages that membership incurs.

Across the globe women are disadvantaged in access to resources and power when compared with men of the same race, class, or ethnic group. Women may also often suffer double exclusion. Women living in minority ethnic communities, for example, can be discriminated against on account of their race and their gender. People's social roles and responsibilities are central to their experience of citizenship. Men's and women's roles and status vary from society to society. However, in the majority of societies women take a far greater role in home-making and care work, and participate less in formal politics and possibly less in wage earning. Ideas of women's lesser status and men's superior status are ingrained so deeply as to make this relation between women and men seem natural, even to women themselves. Struggles for gender equality that work to redress the imbalance of power and resources between women and men, can do so through questioning and challenging these roles. Citizenship can be a dynamic concept incorporating negotiations over membership, exclusion, roles, values, power and equality. Such negotiations can coalesce around struggles to include the roles or activities that are "left out" or under-valued in citizenship—and therefore to include those who undertake such activities. It is important that such struggles do not fix these roles but enable them to be negotiated. People take on a wide variety of multiple activities in society and must be seen as whole and complex beings. Above all, people must be able to articulate how they themselves view their position and their contribution to the groups to which they belong.

Women in Political Arena

A democratic political culture functions and is critical to the advancement of women, primarily, because it encourages political consciousness and action. Consequently, as political alliances are formed and information is shared, power relations within society and the political arena shift, allowing previously marginalized groups (such as women) to identify and fight for their goals. When this point is reached, the social capital (i.e. the relationships, institutions, and norms that facilitate cooperation among various groups) of a country is enhanced, and democracy can then gain a stronger foothold. By building constituencies around particular political concerns, civil society ensures that a range of citizens and interests can gain access to political systems.

There is a growing realisation amongst those working in development that strategies based on economic models have, for many people, failed to bring about genuine, positive change. This has led to the search for new ways of constructing programmes and approaches that look beyond economics, and into the political, social and cultural world. Looking at citizenship means looking at the people who make up a group, community or nation, and how they work within the group to guide the way it functions.

Establishing a participatory democracy is a challenging process that first requires recognition and understanding of the powerlessness experienced by individuals under the prevailing political systems. The next step is to work with citizens in such a way as to encourage political consciousness, organization, and advocacy.

Women Reservation Bill

India may have missed the symbolism of passing the women's reservation bill on the hundredth anniversary of international women's day but the delay does not drop the Rajya Sabha's decision of its historic and global significance. There is hardly any example of such a bold and progressive measure to improve the representation of women anywhere in the world, least of all in a society plagued by pervasive gender in quality, discrimination and violence.

The proposed legislation to reserve 33.3 per cent seats in Parliament and State Legislatures for women was drafted first by the H.D. Deve Gowda-led United Front Government.[3] The Bill was introduced in the Lok Sabha on September 12, 1996. Though it has been introduced in Parliament several times since then, the Bill could not be passed because of lack of political consensus. In fact, if India were to introduce such reservation by the 2014 general elections, the number of women elected to the Lok Sabha will rise three-fold[4] from the present 59 to 181, and India's global position will move from the present 99th rank to the 18th rank. But, for many reasons the success stories referred to need to be studied further before deciding whether India will indeed benefit from emulating them.

A Note on Women in Panchayati Raj

Once Pandit Jawaharlal Nehru said that if one has to look at the condition of a nation the status of women is very important. The UN

Secretary-General recently issued a '*Guidance Note on Democracy*',[5] which acknowledges that promoting women's rights must form an integral part of any democracy assistance, 'including through explicitly addressing gender discrimination that contributes to women's exclusion and the marginalization of their concerns.'

In India and across the globe the majority of population consists of females but the representation of women in politics, business or even sports in the 21st century is below satisfactory. In politics in India, the representation is negligible and below 10 per cent. Woman since the beginning of civilization has been regarded as a commodity and object of enjoyment. She has struggled to achieve a respectable name for her in the society. She is often subjected to physical abuse and mental torture and is treated as a person who is only capable of reproducing. India achieved its independence 64 years ago and in that achievement Sarojini Naidu, Kamla Nehru and many others laid their lives for getting India its freedom.

Visions of political development stress on democracy and participation as innate to its discourse. In the Indian context the process of democratization with inclusive participation is envisioned through the 73rd Amendment Act, 1993 to Constitution of India. The Act fosters the strengthening of grassroots democracy by creating opportunities for inclusive participation of the marginalized groups. It provides rights to Scheduled Castes (SCs), Scheduled Tribes (STs) and women to participate in local government. The Act aims at redressing the gender and caste inequities. Thus it provides proportionate reservation to the SC-ST categories based on their population and 33 per cent for women to ensure their participation in local bodies.

Post implementation of the Act that has now passed sixteen years, women's participation in Panchayat has been remarkably visible. This has recently resulted in Union Cabinet approving a proposal of a Constitutional Amendment Bill for increasing quota (50%) for women in Panchayats at all tiers (Panchayati Raj Ministry report).[6] Ministry Seminar Report 2009 estimate more than 1.4 million women to occupy 2,60,768 panchayats in upcoming panchayat elections (Panchayati Raj Ministry).[7] It also states, at present, out of the total elected representatives of Panchayat numbering around 2.8 million, 36.87 per cent are women. The Panchayati Raj Ministry report indicates a significant role played by reservation in bringing women into mainstream. According to this report, Reservation has played a significant role as four-fifths of all the representatives got elected from reserved seats. Reservation facilitated the first entry into politics for most of the elected representatives (83%).[8] Positive impact of entering politics and working as a Panchayati Raj functionary is visible as 79 per cent of women representatives reported better self-esteem; 81 per cent reported confidence building and 74 per cent stated increase of decision-making abilities. Such positive report gives a picture of better and inclusive governance that India is moving towards by applying 'Gender and Development' approach. This step foresees increased active participation of women in public sphere and their empowerment and development.

Women Representation in Rwanda

The biggest marvel in women's representation has no doubt been Rwanda. It is one of the world's poorest countries, still wracked by the horrific genocide of 1994 that left dead about 800,000 people, mostly belonging to the Tutsi tribe. In 2003, Rwanda's new post-genocide Constitution mandated that 30 per cent of seats in Parliament would be kept for women. In fact, in the 2008 elections, Rwanda broke all records: it topped the world with 56.3 per cent women in the lower Chambre de Deputies. Thus it became the only country with more women than men as elected representatives.

In commending Rwanda for the remarkable feat, though, many tend to ignore the demographics—post-genocide, the population of its women was 70 per cent. Most of the 'missing men' had been killed or fled the country. Even according to the latest survey, women constitute 53.5 per cent of the population. This is a figure that is far higher than that of South Asia, and even parts of Sub-Saharan Africa. The resultant increase in the number of women in positions of power may be explained in part this way.

Once they were elected in such heart-warmingly large numbers, though, Rwandan women deputies have often been criticised for not doing more on gender issues. In a study published by Oxford University Press in 2007,[9] *The Effect of Increased Women's Representation in Parliament: The Case of Rwanda*, authors Devlin and Elgie have argued that they have succeeded in passing only one major piece of legislation in the past seven years that seeks the empowerment of women, compared to a slew of legislative measures relating to rape and sexual torture, mothers' rights and the quota for women itself, that were passed in the preceding seven years. Clearly, it is not enough for women to be elected to those positions, they need to be more vocal in order to bring about a change in conditions for the larger woman population.

Social Capital

As a democratic political culture develops, individuals and groups begin to take on new roles and identities, gain self-respect, develop new skills, and adopt values of cooperation. With some energy and effort, spaces in the political culture can be transformed to provide settings in which private lives and public institutions can converge, and where ordinary citizens can claim their rights as citizens with dignity, independence, and vision (Evans and Boyte, 1992).[10] An evolving political culture depends on these spaces for the creation of social capital, which is often defined as the web of relationships, institutions, and norms that help people cooperate and coordinate with one another for the common good. In other words, the level of social capital in a given context reflects the degree of social cohesion that exists, and is the "glue" that holds institutions together and ensures that they function effectively (World Bank, 2000). By enhancing levels of reciprocity, cooperation, and coordination, a web of social capital and the proactive political culture it promotes are instrumental in the development of sound governance, economic prosperity, and healthy societies (Miller, 1994). It determines the extent to which people are engaged in collaboration and information exchange, share experiences, and feel connected to a broad desire for change. People become confident in expressing themselves publicly, draw strength from one another, and recognize that each has unique skills and perspectives to offer. Social capital is therefore the concrete manifestation of a dynamic political culture. Women Reservation Bill certainly will act as a base to create strong legalized social capital for women community.

Key to Access Political Systems

Access to the political system must be engineered. For women, barriers to such access have always existed in the form of functional illiteracy, gender discrimination, and entrenched political norms. The greatest challenges are to gain access to the political system, and then to transform the dominant political culture so that it is more inclusive of previously marginalized groups, such as women.

Unequal participation by women and men in electoral politics is evident in the predominance of men among Parliamentarians, Cabinet Ministers, and heads of government. In most countries (although not all) women and men have equal rights to vote and to stand for electoral office. According to a recent handbook, *Women in Parliament: Beyond Numbers,*[11] the main obstacles stem from political structures, processes and parties:

- Lack of political party support for female candidates particularly limited financial support and limited access to political networks;
- Lack of coordination and networks of women MPs and women's groups with other public organisations such as trade unions, possibly due to lack of awareness of the potential benefits or lack of financial resources for such links;
- Male-oriented norms and structures that mitigate against women's public participation, including Parliamentary schedules that are difficult to reconcile with parental and family responsibilities;
- Insufficient mobilisation of media support;
- Lack of leadership-oriented training and education for women;
- Electoral systems that are not conducive to women's political participation, such as "first past the post" rather than proportional representation systems.

Other obstacles to women's participation include: inadequate financial resources, illiteracy and limited access to education, the double burden of family and work responsibilities, ideologies or cultural patterns opposing women's participation in public life, and unsupportive attitudes on the part of the media. Women may face difficulties securing the support of other women. It is not always just men who are unconvinced of women's right to participate. Equal rights to vote that exist in law can also be denied in practice. For example, in some countries, women's ability to exercise the vote may be restricted by hostility among male community leaders and officials to women's participation. Women may face cultural constraints to public contact between women and men or other limits on their mobility.

With all these constraints in practice it is the duty of the state to make the women community an empowered sector of the society. In that way Women Reservation Bill will act as a key to open the doors of inequality especially with gender related issues.

Conclusions

Achieving equality for women is not only a laudable goal and a human right, it is also good economics, helps deepen democracy and enables genuine long-term stability. The Asia Pacific region has made impressive progress on many fronts, and seems poised to recover from the global economic downturn more rapidly than other regions. Long-term, sustainable progress, however, requires that more support is given to the empowerment of women.

The latest Asia pacific human development report, *Power, Voice and Rights: A turning point for gender equality in Asia and the Pacific,* estimates that the under representation of women in the workforce costs the region about $89 billion each year roughly equivalent to the GDP of Vietnam.[12]

There are large gaps worldwide between the political participation of men and of women. In the Asia Pacific, however, these gaps are among the largest in the world. The Pacific sub-region alone has four of the six countries in the world with no women legislators at all.

It is common for citizens (particularly women) in transitional societies or emerging democracies to be resigned to the idea that they cannot change things or improve their circumstances. Even in instances of entrenched attitudes of powerlessness formed over decades of authoritarian rule, however, tools and knowledge are available for individuals and communities to transform their thinking. Encouraging women's engagement in a vibrant politics is an essential component of democratic development: This process assists women in gaining greater control over the circumstances that affect their lives and their communities—and consequently affords them greater decision-making power. Such methods as advocacy training, consciousness rising, network building, and political and gender analysis are ways for women to combat the fear and apathy that underpin powerlessness and to generate faith in the possibility of transformation. The area of governance demonstrate that the selection and sequencing of methods to promote women's democratic participation vary widely, reflecting the nuances of different cultural, economic, geographic, political, and social contexts.

When women reach or exceed 30 per cent of a deliberative or decision-making body, they are able more effectively to advocate a realignment of public spending priorities to favour gender equality. At a minimum, more women in high-profile positions can have a striking role-model effect, encouraging women and girls to seek leadership roles. Other affirmative action measures might include reform of campaign finance laws to provide special assistance to women candidates, or special protections barring 'hate speech' directed against women.

Men are generally physically stronger because it was generally their job to hunt and perform physical labour. They're genetically engineered to do the harder physical work requiring brute strength. Women typically have a higher pain threshold, and are more emotionally powerful-women are typically better at understanding relationships and using them to their full advantage. The noted political thinker Andre Beteille[13] wrote that "a constitution may indicate the direction in which we are to move, but the social structure will decide how far we are able to move and at what pace". By presenting the women's bill it has been implied that we plan to move towards the bright future for half of the population, whatsoever be the power of the social structure it can be slowly and deeply handled by women by using a strong weapon of democracy called political participation.

NOTES

1. *http://pmindia.nic.in/cmp.pdf*
2. Dywer, Peter, *Understanding Social Citizenship: Themes and Perspectives for Policy and Practice*, The Policy Press, 2004, UK.
3. *http://www.indiatimes.com/The-Womens-Reservation-Bill/The-origin/photostory/5661781.cms*
4. *http://www.editorialjunction.com/?p=4670*
5. *http://www.un.org/democracyfund/Docs/UNSG%20Guidance%20Note%20on%20Democracy.pdf*
6. *http://panchayat.nic.in/data/1227156093695~Study%20on%20EWRs%20in% 20Panchayati%20Raj%20Institutions.pdf*

7. *http://offerings.nic.in/directory/*
8. *http://www.solutionexchange-un.net.in/decn/cr/res06030901.pdf*
9. *http://pa.oxfordjournals.org/cgi/content/abstract/61/2/237*
10. *Journal: Theory and Society*, Publisher: Springer Netherlands, Volume 28, number1/Feb1999
11. *Women in Parliament: Beyond Numbers*, published by Institute for Democracy and Electoral Assistance (IDEA), 2005.
12. *http://www.southasianmedia.net/index_opinion.cfm?category=women&country=India*
13. *http://www.frontlineonnet.com/fl2704/stories/20100226270400400.htm*

7

Empowerment of Women: A Realistic Approach

G. Pankajam

"Woman must not accept; she must challenge.
She must not be awed by that which has been built up around her;
She must reverence that woman in her which struggles for expression."

—Margaret Sanger

In an ever challenging and changing society, empowerment of women has been a matter of great concern to everyone. When we are observing the 100th year of Women's Day we are still talking about women empowerment and try to find a balance in gender equality. Article 1 of the Constitution of India says "all human beings are born free and equal." Article 2 provides "freedom without any discrimination." Article 3 assures that 'everyone has the right to life, liberty and security". Article 5 of the Constitution proclaims that "no one shall be subjected to torture, cruel, inhuman or degrading treatment". And Article 6 states that "everyone has the right to recognition everywhere as a person before law." But discrimination seems to be a never ending phenomenon. Prejudice is the cause of this ignorance and injustice.

After observing Women's Day for a century, 9th March, 2010 has been made a memorable day in the history of India by introducing in Rajya Sabha the Bill of Reservation of 33 per cent to women, both in Parliament and in State Legislative Assemblies with lot of objections. Media say that it was a historic and giant step. Of course, it is a great move after 73rd and 74th Amendments to the Constitution of India which brought the women to politics by contesting in Panchayat elections, winning and discharging their duties as Presidents and members and made people feel not to underestimate the power of a woman, through their functioning with all the inputs they had in the capacity building training programme.

"There will never be a true democracy until every responsible and law-abiding adult in it, without regard to race, sex, colour or creed has his or her own inalienable and unpurchasable voice in government", says Carrie Chapman Cattti. Though Women comprise of the fifty per cent of the world population there is still denial in many aspects of their life quoting the culture. It is not gender which is destroying our culture…. it is our interpretations of culture which has destroyed gender equality. A woman from Madurai recalls and says that "in our culture we never allowed our women to go out and study. But we have to work ourselves and depend on ourselves." As Jane Galvin Lewis says "you don't have to be an anti-man to be pro-woman". To feel and make women equal we have two ways either we have to be like the candle that spreads the light or the mirror that reflects the light.

When there is realization that a woman is the full circle and within her we find the power to create, nurture and transform it will make everyone to have the feeling of gender equality and live in harmony. Peace and contentment in life comes only when we look at what we have in our life, we will always have more. If we look at what we don't have in life, we will never have enough. We must learn to respect each other and we must learn to listen to each other to live together. It is the time that every woman realizes that our own words are the bricks and mortar of the dreams that we want to realize; our words are the greatest power we have. There is a growing strength in women. All are capable of achieving what they desire and decide for which there should be encouragement and support.

Indicators of Women Empowerment

There are women activists throughout the world who articulate and voice the concerns and issues so that the issues of women could be heard loud and made clear. It is not just raising the voice that will bring about change and empower the womenfolk. Systematic efforts, though sporadic, has brought changes in the life of women and empowered them which could be observed in their behaviour pattern.

The following are some of the indicators of the empowered women. A positive self-image and self-confidence, ensuring equal participation in bringing about social change, ability to think critically and creatively, exhibition of the ability to build group cohesion and lead, courage and commitment to foster decision-making and encourage group action in order to bring about change in the society by providing the wherewithal for economic independence through employment and the right to property are considered as the characteristics of empowered women. Men and women should play complementary roles in the process of empowerment, they cannot be separated.

Empowerment has four components—cognitive, psychological, economic and political. Cognitive component involves acquiring new knowledge to create a different understanding of gender relations and destroying old beliefs of structure of gender ideologies. The psychological component stresses on development of feelings and emotions that women can develop to improve their conditions. The economic component stresses that women should be able to engage in any productive activity that will lead them to financial autonomy. Access to work increases a woman's economic independence and with it a greater level of general independence is created. As Hall (1992) notes, economic subordination must be neutralized for women to be empowered. The political component of empowerment promotes the ability of women to analyze the political and social environment and mobilize social change in the political arena. Only when a woman gets up and comes out of the shackles of the tradition she can assure of her empowerment.

All these will lead to a complete and comprehensive development of women, enabling them to be active participants in development activities in the society. Female Workforce participation is needed for empowerment. In General, the gender gaps in labourforce participation have been shrinking and women's entrepreneurship development has been impressive. This participation helped women to build up positive self and confidence in them. Women, therefore, require education to acquire skills and knowledge to increase their value in labour markets and to get social status.

Action Plan

The principle of gender equality enshrined in the Constitution of India should not be only a constitutional provision; it is to be ensured that there is really gender equality in all the dimensions of life of the women: education, employment, political and social. The critical mass should be in a position to understand, feel and act to achieve their goal in life. Gender disparity is seen in various forms, the most obvious being the decline in female ratio during the last few decades both in urban and rural area. Social stereotyping and violence against women at the domestic and societal levels are some of the other manifestations that are very obvious in the society. Discrimination against girl children, adolescent girls and women persists everywhere, that need immediate attention to make them have equal participation. Providing equal rights, opportunities and responsibilities to women, will go a long way in removing the existing gender discrimination. To empower women to play their role effectively in nation building activities as equal partners, efforts are to be taken in the following dimensions. The State should formulate policies and programmes that will reduce the poverty and vulnerability to risks of women. Social status of the marginalized women should be enhanced by promoting and protecting livelihood and employment, protecting against hazards and sudden loss of income, and improving their capacity to manage risks.

Employment, education, health, media images, place of residence, household chores, women's participation in social and political activities, and their legal status in terms of marriage, divorce and inheritance of property decide their status in the society. The recent move of reservation of 1/3 seats for women in the Lok Sabha and in the State Legislative Assemblies will ensure adequate representation of women in decision-making; to adopt an integrated approach to both women-specific and women-related sectors; to adopt a special strategy of 'Women's Component Plan' to ensure funds/benefits flow to women from other relevant sectors; and to organize women into different organizations like Self-Help Groups and Federations that will mark the beginning of a major process of empowering women.

Women should be made to realize as Gloria Steinem says, "Power can be taken, but not given. The process of taking is empowerment in itself". Creating an environment through positive economic and social policies for full development of women will enable them to realize their full potential. Equal access to women to health care services, quality education at all levels, career and vocational guidance, employment, equal remuneration, occupational health and safety, social security and public affairs will facilitate empowerment of women. Women empowerment could also be promoted by encouraging the women to form their own women's organisations; by providing support systems for women; making available women-specific data and other relevant information; adequate funds; women leadership; networking; favourable media coverage and making available favourable policy climate.

Education remains the key to both economic and political empowerment. Empowerment through education is an ideal action as it is a continuous holistic process with cognitive. Education remains the key to both economic and political empowerment. Empowerment through education is an ideal action as it is a continuous holistic process with cognitive, psychological, economic and political dimensions in order to achieve emancipation. Gender sensitive curricula need to be developed at all levels of educational system in order to address sex stereotyping as one of the causes of gender discrimination.

IFAD supported Tamil Nadu Women's Development Project in 1999. Identified as the main processes that could lead to women's empowerment: changes in women's mobility and social interaction; changes in women's labour patterns; changes in women's access to and control over resources; and changes in women's control over decision-making. The study also has suggested the action programme and key initiatives for bringing about these changes.

Women are to be considered as key change agents. Women bear all the responsibilities at home for meeting basic needs of the family, yet there is denial in providing adequate and needed resources, information and freedom of action to fulfil this responsibility. Equally women also take up jobs outside to earn their livelihood or to supplement their family income. When women are denied adequate nutrition, health care facilities, the children are born mal- and under-nourished. When women are not provided with the opportunity for education the children also suffer of illiteracy. When women are empowered and are supported it lead to a healthy family and empowered nation.

Conclusion

As stated in Beijing Platform for Action, Fourth U.N. World Conference on Women, 1995, "The advancement of women and the achievement of equality between women and men are matters of human rights and conditions for social justice and should not be seen in isolation as women's issue. They are the only way to build a sustainable, just and developed society. Empowerment of women and gender equality are prerequisites for achieving political, social, economic, cultural and environmental security among all peoples."

In the goals of National Policy for Empowerment of Women it is stated that we should create an environment through positive economic and social policies for full development of women to enable them to realize their full potential and encourage them to be equal partners in nation building activities. As Mahatma Gandhi says: "Intellectually, mentally, and spiritually, woman is equivalent to a male and she can participate in every activity." This approach towards women empowerment will enable a prosperous and progressive world to emerge. Let the world move towards that direction and show a new and bright dawn to the generation to come.

REFERENCES

Pankajam G. *et al.* (Edited). *Women in India Today, Their Status*, Kanyakumari Justice and Peace Publication, (2008).

Pearls of Wisdom. Empowering Women Quotes.www.s.appyr.net

The Hunger Project, 5 Union Square West, New York, NY 10003.

The Republic of India: Tamil Nadu Women's Development Project Completion Evaluation, *Report 340-IN*. Rome, IFAD/OE, April. 2000.

Times of Madurai, Published by Projects Abroad, Madurai, March. Issue no. 4.

8

Political Representation: The Promise for Women

Suganda Ramamoorthi

The capacities of the states to deliver on policy promises are fundamentally shaped by politics as are the outcome of economic, social and governance reforms. It has been universally accepted that the participation of women on equal footing alone will ensure full-fledged achievement of the agenda for development. One of the resolutions of the Beijing Platform for Action 2005 was the call for women's greater access to public office. The average proportion of women in national assemblies across the globe had increased from 9 per cent in 1995 to 16 per cent in 2004. Although this is not the "critical mass" that could make a dent in the reforms and it does call for celebration. Yet one should not get the impression that numbers alone matter. The number of women found in formal politics is not the best indicator of either of the intensity of women's political participation, or of its effectiveness in orienting policy making particularly towards gender concerns. In fact, a far better indicator would be the numbers of active women's organizations in a country. Nevertheless, there is the outlook for a critical mass because it is indeed believed that this critical mass would and could change the culture, practices and outcome of politics. It implies an automatic and even irreversible, causal sequence between increased numbers of women in politics and better policy outcomes for women. Social reconstruction generally takes place through polity.

Since the 1990s, an important focus of governance reforms has been the strengthening of local government by the decentralization of powers, resources and responsibilities to municipal councils and other locally administered bodies. Local government is regarded as a significant political apprenticeship arena for women. Barriers to their entry such as the need to travel and spend time away from home, a large disposable income, a reasonable level of education, experience of political competition and social connection etc. are low at the local level. Local governments are also considered appealing to women participants because of the focus on basic community services. The geographical area too is small. Women are generally engaged in informal community management and hence it is believed that their participation in local planning and management will bear fruits.

The 1990s saw a number of legal and constitutional innovations around the world designed to enhance women's participation in local government like quotas and other measures to bring them into local office. These actions were supported and promoted by the 'International Union of Local Authorities', which in 1998 issued a Worldwide Declaration on Women in Local Government to encourage national support for affirmative action at the local levels.

In India, rural transformation has undergone a metamorphosis after the introduction of the new governance at the grassroots through the 73rd Amendment to the Constitution. A new participatory culture of governance with gender justice has been created. It has enabled women to find a legitimate space in the political sphere in rural areas. This was designed to overcome social resistance to the public participation of previously excluded groups in local affairs. It has successfully put about a million women in local government.

The participation of women in Panchayati Raj Institution is considered essential for ensuring political participation in the democratic process and also for realizing the development goals of women today. Their participation opens an avenue for them to make their voices heard and bring action for development. It will have a profound impact on women's prospects of bringing weight in decision making councils.

Yet, women hesitate to take part in politics as if the space is for men alone. In the Indian context, empowering women seems like a Herculean task as social and cultural moorings have established strong roots in the belief systems of the people. Power to women would mean a sense of internal strength and confidence to face life, the ability to influence the social process that affects the lives of women as well as the direction of social change. Empowering women has become the greatest challenge in India. Presently, NGOs have been playing a proactive role by providing training programmes to build women leaders' capacity to engage in local decision making.

Although there are constitutional provisions for the easy entry of women in grassroots politics, it is found that the effective participation of women is rather low. A very common and commonsense explanation for the low numbers of women in politics is that their resource endowments for public life are less. Resource here would mean their education levels, employment, spare time, no networking, learnt to live in the private domain etc. They are lower than men. However, it is difficult to establish a hard and fast correlation between the levels of women's education or economic activity and their political participation. Women's participation is culture specific. Women are dominating the agricultural and the organized sectors in the rural areas. Their economic participation is very high and visible unlike in governance. In India, factors like literacy, poverty, lack of managerial skills, self-confidence, etc. keep the women away from politics. Their role is limited only to voting and often even this is decided by the menfolk at home. The reservation system has forced the village mass to provide political space for women and encourage them to participate *per se*. Of course, their level of participation is a matter of contention. India has a dichotomous division of society where the private world has narrow restricted boundary for women. She is nurtured within the four walls of her home. The socialization process deprives her of exposure to the outside world. This could be a plausible explanation for the reluctance on the part of women to participate actively in public life.

There are two issues associated with women in politics. One is their visibility/invisibility in governance and the need to understand their concerns and two the need to initiate an enabling process so as to help them to participate proactively and contribute to an inclusive growth and development of the economy. This chapter focuses on the performance of women leaders in Madurai district.

A study on women leaders was done in Madurai district to understand the issues of women in grassroots politics that is elected women leaders. For the study, East and West Panchayat Union of Madurai district were selected. In Madurai East, there were 13 women elected Panchayat Presidents and in Madurai West there were 11 women Presidents. Out of the 24 women 18 of them were selected which forms 75 per cent of the total women Presidents in the two zones. These women were interviewed to understand the various issues that surround these women who have chosen to enter a non-traditional profession. Of course, it is also pertinent to know whether they chose it or were forced into it due to the quota system of the government. Women are wrapped and cordoned into the culture, society, economy and polity. This chapter gives an insight into the personal and professional face of the women leaders.

Profile of the Women Leaders

To assess the nature of participation of women leaders in politics, it is necessary to understand their background. The influence of demographic and social factors directly affects the degree of political involvement and participation of women. The study showed that women entered politics in the prime of their youth. Fifteen women were within the age group of 24-25. Only one women was above 45 years of age. It is generally believed that women in that age are burdened with familial responsibilities, care of children etc. and will not be able to allocate time for public affairs. But the study has proved otherwise. The indication that younger women are jumping into the fray does indicate an encouraging sign and direction for new era. Catch them young to shape them. There is also the lurking suspension that the men behind are the persons choosing these women for want of contestants.

Education widens the horizon of people offering new avenues of knowledge and development. There is a positive correlation between education and opportunities. But for a women it need not necessarily be so since it is her environment which decides her status, role and duties in the society.

Table 8.1: Level of Education

S. No.	*Level of Education*	*No. of Respondents*	*Percentage*
1.	Illiterate	1	5
2.	Up to 5th Class	2	10
3.	6th-10th Class	13	75
4.	Graduate	1	5
5.	MA BL	1	5
	Total	18	100

Source: Primary data.

Educational qualification is not a criterion for a person to enter politics but it does have a bearing on performance. It is evident from Table 8.1 that 16 of them are barely educated. Only two have entered the portals of a college. As expected their education levels are very low. It is important to note that low levels of education need not necessarily imply poor performance. The duties in grassroots politics is so much intertwined with their day-to-day life that it becomes an extension of the duties they perform at home. The only difference is that one is in the public domain and the other in the private domain.

It was found that 8 of them belonged to Scheduled Castes and 10 to backward community. Among the 18 women 17 were married and only one was unmarried. All the 17 had children which implied greater responsibility at home and less time for public affairs.

Political Factors

The 73rd Amendment has ensured that women are pushed into the political arena. But in reality these women have no or little political socialization. All of them were experienced and amateur. The reservation system has opened opportunities galore for women who never believed that a time would come in their lives when they would lead and not follow.

An important factor is the source of backing. Among the 18 women only 6 faced the election under a party banner and 12 of them stood as independents. This is indeed an interesting revelation. Among the six it was found that five of them stood under the banner of AIAMK and only one on behalf of DMK. It could be carefully construed that in grassroots politics the state and national parties do not play a major role or it can be inferred that women find it easier to take up leadership roles at the grassroots levels because of its rather small boundaries and as an extension of the family role.

Age of entry into politics is an indication of the maturing of the political process. Among the 18 women four were elected when they were quite young that is between the age of 18-25 and 13 of them between the ages 26-45. Get them young is an important criteria for creating gender equity. Grassroots politics provides the right climate for women.

Often, women who are naive and unexposed to the outside world are exploited because of the reservation system. The menfolk find it convenient to push their wives or daughters and use them to hold on

Table 8.2: Source of Motivation

S. No.	*Motivation Person*	*No. of Respondents*	*Percentage*
1.	Parents' family	9	50
2.	Husband	5	30
3.	Community	3	15
4.	Party	1	5
	Total	18	100

Source: Primary data.

to power keeping them in the forefront. It is pertinent to know whether these factors have had a bearing on their performance. This study found that 50 per cent of the respondents did not have any relatives who were actively involved in politics or in the Panchayat. This indeed is a good sign. Of course, this takes one to the next question that is who then motivated them to enter into the fray. These women are not educated and yet they summoned enough courage to enter politics. It is evident that political party did not have a very great role in encouraging them. Nine of them revealed that it was their parents' family who motivated them. Husbands too have played an important role. Five of them said that their spouse had encouraged them to assume public office. Three of them said that the community was behind them and only one revealed that political party invited her. Here the point to be noted is that although 17 women are married, 9 women were backed by their parents' family and not their husbands. Contesting election has financial implications. A society where investing in education of a girl child is considered a waste, financially supporting women for election is a greater risk. Not many would be willing to do so unless the probability of winning is very high. It could be seen that the decision to stand for elections was not theirs but the external factors were more forceful.

A women's life is centred on her family as she is the caregiver of the family. Most of the women's decisions are taken by her nearest and dearest. The empowerment of women even in her family leaves much to be desired. The question of her decision taking capacity in public life arouses many doubts.

The study of the 18 women revealed that 11 of them contested mainly because it would enhance their family prestige. Unfortunately, only four of them opined it would help them serve the people. Three of them expressed that it was in their personal interest. It would further

Table 8.3: Purpose of Contesting the Election

S. No.	Purpose of Contesting	No. of Respondents	Percentage
1.	To serve the people	4	20
2.	For family prestige	11	65
3.	Personal interest	3	15
	Total	18	100

Source: Primary data.

their self-interest. Of course, it does show their ignorance and innocence as they were quite honest in answering this question. Whatever the source of motivation, they have entered the fray and have donned the role of a leader and a benefactor. It is now their duty to adapt to the new circumstances and take new responsibilities. They have to move from a protected family environment to a public sphere. This new role requires political efficacy. They have to attend office and meetings regularly and perform their role and functions assigned effectively and efficiently. It was of interest to know whether they attended meetings alone or were accompanied by someone.

Table 8.4: Persons Accompanying for Meetings

S. No.	Accompanying Person	No. of Respondents	Percentage
1.	None	2	10
2.	Husband	13	75
3.	Son	1	5
4.	Father	1	5
5.	Party Member	1	5
	Total	18	100

Source: Primary data.

It is evident that only two of them attend meetings without escort. The remaining 16 of them go along with someone. Patriarchal grip is so strong that she is unable to slip out of its clutches. It is believed that she requires support particularly when she goes out. The same is emulated when she assumes public office as an elected leader, representing the people. This is a point of ponder. The overbearing figure of the males in the family of otherwise negates the opportunity for the women to exhibit her capacities and actively participate in the affairs of the Panchayat. They belittle her role.

It is believed that when women are involved in grassroots politics, the issues and concerns of women will get a greater representation leading to gender equity. Among the 18 leaders, 16 of them said that they freely participated in the meetings and expressed their views. Only 2 said that they could not actively participate due to the domination of male members and they were silent spectators. All the women leaders expressed that they regularly visited their wards and when there was some problem in their wards they visit the place and discuss the problem with the people.

Problems Faced by Elected Women

In spite of having entered the political arena, women are not freed from the stereotyped roles assigned by the society. She is burdened by the traditional role expectation. Some of the problems faced by these women were:

Increased Workload: The moment the women filed their nomination their workload increased doubly and so did the constraints. Her family commitment and her public commitment cows her down.

Varied Concerns of Women Leaders: Politics has its own ramifications and dimensions whether it is state politics or national politics. From silent voters to active leaders has created role conflicts in their lives.

Illiteracy: Illiteracy and poor education levels are some of the basic problems of the women leaders. They are not able to function effectively as they are unable to read the government orders, their level of confidence dwindles etc.

Usual Shyness: Having been brought up from childhood secluded from society, they find it difficult to interact with men in the office. As they have had no previous experience, they feel inhabited. When Gram Sabha meetings are convened, they have to conduct the proceedings as chairpersons. They expressed that they find it difficult to do so.

Domination by Men: The elected women representatives do not have the freedom to act by their own family members as also from the other men leaders. But after attending training programmes organized by NGOs they expressed that they are much more confident.

Forced not to Raise Women's Issues: Often, the issues raised by them in meetings are not taken seriously. This is so particularly with regard to women's issues. Even the officials have a negative attitude.

They do not encourage women's participation. They feel that women are present only due to the reservation policy and hence they cannot contribute effectively.

Domination by Family Members: The family members particularly the husbands sideline the women and assume office as if they are the elected leaders. This renders them inoperative. Women are dissuaded from learning and participating. Even the villagers approach the menfolk and not the women. Hence their opportunity to involve themselves is very minimal. These are some of the problems that they encounter in their day-to-day life as a leader.

One important indicator suggesting that these leaders are self-contained and find satisfaction in undertaking duties of governance is their willingness in continuing in office. It was found that 15 of them answered that they would contest elections again if given the opportunity. One said she would not stand and 2 said that they were not sure. Thus it is evident that most of them have not found this new experience unpleasant.

Suggestions: Presently, the 33 per cent reservation has increased to 50 per cent. It is time for the community to face the reality and accept that women are going to be active participants and partners in political life. Women too need orientation to discharge their duties effectively. Some suggestions have been put forth to improve their performance:

- Proper orientation has to be given to the elected women representatives by way of periodic training.
- Adult education scheme should be extended to them.
- Capacity Building workshops for women leaders.
- Disallowing family and other members from accompanying the women leaders for meetings.
- Enabling women's voices to be heard.
- Creating a climate for gender sensitive spending.
- Incentive could be given on officials to respond to the concern of women.
- Ensuring gender budgeting at the local level.
- Conducting regular meetings for women leaders which would be a forum for them to share their experiences, concerns and problems.

Conclusion

In spite of the significant obstacles to women's local political effectiveness, there is evidence from decentralization experiments in all parts of the country that women do manage to articulate priorities in local planning and decision making and also their decisions happen to be different from the men's decisions. It has been observed that the levels of corruption had come down and the usage of common resources has been channelized. Despite the handicaps they face in terms of education and prior experience, weak leadership etc. they have been able to make a significant impact on policy decisions. Issues like drinking water, health facilities, provision of essentials, education etc., has been given priority. There is ample evidence to show that women responsive politics and policy making require changes to the conduct of politics and system of governance that reach beyond simply putting more women in office. Strong and autonomous women's movements are needed to debate priorities to legitimate feminist policy demands, and press them upon political parties and government leaders at local, state and national levels. Women's participation in the political arena is something that has to be watched over in the next few decades as they will be the major players in governances.

REFERENCES

Devi, Lakshmi, *Women in Politics: Management and Decision Making Process*, Anmol Publications, New Delhi, 1998.

Gender Equality Striving for Justice in an Unequal World, United Nations Research Institute for Social Development, France, 2005.

Jha, Ashok Kumar, *Women in Panchayati Raj Institutions,* Anmol Publications, New Delhi, 2004.

Mehta, G.S., *Participation of Women in Panchayat Raj System,* Kaniska Publishers, New Delhi, 2002.

Palanithurai, G, *Process and Performance of Gram Panchayat Women and Dalit Presidents.* Concept Publishing Company, New Delhi, 2005.

_____, *Empowerment of Women, Experience of the Elected Women Representatives in Grassroots Institutions,* Rajiv Gandhi Chair for Panchayati Raj Studies, Gandhigram, 2002.

Pitam Singh, *Women Legislators in Indian Politics,* Concept Publishing Company, New Delhi, 2003.

Rajalakshmi, V., *The Political Behaviour of Women in Tamil Nadu,* Inter-India Publications, New Delhi, 1985.

9

Capacity Building of Elected Women Representatives

V.R. Vanajaa

Background

The passage of the 73rd and 74th Constitutional Amendment in 1994 provided the entry point for the women to participate in the local governance. The amendment mandated reservations of positions in village panchayats for women and for individuals from two traditionally disadvantaged groups: Dalits and Adivasis. But the legal structure failed to provide concrete structure that would facilitate dalit and women elected representatives to function to their optimum period in more efficient manner. Though women occupied 32,638 seats out of 97,458 seats allotted for village Panchayats in Tamil Nadu, with the help of the Constitutional provisions, the effective functioning of women elected representatives is always remains the dreams owing to many factors. The major constraints which limits women participation in governance were—

- Lack of gender sensitivity for the women itself, husband and family members, Government officials and the community.
- Absence of legal structures and mechanisms.
- Absence of proper capacity building with specific focus to women.
- Caste system and cultural background.
- Level of literacy etc.

With the above gaps as the key points, this chapter intends to analyse the need and importance of effective capacity building strategies with more gender specific to the women elected representatives.

Objectives of the Programme

1. Marginalized people—women, Arundhathiyars, and other dalit—will achieve greater political and human rights and reduce discrimination on the grounds of gender, caste, health status or sexual orientation.
2. The Quality of life for a population of 40 Panchayats improves as a result of effective functioning of Panchayats and their standing committees in the fields of health, education, welfare and development.

Strategies

- Capacity Building of communities, People's Organizations, Federations of Elected Women Representatives, and Elected Women Representatives
- Gender sensitization programmes
- Influencing Opinion
- Networking/Collaboration
- Participation

Table 9.1: Coverage

Block	*Total Number of Potential Panchayat*	*Total Number of Working Panchayat*
Aundipatty	13	15
Myladumparai	9	6
Uthmapalayam	4	—
Chinnamanor	7	7
Periyakulam	3	5
Theni	9	9
Total	45	42

2006 Election

Before Election Activities

- Future candidates motivation
- Federation motivation
- Election camp-posters notice
- Panchayat-wise SHG meeting
- Panchayat support committee motivation
- Culture programme
- Conducting village meetings

Table 9.2: Outcome: President

Process	*Women*			*Men*			*Total*
	AR	*SC*	*BC*	*AR*	*SC*	*BC*	
Selected	3	4	10	12	11	15	65
Trained	2	7	7	4	2	1	23
Nominated	3	14	8	12	11	15	63
Dropout	0	1	1	0	0	1	3
Winner	1	5	0	5	6	10	27

Out of 60 candidates contested the election 27 (45%) won the election including both women and men. Out of the 27, the women who won the election is only 6, i.e. 22 per cent. Initially capacity building has been provided for 25 women and the canvassing with support of women federation has been done. From Table 9.2 it is evident that out of 25 women only 6 (24%) have won the election. Again when it is analysed based on caste, out of 3 Aruthathiar women who nominated only one (33%) could win; out of 14 SC women nominated 5 (36%) had won and out of 8 BC women nominated no one had win the election.

It is seen that at least dalit women could occupy seats only because of reservation and BC women could not succeed. But in the case of men out of 15 BC candidates nominated 10 (20%) had won. This fact clearly shows that there is a serious need for gender sensitized capacity building.

Out of 361 candidates who contested the election, 218 (60%) won the election. In the 218 elected representatives 85 (39%) were men and 133 (61%) were women. In the case of women we could see

Table 9.3: Ward Member

Process	*Women*			*Men*			*Total*
	AR	*SC*	*BC*	*AR*	*SC*	*BC*	
Selected	33	99	134	25	52	59	402
Trained	23	61	91	6	18	40	239
Nominated	32	98	131	25	52	59	397
Dropout	2	11	14	0	2	7	36
Winner	15	50	68	15	28	42	218

that out of 30 Aruthathiar contested 15 (50%) won; out of 87 SC women contested 50 (57%) had win; and out of 117 BC women contested 68 (58%) women had win. This figure is fair for both dalit and BC women. And it is also seen women had surpassed men in this ward member position. This is because the ward member position is of less power when compared to the President position and so the opposition from men and dominate caste is less.

Summary

(a) Among 411 trained potential candidates 246 candidates were elected.
(b) Winning of Dalit—50.40 per cent
(c) Winning of BC—49.59 per cent
(d) Winning of Women—56.91 per cent
(e) Winning of Men—43.08 per cent
(f) Winning of Dalit Women—50.71 per cent (AR-21.21%)
(g) Winning of BC Women—49.28 per cent

Major Constraints

1. Since election date was announced in short period the activities planned for the election work could not be carried out to the maximum.
2. Due to reservation changes, heavy pressure from political parties, and other caste people were witnessed.
3. More than one member from our SHGs being interested to contest.
4. The selected candidate faced more problems from their families and relatives.

After Election

Major Activities

1. To train elected representatives to become active and improve their fund raising and managerial capacity.
2. To sensitize elected representatives in gender and gender related issues.
3. To sensitize elected women representative's husband in gender concept.
4. To sensitize Panchayat clerk in gender concept and decentralizing the power.
5. To motivate the Presidents thereby reducing the domination.
6. To strengthen Gram Sabha quorum and functioning through Panchayat support committee and federation.
7. To strengthen Federations and increase AR membership.
8. To motivate the standing committees.
9. To address and solve issues related to violence against women, infanticide, foeticide, discrimination, domination etc. through block level solidarity committees.
10. To create awareness among the general community on sex ratio, discriminations, violence and gender.
11. Advocacy and lobbying with district and state government.
12. District level network of likeminded Presidents.
13. Federations and other people's organization independently network.
14. NGO and CBO networks established within the district, with surrounding districts and at state level.
15. Establishing Arundhathiyar network in three districts.
16. To improve staff attendance and reduce dalit children drop out in primary schools.
17. To improve the functioning of PHCs with adequate drugs, posted and committed staff, following best practice in fields of AIDs, TB, mother and child care, STI.

Level of Performance of Elected Representatives

867 elected representatives were studied by recording inputs given to them and their level of activity in the Panchayat and in the project. Some of the indicators assessed in the study include:

1. Schemes: what the Panchayat has received, what steps they have taken if not received, what is their plan, who have been benefited through the schemes.
2. Accounts and system—transparency both in Panchayat and Gram Sabha.
3. Relationship with NGOs.
4. State Finance Commission.
5. Other than population, whether they have done anything to the vulnerable population.
6. Trainings they have undergone till now.
7. Level of understanding of Panchayat system.
8. Independency, domination etc.
9. Gram Sabha—What is the attitude of Panchayat towards this.

The assessment shows the following results:

- *87 Presidents* (*33 women, 54 men*): 62 (56%) are active—70 per cent of the men and 30 per cent of the women.
- *87 Vice-Presidents* (*25 women, 62 men*): 69 (61%) are active—75 per cent of the men and 25 (23%) of the women.
- *694 Ward members* (*293 women, 401 men*): 62 (52%) are active—60 per cent of the men and 40 per cent of the women.

Standing Committee

537 Standing Committee members were trained—64 Arunthidiyars, 150 Dalit, 323 other castes. Of these 48 per cent were women. There was a good response from Dalit and Arunthidiyar members. In 49 Panchayats the importance of Standing Committees and their roles were discussed as a special issue in Gram Sabha.

There are 435 mandatory Standing Committees in the 87 Panchayats but in only 6 Panchayats they function properly. In a many others the education committee functions due to Central Government's Sarva Shiksha Abhiyan Scheme for education.

Gram Sabha

There is a strong impact on Dalit attendance which comprises 45 per cent of the attendance compared to around 33 per cent in the population of the Panchayats assessed. The January attendance was

Table 9.4: Gram Sabha comparison for three years (2006 to 2009)

Attendance	*Year-1*	*Year-2*	*Year-3*
Dalit Men	4,760	4,467	3,751
Non-Dalit Men	6,825	9,478	9,044
AR-Men	425	2,329	2,613
Dalit Women	2,882	4,237	4,665
Non-Dalit Women	3,867	6,757	7,207
AR-Women	242	2,422	2,797
Total	19,001	29,690	30,077

high because the agenda included government schemes, pending works and selection of beneficiaries.

Beneficiary Selection

The current assessment finds that 19 Panchayats select beneficiaries openly and transparently and another 18 do so partially.

In three Panchayats in Myladumparai area additional poverty list details were collected and presented in the Gram Sabha. In five Panchayats, Gram Sabha joint meetings were conducted, beneficiaries were selected and a petition was given to the President. In Endapuli, malpractice in beneficiary selection was reported to the President who took no action, but use of the Right to Information Act and Gram Sabha resolutions forced a change. In two Panchayat houses were allotted to real beneficiaries previously omitted from the poverty list.

Support Committee

Support groups formed by the project have been found to be effective and 87 (target 35) are functioning—48 function very well and the others are at a medium level. The project documented 49 issues taken up by them—untouchability, illegal sand mining, health and waste management (2 each); below poverty line list (8); basic needs (12); condoms, illegal high interest loans, land documents, encroachment (1 each); burial ground and drainage (3 each); toilet facilities (6); ration shops (3).

Solidarity Committee

Solidarity committees have been formed in Five Blocks. They are composed of elected members, women's federation representatives and other interested people. Each has between 10 and 15 members with Dalits and Arunthidiyars predominating. Among the five groups, 37 out of the 67 members are very active. Training was given on running a Panchayat and Dalit and gender concepts. The long-term idea is that the solidarity committees should take an overview and critique of their individual Block identifying successes and needs which can be addressed by Panchayats. They have close links with the support committees. They have taken up sensitive issues which are sometimes difficult to address without support such as untouchability, Arunthidiyars not being permitted to sit equally in the Gram Sabha, Dalit burial ground issues and encroachments. The solidarity committees helped in instances when the Gram Sabha was not held. They were active in a number of other issues regarding drinking water, encroachment, use of common property and child labour. They were also involved in a number of employment guarantee scheme issues and lobbied for a higher daily wage.

Women Issues Discussed in Gram Sabha

53 women issues were discussed in Gram Sabha and 91 women issues were discussed in the Panchayat meeting, with only 16 discussed in male dominated open forums. This good result has been achieved through federations and support and solidarity committees, which have been given strong gender inputs. It is becoming increasingly easy to introduce local agendas in the Gram Sabha due to rapport with Presidents and the support of the District Presidents association. Issues discussed were girl school dropouts (15), dowry harassment (10), a record 32 domestic violence, three cases of female infanticide/ foeticide. The issue of husbands dominating their elected wives was discussed in 10 Gram Sabhas.

Untouchability

During the year 16 Panchayats reduced discriminatory tea shop double tumbler system, caste based abusive language, restrictions on clothing and access to facilities including temples, reduction in manual handling of excreta, and increased access to burial grounds.

Burial ground issues were taken up in 68 villages and succeeded in 50 villages. in the 15th August, 2008 Gram Sabha resolutions were passed calling on the authorities to sanction burial grounds.

Positive Speakers

There were 24 positive speakers in Gram Sabha and 16 spoke in their own Gram Sabhas. This year 34 spoke, with 23 speaking in their own Gram Sabhas. They created awareness on prevention of HIV/AIDS and spoke out against discrimination. The District Collector was lobbied that Gram Sabhas should take oath regarding HIV/AIDS prevention and care. Through these activities a number of PLHIV obtained benefits from government schemes and the number of condom outlets has increased.

Panchayat and Health

Instances of Panchayats being more involved in health are on the increase. Case histories reported included—general health discussions (7), Village Health Nurse problems (3), support to health camps (16), cervical cancer screening (3), referral of HIV/others (9), sanitation/ water contamination, provision of toilet facilities (9).

Seven Panchayats were identified as the best:

- Thangammalpuram—care and support, TB awareness, petitions to prevent diarrhoea;
- Poomalaikundu—cervical cancer awareness, identification and referral, health camps;
- Dharmapuri—TB and PLHIV identification and referral, good and effective health camps, improved VHN services;
- Thekkampatty—425 benefited through medical camp, preventative health, drainage and sanitation, HIV issues openly addressed in Gram Sabha, benefit to PLHIV;
- Kanniservaipatty, Iyampatty and Pulikutti received Nirmal Gram Puraskar Award given for a clean and hygienic Panchayat. This was achieved with the help of support and solidarity committees, NGOs and women's self-help groups.

District Presidents Association

The District Presidents Association (DPA) was unexpectedly formed early in the first year. In the second year there were some problems but in the past year the association has regained strength. It addressed a number of issues concerning implementation of NREGS (employment guarantee scheme): higher wages and a monitoring team were lobbied for and obtained.

The District Collector sent a notice to the Woman President of Nagalapuram under Section 205 of Tamil Nadu Panchayati Raj Act. During his monitoring visit to NREGA (work guarantee) scheme he found only 8 people were working (it was at the height of the agricultural season). This issue was taken up by the Theni District President's Association. The reply to the notice backed up by representations explained the situation and the notice was withdrawn.

The central legislation mentions 29 powers which *may*—rather than *must* be devolved to Panchayats (education, welfare, agriculture, health etc.). Tamil Nadu state has a very poor record compared with neighbouring Kerala which has made good inroads into poverty reduction through the Panchayats. Much emboldened, the DPA is taking legal advice on registering public interest litigation on matters such as District Collectors' power, power to takeover the encroachments, Block Development Officer interference, wrong inclusion in poverty list, NREGS implementing problems and lack of or encroachment of burial ground etc.

Constraints

- The District authorities discourage the involvement of the NGOs who are seen as subversive.
- Women though given intensive training still find it difficult to function independently.
- Standing committees are not yet started functioning.

Case Studies

1. Model Dalit Women Panchayat President

Surliammal of Thimminayakanpatty village is the President of Pottippuram Panchayat. With no previous experience, but charismatic and empowered through education, training and NGO association, Surliammal has been able to overcome all the hurdles and pilot a well functioning Panchayat, setting an inspiring model not only to dalit women Panchayat Presidents, but to all Panchayat Presidents. It goes to her credit to have transformed elected members belonging to rival political parties into a well-organized team for implementing several developments as well as welfare schemes in the Panchayat. She is capable of analyzing problems, identifying proper remedies and taking appropriate decisions. After attending a training course in KILA in Kerala and seeing replicable models there, she introduced the practice of conducting ward meetings, prior to the G.S. meeting, giving an opportunity to everyone in the ward to participate in discussions. She also took the bold initiative of raising jatropa plants in more than 300 acres of land belonging to the Panchayat, with a view to generating own funds for the Panchayat. Apart from personal charisma, education, experience of working in NGOs, support from husband, economic security etc. have contributed to her success.

2. Positive Woman Member

Easwari, an HIV positive woman in Kodangipatti Panchayat, has made history by contesting in the Panchayat election against 10 contestants and winning by a margin of 220 votes. Today she is an active elected member, confident and outgoing as well as wanted and respected by the people. Her example has boosted the morale of the positive people.

3. Tackling Male Domination

In Singarajapuram Panchayat, the President, Ms. Vasanthi, a BC woman has been completely overshadowed by her benami husband, who used to sit in the President's chair and conduct the meetings. Once a male ward member raised the issue and remarked that the President should occupy her chair and conduct the meeting. But the husband did not budge. Then the ward member lodged a complaint with the ABDO. ABDO asked the husband to vacate the seat and allow the President to occupy her legitimate seat. In response the lady President and her husband left the place in a huff. The Panchayat meeting was conducted by the ward members with the Vice-President in the chair. All the ward members boycotted the next Panchayat meeting, because the President's husband came to conduct the meeting. Finally, the Panchayat meeting in October 2008 was conducted independently by the woman President.

In Nariyuthu Panchayat, initially, there were two proxy Presidents: one, the husband of the real President, the other, a village leader, belonging to BC community. Slowly through orientation, training, counselling and persuasion the proxies dropped out and now the real President is functioning.

In Thangammalpuram Panchayat, initially, the Vice-President's husband acted in her place, but slowly he has retreated. When the husband of the Vice-President of Koilparai started acting as the Vice-President, the people shouted: "You are not the Vice-President, please go back and send your wife to the Panchayat". He went back and never again acted in the place of his wife.

Future Focus

A. State Level Convention of elected representatives.
B. Advocacy and lobbying with district and state governments.
C. Expand our network and collaboration state-wide.
D. Promoting model Panchayats.
E. Future candidate selection and training for election 2011.

10

Women's Empowerment through Gender Budgeting

R.V. Pole

"Gender Budgeting" is now recognized as a tool for empowering women. This chapter gives a broad overview of the gender budgeting initiatives in India, highlighting certain related issues that need to be addressed for making gender budgeting an effective tool for women's empowerment, in the Indian context. It explores the query—how effective has gender budgeting been as a tool for women's empowerment, in its present form, in the Indian context. While no direct solutions are offered, an attempt has been made to bring certain pertinent issues into focus along with suggestions on alternative strategies.

Definition and Concept

The term "gender budgeting" has become a catch all phrase to describe various government initiatives that seek to address gender issues in the domain of public expenditure and policy. Two definitions are quoted to introduce the concept.

" 'Gender-sensitive budgets', 'gender budgets', and 'women's budgets' refer to a variety of processes and tools aimed at facilitating an assessment of the gendered impacts of government budgets. In the evolution of these exercises, the focus has been on auditing government budgets for their impact on women and girls. This has meant that, to date, the term 'women's budget' has gained widest use. Recently, however, these budget exercises have begun using gender as a category of analysis so the terminology 'gender-sensitive budgets' is increasingly being adopted. It is important to recognize that 'women's budgets' or 'gender-sensitive budgets' are not separate budgets for women, or for men. They are attempts to breakdown, or disaggregate, the government's mainstream budget according to its impact on women and men, and different groups of women and men, with cognizance being given to the society's underpinning gender relations" (Sharp, Rhonda: 1999).

"Gender budget initiatives analyze how governments raise and spend public money, with the aim of securing gender equality in decision-making about public resource allocation; and gender equality in the distribution of the impact of government budgets, both in their benefits and in their burdens.

While presenting the Union Budget 2007-08, Finance Minister in his budget speech made a special reference to Gender Budgeting Cells. It was noted by Finance Minister "there is growing awareness of gender sensitive of budgetary allocations. 50 Ministries/ Departments have set up Gender Budgeting Cells. For 2007-08, 27 Ministries/Departments and 5 Union Territories covering 33 demands of grants have contributed to a statement placed in the budget papers. The outlay for 100 per cent women specific programmes is Rs. 8,795 crores and for schemes where at least 30 per cent is for women specific programmes is Rs. 22,382 crores. The statement being referred to by the Finance Minister in his speech is Statement 20 of the Expenditure Budget Vol. I, 2007-08. This is a statement on Gender Budgeting initiatives of the government and before we embark upon an analysis of this statement it is very important to get an insight into the concept of Gender Budget initiatives.

What it is?

Gender responsive budget initiatives are the various terms, which loosely describe the Government's commitments towards gender concerns translated into monetary terms. Contrary to popular perception, Gender Budgets are not separate budgets for women or men. In the words of Rhonda Sharp, leading feminist economist, "They are attempts to breakdown or disaggregate the Government's mainstream budget according to its impact on women and men with cognizance being given to the societies underpinning gender relation". Gender budget initiatives analyze how governments raise and spend public money, with the aim of securing gender equality in decision making about public resource allocation and gender equality in the distribution of the impact of government budgets, both in their benefits and their burdens (IDRC, 2001). The Council of Europe Informal Group of Experts on gender budgeting defines gender budgeting in these words.

"Gender budgeting is an application of gender mainstreaming in the budgetary process. It means a gender-based assessment of budgets, incorporating a gender perspective at all levels of the budgetary process and restructuring revenues and expenditures in order to promote gender equality." Gender budgeting examines the resource allocation through gender lens and stresses on re-prioritization rather than an increase in public expenditure.

Determinants and Types of Gender Budget Initiatives

The various Gender Budget initiatives can be classified based on location, scope of exercise, report format, political dynamics etc. However, these determinants are not mutually exclusive and a country may adopt a combination of determinants to define its gender budgeting policy.

There are three types of gender budget initiatives based on who initiated them:

1. *Government Initiatives*: The Government initiates the exercise and takes steps to institutionalize the same. The primary focus of government initiatives is on allocation of resources, monitoring, reviewing and auditing.
2. *NGO Initiatives*: Civil society organizations, which focus on women upliftment and empowerment, have launched gender-sensitive budget initiatives outside the government. These initiatives tend to be focused on the demand for better policies and greater democratization of policy. They focus on influencing the national budget and its budgetary processes to adopt gender interpretation.
3. *Joint NGO and Parliamentary Initiatives*: Some non-governmental initiatives have been launched by civil society organizations in cooperation with Parliamentarians to make fiscal policy more responsive to the needs of women. Elected representatives like Parliamentarians play a role in outside

government initiatives as well as those initiated within governments.

Tracing the Footsteps

The various Governments at the Centre have tried to tackle the issues of poverty, population, unemployment, health, education, inequitable growth, etc. through their focus on the national budgets. For example, to eradicate poverty and reduce unemployment, government may launch employment guarantee schemes funded by government. Similarly, there are schemes, which try to tackle the literacy gap between girls/boys or focus on universalization of education or target reproductive and child health as its goal. There is an increasing awareness that due attention needs to be paid to women, as evidence suggests that the economic gains of gender equality lead to increased output and better development of people's capacities. Women's economic empowerment could provide the possibility for all countries to have some combination of increased productivity, less stress and better overall health. Recognizing the importance of budgetary allocations in the socio-economic development of the country, the successive Governments, over a period of time, have also tried to build in gender perspective in the planning process and successive national budgets. The gender perspective on public expenditure has been gaining momentum over the years and is reflected in the evolving trends on the subject:

- The Seventh Five Year Plan introduced the concept of monitoring of 27 beneficiary oriented schemes for women by Department of Women and Child Development.
- The Eighth Five Year Plan (1992-97) highlighted for the first time the need to ensure a definite flow of funds from the general developmental sectors to women. The plan document made an express statement that "... the benefits of development from different sectors should not bypass women and special programmes on women should complement the general development programmes. The latter in turn, should reflect greater gender sensitivity."
- The Ninth Five Year Plan (1997-2002), while reaffirming the earlier commitment adopted Women Component Plan (WCP) as one of the major strategies and directed both the

Central and the State Governments to ensure that. "Not less than 30 per cent of the funds/benefits are earmarked in all the women's related sectors."

- The Department of Women and Child Development as the nodal advocacy Department in Union Government spearheading the gender budgeting initiative in 2004 defined a broad strategic framework for gender budgeting and defined "Budgeting for Equity" as the mission statement.
- Expert group constituted by the Government of India on "Classification System of Government Transactions" whose terms of reference included Examining the feasibility of and suggesting gender budgeting and economic classification, recommended a gender sensitive budget aimed at examining budgetary associations through a gender lens. The group recommended a dissection of the budget to translate gender commitments into budgetary commitments with a view to ensuring effective targeting of public spend.
- The gender concerns were institutionalized by the introduction of Gender Budgeting statement in the Union Budget for the year 2005-06.
- Instructions and checklists issued regarding setting up of Gender Budgeting Cell in various Ministries/Departments with effect from 1st January, 2005.
- Ministry of Finance in March 2007 issued guidelines regarding the composition and functions of the Gender Budget Cells to ensure that uniform approach is adopted by all Ministries/Departments. The GBCs are envisaged as a cohesive group of senior/middle level officers from policy, coordination, budget and accounts that will direct the gender budgeting policy in the Ministry/Department based on the guidelines issued on the subject.

The guidance sheet series produced by United Nations Development Fund for Women's (UNIFEM) Gender Responsive Budgeting Programme aims to assist government officials and gender equality advocates in their efforts to make gender responsive budgeting a reality. Debbie Budlender, specialist researcher with the Community Agency for Social Enquiry (CASE) South Africa, in Guidance Sheet Series No. 1, January 2007 describes two tools that can be used by government officials in their task. The first tool, the call circulars are the official notices that are issued by Ministry of Finance, Planning Commission or similar agencies near the beginning of each budget cycle. The call circulars describe government priorities that should be addressed in the coming year's allocation. One way in which call circulars can be made more gender responsive is for them to state explicitly that gender should be reflected in submissions.

Ministry of Finance has introduced a separate gender budget statement in Union Budget from 2005-06 onwards. Statement No. 20 Gender Budgeting-Expenditure Budget Vol. I reflect the budget provisions under the various programmes and schemes administered by the different Ministries/Departments that target the socio-economic welfare and empowerment of women as a key objective of these schemes. This statement indicates in two parts, the budget provision for schemes that are substantially meant for the benefit of women. Part A details schemes in which 100 per cent provision is for women. Part B reflects schemes where the allocations for women constitute at least 30 per cent of the provision. Both the tools as explained in the Guidance series sheets are being used in the Indian context and it reflects a serious commitment on the part of the Government to strengthen the gender budgeting initiative in Indian milieu.

It is evident that the perspective on gender budgeting in India has evolved over the last few years from the passive statistical exercise to an active one which seeks to establish not only the quantum of resources allocated for the development needs of women but also to analyse the actual amount spent and link with the outcomes.

Growing Relevance in India

Progress on the social sector front continues to be slow in the country as reflected in India's latest Human Development Report (HDR) for 2008. It ranks India in terms of the HDI at 134, up one rank from last year among the countries with medium human development out of 177 countries of the world. In terms of the Gender Development Index India ranks 96th which is a marked improvement from the 105th rank in 2000. The first HDR prepared by the Planning Commission of India reveals that gender disparity across the states has declined. The report has given Gender Equity Index (GEI) in which Bihar has the most abysmal record of 0.49. GEI of UP and Assam is between 0.5-0.59. Maharashtra, Orissa, Rajasthan, West Bengal figure in the GEI bracket 0.6-0.74. The group in the topmost bracket, i.e. 0.75 + is composed of the North Eastern States except Assam, Southern States and Himachal Pradesh. The HDR has not seriously taken into account, the declining sex ratio, especially the juvenile sex ratio (0-9 years) while estimating various development indices. The report has used 8 indicators to map the human development of states. It has provided diagrammatic representation of human development in the form of development radars comprising of 8 indicators, namely: incidence of poverty, per capita consumption expenditure, life expectancy at age one, infant mortality rates, intensity of formal education, literacy rates, access to safe drinking water, proportion of households with *pucca* houses. The central thesis of HDR has been economic prosperity in terms of high per capita income does not necessarily lead to overall human development. Declining sex ratio in the prosperous states like Punjab, Haryana, Gujarat and Maharashtra prove the point. There is a need to focus more on the impact of budgetary allocations on women's well-being and women's development.

Table 10.1: Human Development Index

Year	*Human Development Index*	*Gender Development Index*
2006	0.648	0.633
1996	0.584	0.568

The approach to the Eleventh Plan specifically talks about gender equity. "Gender bias is deeply ingrained in our social psyche and this is reflected in indicators such as sex ratios, literacy and health gaps of boys and girls, Maternal Mortality Rates etc. These data, however, do not fully reflect the discrimination against women. The Eleventh Plan strategy for gender equity must pay attention to all aspects of women's lives. It must ensure that women live and live with dignity."

"The impact of government budgets on the most disadvantaged groups of women is a focus of special attention." (IDRC, 2001). The above definitions underline the fact that gender budgeting is now seen as a socio-economic tool for ensuring gender equity in the development process and lays a strong emphasis on engendering public expenditure and policy. Critical activities constituting the gender budgeting exercise would include:

(a) Addressing gap between policy commitment and allocation for women through adequate resource allocation and gender sensitive programme formulation and implementation.

(b) Mainstreaming gender concerns in public expenditure and policy.
(c) Gender audit of public expenditure, programme implementation and policies—relating to public expenditure, fiscal and monetary matters etc.

Budget impacts women's lives in several ways. It directly promotes women's development through allocation of budgetary funds for women's programmes and reduces opportunities for empowerment of women through budgetary cuts. Structural adjustment programmes and globalisation policies have directly increased women's unpaid work burden, thereby increased women-provided subsidy in the economy. Devaluation of income for the majority of masses as a result of new economic policy coupled with price rise, erosion of public distribution system and reduction of services offered by the public health system have made women bear disproportionate share of burden, because in the patriarchal families women have to shoulder responsibility of providing meals and looking after the sick family members. Hence women have high stakes in preventing an increase in the proportion of indirect taxes on essential commodities and in budgetary provisions to guarantee food security and health care. Hence, careful study of the working of PDS and local taxonomy on food security and impact on nutrition, health and health services of budgetary allocations is a must (Patel, 2002):

Table 10.2: Public Distribution System

Year	*Part A*	*Part B*	*Total*	*%*	*%*
	(100% allocation for women)	*(30% allocation for women)*		*Allocation in Part A*	*Allocation in Part B*
2004-05 (RE)	—	—	10574.16	—	—
2005-06 (RE)	8273.88	15966.33	24240.21	34.13	65.87
2006-07 (RE)	4618.95	17362.46	22251.41	20.75	79.25
2007-08 (BE)	8795.47	22382.44	31177.96	28.21	71.79

Source: Expenditure Budget, Volume I.

Women's Component Plan and Gender Budgeting

The Planning Commission of India has always focused on women's issues as per the perceptions of their members on women's status within the economy. The First Five Year Plan (1951-1956) set up Central Social Welfare Board in 1953 to promote welfare work through voluntary organisations, charitable trusts and philanthropic agencies. The Second Five Year Plan (1956-1960) supported development of Mahila Mandals for grassroots work among women. The Third, Fourth and Interim Plans (1961-1974) made provision for women's education, pre-natal and child health services, supplementary feeding for children, nursing and expectant mothers. The Fifth Plan (1974-1978) marked a major shift in the approach towards women, from welfare to development. The Sixth Plan (1980-1985) accepted women's development as a separate economic agenda. The Multidisciplinary approach with three-pronged thrust on health, education and employment. The Seventh Plan (1985-1990) declared as its OBJECTIVE TO BRING WOMEN INTO THE MAINSTREAM OF NATIONAL DEVELOPMENT. The Eighth Plan (1992-1997) projected paradigm shift, from development to empowerment and promised to ensure flow of benefits to women in the core sectors of education, health and employment. Outlay for women rose from 4 crores in the First Plan to Rs. 2,000 crore in the Eighth Plan. The Ninth Plan (1997-2002) stated that Empowerment of women was its strategic objective. It accepted the concept of Women's Component Plan to assure at least 30 per cent of funds/benefits from all development sectors flow to women. The Tenth Five Year Plan (2002-2009) has suggested specific strategies, policies and programmes for Empowerment of Women. They are as follows:

- Measurement of development has to go beyond achievement of GDP growth to indicators of distributive justice and their monitoring.
- Women headed households have to be specifically targeted, identifying added disadvantages in the rural and urban locations with reference to different parameters of deprivation. Formulation of Gender Development Indicators to measure Human Development and their use as a tool for monitoring development needs to be hastened.

The Component Plan approach, which did not address compartmentalisation of government functioning should be replaced with a mandated approach of convergence of services at all levels of governance, through intersectoral committees of all Ministries/ Departments at the Centre and the States with specific responsibility given to the Panchayats and Municipalities to administer at the grassroots level.

Earmarking of funds for women under all major poverty alleviation programmes and maintenance of gender disaggregated records of implementation of all poverty alleviation programmes. Mandatory registration of all assets provided under government programmes (land, house, animals, production units) in the joint names of husband and wife. Intensified focus on rights education and capacity-building interventions for women in all strategic sectors, including health and reproductive health, agriculture, natural resource management, technology (including information technology) and legal awareness. Revision of regulatory framework to allow women's collectives to access institutional credit, obtain medium-term leases for cultivation on wastelands and common lands, bid for contracts for collection and sale of minor forest produce and other collective activities that will ensure household food security while regenerating the natural resource base.

Women's groups have demanded allocations for women-specific programmes of strategic nature to arrive at the desired goals in a shorter time span. They should target women of different age groups in terms of strategic interventions to take specific notice of adolescent girls, older women and women in difficult circumstances. Strategic gender tools like gender audits, gender impact assessments, gender analysis and gender budgeting to monitor implementation and impacts must be developed. Gender audit of plans, policies and programmes of various Ministries with pro-women allocations has to be a part and parcel of the monitoring process.

There is a need for provisions in the composite programmes under education, health and rural development sectors to target them specifically at girls/women as the principal beneficiaries and disaggregated within the total allocation. It may also be necessary to place restrictions on their reappropriation for other purposes. To effectively attain population stabilization, policies and plans need to empower women, promote their reproductive rights and involve men in reproductive decision-making and household responsibilities. Particular attention should be given to improve women's access to quality reproductive health services, including adolescent girls to counselling on reproductive health and sexuality issues.

The strategy of organising women in self-help groups in the Ninth Plan period has paid good dividends for expanding micro-credit. This should be extended not only for reaching larger numbers of women but also for increasing awareness of and access to social development, apart from encouraging a process of convergence in the delivery of services in a decentralised set up.

It is important to empower women's organisations and citizens groups to monitor enforcement of equal and minimum wages legislation by State Governments, and the adherence to norms in poverty alleviation programmes. Professional Organisations including Universities should be included for undertaking monitoring, evaluation and research studies for identifying issues requiring special attention.

To engender budget at the National level, it is important to make thorough study of the Five Year Plans, Economic Survey, National Human Development Report and other important policy documents such as Towards Equality Report (1974), Shram Shakti Report (1988) and Women Empowerment Policy (2001) published by the Government of India and the State Governments policies that guide programmes and budgetary allocations. This exercise helps us understand the working of macro policies in determining the fate of social sector under which budgetary allocation for women falls.

Way Ahead

The inclusion of Gender Budget Statement in the Union Budget document demonstrates the growing concerns of the government, its commitment and openness to make available the public expenditure figures for analysis. Gender budgeting initiatives in India are still in their nascent stage and the process will get refined and strengthened over a period of time.

In Indian context, there is a growing relevance of gender budgeting initiatives keeping in view the position of women *vis-à-vis* various socio-economic indicators. Therefore, the ultimate outcome of the gender budgeting initiatives is the improvement in the socio-economic indicators where women/girls are concerned. There is also a need to spread awareness among various stakeholders involved in the process. SHGs and NGOs can play a crucial role in sensitizing the beneficiary group. Advocating for grassroots linkages of various schemes and facilitating independent evaluation of various schemes.

Corporate sector is also playing a crucial role in the development of economy and women are contributing their mite by working in private sector. The scope of extending employment opportunities is more and secure work environment need to flow to women employees.

Gender budgeting initiative may have started as a strategy for examining the public expenditure through gender lens but it can evolve into a powerful tool for participatory development, it can be used for re-examining the existing schemes. Reprioritization of resources and training new schemes with clearly defined quantitable goals. The present limited analysis also shows that there is a need to increase the resource allocation in education, economic empowerment initiatives, alternate fuel technology, sanitation and nutrition. These areas directly impact women and can have a cascading effect in the overall growth of the economy.

Conclusion

Budgets gain resources through the taxation policies and allocate resources to different sections of the economy. The Budget is an important tool in the hands of state for affirmative action for improvement of gender relations through reduction of gender gap in the development process. It can help to reduce economic inequalities, between men and women as well as between the rich and the poor. (NCAS, 2003). Hence, the budgetary policies need to keep into consideration the gender dynamics operating in the economy and in the civil society. Serious examining of budget calls for greater transparency at the level of international economics to local processes of empowerment. There is a need to provide training and capacity building workshops for decision-makers in the government structures, *Gram Sabhas,* Parliamentarians and audio-visual media. There is a need to highlight participatory approaches to pro-poor budgeting, green budgeting, local and global implications of pro-poor and pro-women budgeting, alternative macro scenarios emerging out of alternative budgets and interlinkages between gender-sensitive budgeting and women's empowerment.

REFERENCES

Bandopadhyaya, D., "Panchayats in Karnataka", *Economic and Political Weekly,* Vol. XXXVII, No. 35, August 31-September 6, 2002, pp. 3572-3573.

Bandyopadhyaya, S., *Non-farm Employment and Role of Panchayats: Some Experiences,* Department of Economics with Rural Development, Vidyasagar University, Midnapur, West Bengal, 2002.

Carr, M., Chen, M., Jhabwala, R. (ed.), *Speaking Out, Women's Economic Empowerment in South Asia,* Vistaar Publications, New Delhi. Centre for Social Medicine and Community Health (1998), *Reproductive Health—India's Primary Health Care,* School of Social Sciences, Jawaharlal Nehru University, New Delhi, 1998.

Das, P., Bandyopadhyay, S. and Majumdar, T., *Panchayat Finance: A Study of Some Gram Panchayats with Special Focus on Own Source Fund,* Department of Economics with Rural Development, Vidyasagar University, Midnapur, West Bengal, 2002.

Das, P., Bandyopadhyay, S. and Majumdar, T., *Panchayati Raj System and Rural Development in West Bengal: A Study Based on Household Survey of Some Villages of the District of Midnapore*, Department of Economics with Rural Development, Vidyasagar University, Midnapore, West Bengal, 2002.

Department of Distance Education, SNDT Women's University, 1995.

Desai, N. and Thakkar, U. *Women in Indian Society,* National Book Trust, Delhi, 2001.

Gopalan, S. and Shiva, M., *National Profile on Women, Health and Development*–Country Profile—India, Voluntary Health Association of India and World Health Organisation, 2000.

Gupte, M. and Shatrughana, V., *Shrama Shakti Report,* GoI, 1988.

Jain, D. "Valuing Women's Work: Time as a Measure", *Economic and Political Weekly,* vol. XXXI, no. 43, October 26, WS46-WS 57, 1996.

Kapur Mehta, A., "Recasting Indices for Developing Countries: A Gender Empowerment Measure", *Economic and Political Weekly,* October 26, WS80-WS86, 1996.

Kramarae, C. and Spender, D. *Routledge International Encyclopedia of Women: Global Women's Issues and Knowledge,* Vols. I, II, Routledge, New York, 2000.

Krishnaraj, M. (ed.), "*Women in the Data Systems*", Research Centre for Women's Studies, SNDT Women's University, Mumbai. KWIRC (2002), Building Budgets From Below, Banglore, p. 3, 1991.

Lahiri, A. Chakraborty, L. and Bhattacharya, P.N., *Gender Budgeting in India,* The National Institute of Public Finance and Policy, New Delhi, 2002.

Mahajan, R., *Maharashtra Human Development Report,* State Planning Board, Maharashtra, 2002.

Mishra, N., *Poverty in South Asia,* Authors Press, Delhi, 2001.

Moser, C., *Gender Planning and Development,* Routledge, London, 1993.

Mujumdar, N., "Rural Development: New Perceptions", *Economic and Political Weekly,* Vol. XXXVII, No. 39, September 28, 2002.

Mukherjee, M. "Towards Gender-Aware Data Systems: Indian Experience", *Economic and Political Weekly,* Vol. XXXI, No. 43, October 26, WS63-WS71, 1996.

Murthy, R.K. *Building Women's Capacities, Intervention in Gender Transformation,* Sage Publications, New Delhi.

NCAS (2003), *Parliament Digest For the People,* National Centre for Advocacy Studies, Pune, 2001.

Nerulkar, A. and Patel, V., *Women and Development,* Text Book for MA Parts 1 and 2.

Nussbaum, M., *Women and Human Development: The Capability Approach,* Kali For Women, Delhi, 2000.

Pal, M., "Empowerment at Grassroots", *Economic and Political Weekly,* Vol. XXXVII, No. 38, September 21, 2002, pp. 3923-3924.

11

Empowering Women: Some Aspects of the Karnataka Experience

K. Subha[1] and *B.S. Bhargava*[2]

Empowerment is a widely used but a complex concept. Since the 1970s, the feminist literature and the Gender And Development (GAD) discourse have shed considerable light on the concept of empowerment and has addressed several important questions like what constitutes empowerment? Who empowers whom? What are the goals and strategies of empowerment as well as the process of disempowerment? The notion of empowerment is thus multifaceted. It is very much reflected in the following, as given in the Ninth Plan Document, the NPEW:

> "Empowerment is manifested as a redistribution of power, whether between nations, classes, castes, races, genders, or individuals. The goals of women's empowerment are to challenge patriarchal ideology (male domination and women's subordination); to transform the structures and institutions that reinforce and perpetuate gender discrimination and social inequality (the family, caste, class, religion, educational processes and institutions, the media, health practices and systems, laws and civil codes, political process, development models, and government institutions); and to enable poor women to gain access to, and control of, both material and informational resources."

These components outline the inclusive elements of empowerment. In addition to the different levels of empowerment, the 1990s trend was also toward a synthesis of power over resources and power to make decisions. This definition of empowerment is captured effectively in the definition of empowerment used in the United Nations (UN) system. It includes the following components: women's sense of self-worth; their right to have and to determine choices; their right to have their power to control their own lives, both within and outside the home; and their ability to influence the direction of social change to create a more just social and economic order, nationally and internationally.

Empowerment occurs most definitely when women mobilize themselves and take leadership positions in work settings and in the community. An essential element of empowerment is self-empowerment and grassroots activism. India is a Parliamentary Democracy. The Constitution of India makes commitment not only to equality but also to providing special opportunities for the advancement of women. Chapters 3 and 4 of the Constitution of India have many provisions in regard to equality between men and women. For instance, political equality is provided through adult franchise. Article 14 provides for equality—substantive as well as procedure. Article 15 prohibits any kind of discrimination. Article 16(2) forbids discrimination in respect of 'any employment of office under the state' on the grounds of '*religion, race, caste, sex, descent, place of birth, residence or any of them*'. The Directive Principles of State Policy enunciated in Chapter 4 of the Constitution embody the major policy goals of welfare state. Some of them concern women indirectly or by necessary implication.

Some of the provisions highlight the different implications of empowerment for women in unique contexts of development and social change. Laws and policies enable women to have greater self-confidence and freedom from violence and oppression and also empower women to take leadership in other spheres of their life.

It is interesting to trace the differences in empowerment experiences in different regions and levels at which they occur. Our country is taking rapid strides in empowering women and it would be appropriate to share some of the experiences in Karnataka. Looking back in a historical mode (in different periods), in brief, is rather an imperative to understand the present status. As it is very well known that the status of women in India is intertwined with socio-economic and political hierarchies. Since the Vedic times, women have received different status depending on class and caste hierarchies.

It is widely believed that in the Vedic period, women were relatively more independent and were allowed to participate in the socio-economic and political activities. Later on, towards the end of the early Vedic period and the beginning of the later Vedic period their position began to decline. This situation continued for centuries and further deteriorated in the mediaeval period. As a result, the social reformers started a powerful movement to improve the position of women. Several reform societies and religious organizations worked hard to spread education among women, to encourage widow remarriage, to prevent child marriage and other related matters.

Kitturu Rani Chennamma (1778-1829) was the queen of the princely state Kittur in Karnataka. In 1824, thirty-three years before the 1857 war of independence she led an armed rebellion against the British. The resistance ended in her martyrdom and she is remembered even today as one of the earliest Indian rulers to have fought for independence. Along with Abbakka Rani, Keladi Chennamma and Onake Obavva, she is much venerated in Karnataka as an icon of bravery and women's pride. Akkamahadevi established gender equality, was a poetess of great literary and spiritual merit who composed Vachanas. Nearly 40 women composers of the Vachanas are among the earlier poetesses in Kannada. This indicates the achievement in the emancipation of women.

A number of political events which were taking place in British India at that time had their repercussions in Mysore (now Karnataka). Among the women of Karnataka, Bellari Siddhamma's name stands out prominently as one who not only participated in the fight for freedom but also played an important role in the formation of integrated Karnataka. Ordinary women formed the rank and file of fighters and put up a brave struggle. In Mysore it was in 1930 that, for the first time some women took their seats as members at the Budget Session of the Representative Assembly.

Though there was almost no change in the socio-economic position of Indian women in general, by 1937 India was the third country in the world in terms of the number of women legislators. With Independence in 1947 and the framing of the Constitution, many of the demands of the women's movements were incorporated. This special attention given to the needs and problems of women as one of the '*weaker sections*' of Indian society, and the recognition of political equality was a radical departure from the norms prevailing in traditional India.

It has led many scholars to describe the Constitution of India as a manifesto of social revolution. The attainment of independence in August 1947 followed by the establishment of a republican form of state in 1950, brought to women the promise of adult franchise and complete equality of opportunity in all spheres. Widening of Women's participation in all areas of social activity—economic, social and political—was the aim of many provisions (as referred to earlier) incorporated in the Constitution. This radicalism of the Constitution and the departure from the existing social system was the result of the assumption that every adult woman, irrespective of her social status, would function as a citizen and as an individual partner in the task of nation building.

The message of the Report of the Committee on the status of Women in India (1974), International Women's Year 1975, National Plan of Action for Women and International Women's Decade (1976-1985) was clearly to bring women to the forefront of development concerns and reassured the commitment to gender equality enshrined in the Constitution of India.

A sustained women's movement over the years has led to changes in various fields. With '*women*' having became a legitimate subject or field of academic enquiry, there has been a fairly rapid increase of women studies centres in Universities and Colleges.

One of the fundamental aspects of empowerment is equity. Relatively, Karnataka seems to have performed better in gender related developments. Yet demographic and health indicators reveal unequal access to facilities owing to the belief in secondary status of women. This devalued status and its extreme implications led to a gradual shift in the government's perception of women as beneficiaries of programmes and services to women as '*critical agents of change*'.

Programmes of the state concentrated on increasing women's incomes by setting up suitable training and production units. The Karnataka State Social Welfare Advisory Board was the first official institution, set up in 1954 to reach women. A Department of Rehabilitation and Aftercare Services was established in 1956 which was converted into the Department of Women and Child Welfare in 1975 following the announcement of the International Women's Year. The Women's Development Corporation was set up in 1987 to fund income generating programmes for women. These departments and bodies focused on the care and welfare of destitute women and children on the one hand and training and financing income earning projects for poor women on the other. Social welfare schemes for poor and destitute women are also being administered through different departments. Special programmes cover selected areas like *devadasi* rehabilitation.

Despite several attempts there is still difficulty in pushing through the agenda for a woman-oriented perspective. What is required in this and other programmes is therefore a bottom up approach which starts with identifying what women need and understanding how they can be strengthened by appropriate training and awareness programmes (including awareness and sensitization programmes for officials and other persons). The strategy of self-help groups first tried out by NGOs has succeeded in actually reaching rural women and improving their lot. Self-Help Groups (SHGs) in Karnataka are functioning in an efficient manner and the SHG Movement was spreading at a fast pace to other parts of the country. It is reported that Karnataka alone has 4,56,000 SHGs out of a national figure of 40 lakhs. The credit flow to SHGs in the country is over Rs. 4,200 crore and Karnataka's share was Rs. 1,004 crore which amounts to nearly 24 per cent (Deccan Herald, January 20, 2009). Thus women have found their voice in exclusive women's sanghas and Self-Help Groups. An encouraging trend is the significant number of women who belong to a '*Local Mahila Sangha*' or women's group.

Increasing the proportion of women in local bodies is certainly a welcome step but the nature of participation has to change. Facilitation programmes assume crucial significance in such circumstances. With greater experience and self-confidence, we can expect women representatives to gradually develop into a powerful pressure group for improving the status of women. Already, there are cases of women panchayat members effectively increasing allocations for anganwadi buildings and advocating women's issues at the local level.

Participation of the citizenry in governance has long been a cherished goal. That everyone has the right to take part in the government of his/her country is expressed in the Universal Declaration of Human Rights. True democracy can exist only when there is participation of women in governance and developmental programmes. The 73rd and 74th Constitutional Amendments have provided for women's inclusion in politics and administration at the grassroots level. This was the starting point for the revolution in the field of decentralization and recognition of the principle of '*gender equality*'. This change is hailed as the most important development in the history of democratic governance in India and as the greatest event for women's empowerment as one-third of the seats are reserved for women. Karnataka can very well take the pride in the fact that before the 73rd Constitutional Amendment, 25 per cent of the seats were reserved for women in the local bodies like panchayats and municipalities. These institutions have brought governance closer to people in general and women in particular.

Karnataka is considered a pioneer in enacting legislation reserving substantial seats for women in elected local bodies. Although the Karnataka legislation only stipulates a minimum one-third reservation for women, exact figures of the elected women representatives in Panchayti Raj Institutions, emerged after 2005 Panchayati Raj elections, are given below:

Table 11.1: EWR Panchayati Raj

S. No.	*Gram Panchayats*	*Taluk Panchayats*	*Zilla Panchayat*
1.	SC—19%	SC—18%	SC—18%
2.	ST—11%	ST—9%	ST—8%
3.	BC—33%	BC (A+B)—34%	BC—38%
4.	General—37%	General—39%	General—36%
5.	Women—43%	Women—41%	Women—37%

Source: Computed.

Karnataka had 3 rounds of Panchayati Raj Elections after the implementation of the Panchayati Raj Act, 1993 (conformity Act). In these elections, in many cases women have had captured 45 per cent of seats. It can be observed from Table 11.1 that training for the elected members of the Panchayati Raj Institutions is a tremendous task because of its spread and number.

This chapter also examines *a very innovative and novel method of capacity building, programme being organized by Abdul Nazeer Sab State Institute of Rural Development (ANSSIRD), Mysore, to impart training through satellite.*

The main concern since 1993 is to train the rural leadership in the art of running these institutions, so that the rural local government is strengthened and it becomes viable enough to deliver the goods as desired by the objectives of Panchayati Raj and sustain the values of the system. This is more applicable to women leaders as they were new entrants to the field, illiterate and unexposed to the world around them. The need for systematic training and orientation is necessary to empower all elected members specifically the women members to exercise their power and authority. Empowerment gives women the capacity to influence decision making process, planning, implementation and evaluation by integrating them into the rural local political system. Awareness should also be developed in times to come as the fate of the State and National political systems depend on the emerging leadership at the grassroots.

Capacity building actually means, developing adequate skills to perform the given role and function efficiently depending on the capacity of the individual to understand the given situation, to work effectively, to tackle them and prepare future plans.

ANSSIRD is working under the Department of Rural Development and Panchayati Raj, Government of Karnataka. ANSSIRD is primarily responsible for training elected representatives, functionaries, NGO personnel and members of the general public on various aspects of rural development. The training modes include face-to-face training programmes at the premises at Mysore, satellite based training with a studio, earth-station and transmission centre being located at Mysore and more than 210 receiving stations across the state, and cascade mode training for specific applications like computer software, etc. In the cascade mode, resource persons are trained at Mysore who in turn train participants at district and taluk levels across the state.

ANSSIRD has been designated as a nodal institute for undertaking training and capacity building of Panchayati Raj members. However, the planning for the training and capacity building programme was district specific. It also conducts capacity building programmes for officers of various development departments, representatives of voluntary organizations and Bank Officials. Conducting training research activities, evaluation and assessment of impact of various Rural Development Programmes are also being undertaken.

The focus of training programme was largely on local issues; the programme was the largest one of its kind held for the grassroots level leadership, encouraging them to contribute to mainstream development.

This training and interaction programme was of particular significance because of its innovative use of modern communication technology coupled with participatory training methodology to reach out to people spread over great distances.

The objective of this interaction, which has been the outcome of months of intensive planning and preparation, was to create a ground for democratic decentralization through people's participation in local planning. It aimed at provoking Gram Panchayat members, especially women and representatives of disadvantaged groups to take a deeper look at their own situations and struggling, to find solutions to their problems, as also to enable them to think constructively—i.e. in terms of small but constructive activities that they can initiate individually or as collectives.

The Satellite based Training and Communication (SATCOM) Centre was established and commissioned in April 2002. The advantage of reaching out to large numbers simultaneously at low costs is unmatched. The Satellite based Training and Communication System comprises an earth station, digital transmission studio and one-way video, two-way audio communication on INSAT-3B satellite's extended c-band transponder. At the studio, dedicated anchors and panelists conduct live or pre-recorded presentations, discussions and talkback sessions, and transmit them through the earth stations linked to the studio.

To make the participants feel at home, the set is designed to look like a typical panchayat session, where the panelists squat on the floor against a rural backdrop. Considered an effective strategy to ensure participation of women members and those from marginalized sections, the interactive sessions are eye-openers. They dispel ideas that rural folks are ignorant and don't take responsibility for their localities.

One of the main users of the set up is the Rural Development and Panchayati Raj Department—for training the elected representatives across the state. For illustration, 80,000 Gram Panchayat members have been trained for a period of 8 days each during October 2002—January 2005. Besides Gram Panchayat members, Taluk Panchayat and Zilla Panchayat members have also benefited from the SATCOM Centre.

At the outset of the programme out of 175 Taluks, 102 Taluk Panchayats had installed Dish Antennas, i.e. DRS (RX) to receive satellite waves and 47 Taluk Panchayats had purchased T.V. Sets. In other Taluk Panchayats installing of dish and purchasing of T.V. Sets was undertaken. Thus the Taluk Panchayat meeting hall was being converted as training hall. By this procedure training was imparted to maximum number of members at a time.

Objectives of the Training and Capacity Building Programmes

- Enable Gram Panchayat members, particularly women and representatives of disadvantaged groups, to understand their own context and possibilities.
- Provoke them to take a deeper look at their own situations and struggling to find solutions to their problems.
- Enable them to think constructively—i.e. in terms of small but constructive activities that they can take or facilitate others to take.

The Street Plays

As reported in a daily newspaper the Abdul Naseer Sab State Institute for Rural Development (ANSSIRD) has staged street plays in more than 5,000 villages across 44 taluks in the State to create an awakening about the Panchayati Raj System and decentralization of power. The training and capacity building activities were conducted in all the Gram Panchayats of all taluks and in every District of the State. The trainings were conducted in phases.

The street plays are part of a training programme organized by the institute to bring about a qualitative change in the functioning of Gram Panchayats and their members. They are not only aimed at creating an awakening about the Panchayati Raj System among the general public, but also to enable members of Gram Panchayats to understand their context in the decentralization process and inspire them to chart out their role in social transformation.

The artists had been divided into 50 troupes, each comprising 12 artists. The street plays had been specially written by well-known scholars, on the right to information, corruption, conservation of natural resources, accountability, and people's planning and participation in the process of decentralization.

Apart from enhancing the confidence of Gram Panchayat members, particularly women, to enable them to deliver speeches and participate in Panchayat meetings; the programme dwells on issues of social importance such as education, equality, and health.

The Messages through Films

The message through films was considered to be an attractive medium for Gram Panchayat members. These films were developed in the workshop mode, which are neither pre-scripted nor use lectures from experts. They reflect the experience of Gram Panchayat members.

The format of the films included workshop discussions, individual interviews, and dramatized plays. For the training programme, 12 films had been developed with the assistance of UNICEF. Many NGOs had been involved in developing them.

The films were to be transmitted from the SATCOM Centre located at the institute in Mysore and received at district and taluk stations. The Centre has a "*one-way-video and two-way audio*" system.

The film highlights the importance of decentralization, extending power to the people, and issues related to reservation of the vulnerable sections of the rural society. It also seeks to enlighten members of Gram Panchayats about tampering with the allocation or rotation of seats and reservation for the posts of chairperson and vice-chairperson, which often occurs on account of illiteracy, gender, and caste bias. A film related to Gram Panchayat meetings, including notice, agenda, ordinary and special meetings, quorum, sitting fees, recording and reading of resolutions, etc., were also developed.

The films raises the issue whether Gram Panchayats are intended to merely implement the schemes designed and conceptualized elsewhere or whether they have a role in the overall development of the people.

The Outcome of the Programme

It will not be an exaggeration to say that the programme could achieve cent per cent success in meeting its objectives. Though there were some constraints like elections and related activities and extreme climatic conditions like heavy rains, the programme went on well and could be completed involving the required number of members.

In course of conducting capacity building programmes by ANSSIRD since the very beginning, many issues and practical problems have cropped up, which need serious consideration and appropriate remedies. Some of these are given below:

Issues and Problems

(i) The technology is quite expensive.

(ii) Lack of time for interactions with the participants.
(iii) Members have to come to taluk headquarters. In other words, it has not reached each Gram Panchayat.
(iv) Whether the training should be given in the beginning of the term they are elected or after one year of their assuming elected positions.
(v) Power cut, electricity problem at some places.
(vi) Timing of the programme is not convenient for most of the members.

Based on our visits to ANSSIRD at Mysore and attending relay of some programmes in the studio, and discussions with its officials and informal interviews with the elected members of a few Panchayats and reading the scanty materials available in the ANSSIRD office, we developed our perceptions about the organization, its functioning and its impact. Some of the observations may be made as follows:

(i) The elected members have started realizing the importance of decentralization, grassroots governance and people's participation. They have realized that it is through this that the Panchayati Raj Institutions (PRIs) can prepare and formulate schemes in a scientific way by involving the local people. One can surely say that these members have found new meanings to the word '*Participation*'.
(ii) Continuous efforts should be made to train the leadership with a broader perspective than before. Comprehensive and meaningful training programmes have to be designed specifically for rural women so that they perform their constitutional duties and responsibilities as elected members of the PRIs.
(iii) The programme discussed in this chapter could bring out the hidden qualities of women members more so that they gain self-confidence, develop communication skills and raise issues. Still government, NGO, Academic and people themselves should be committed and completely involved in strengthening women's participation in rural local government.
(iv) Participation is needed as a right to create a fair and just society. The 73rd Constitutional Amendment has given the necessary venue for participation for women so that they have a voice in

decisions. The need of the hour is to invest in accelerating human development through capacity building. Only this can integrate the hitherto unexposed sections of society in the process of development and democracy in an effective manner.

(v) The members expressed in one of the interviews that this programme was more effective and they would motivate the other members of their Panchayat who could not attend the training and they stressed that the reservation to women has promoted greater participation and this programme has really strengthened and has made them knowledgeable and articulate to take effective decision.

(vi) Due to the Rotation System as per the Panchayati Raj Act, Karnataka, the same constituency will change and new entrants of elected representatives come in after every five-years term is complete. So Capacity Building has to become a continuous process to strengthen the decentralized governance at the grassroots.

(vii) To cover such a huge programme concerted efforts by the Government and the organizations of the civil society is more important.

(viii) It is one of the innovative programmes and first of its kind in the country and it is hoped that such kind of programme would cover whole of the country.

It is increasingly recognized that '*ANSSIRD's successful blending of technology and training has caught the attention of administrators at home and abroad*'. It appears that technology has taken a wider role though it is more expensive. To us, it should be a continuous process to have success of such an innovative programme.

One of the initiatives towards strengthening decentralization is thus capacity building and training. So capacity building must be given utmost importance and priority. Increased participation in rural government cannot be achieved without capacity building.

The welfare orientation of the government schemes needs to be replaced by a positive campaign for the promotion of equality between the sexes. At present, government programmes are not focused on enabling women to realize their full potential; they only partially compensate for economic and social disabilities. Assistance is also confined to the very poor and is too meagre to significantly improve women's control over resources. Much still remains to be done regarding publicizing the gamut of schemes available for women.

If human development is about enlarging people's choices, the greatest challenge facing us today concerns women. The effort required is immense and will extend over a long period.

The local governments are the best means of promoting participation and efficiency. It is a training ground for leadership and an important channel for women's involvement in the development processes. Karnataka is having number of examples of women legislators (at state level) and Parliamentarians (at national level) who started their political career at the local government levels (both urban and rural). At the local level, Women Panchayat Members have come together to protest against the Panchayati Raj Amendment Bill, 2007 effectively placing Gram Panchayats under the control of MLAs. A forum came into existence called Panchayati Raj Hakkotaya Andolan to take up critical issues in strengthening Panchayati Raj System in the State. The women members under this banner staged dharana, collected signatures and sent out appeals to the governance to withhold the consent. Recently they have also urged the government to reserve 50 per cent of seats for women in the forthcoming (2010) PR elections.

The experiences of quota system for women at the grassroots became so encouraging that in 1996 the Government of India thought of giving reservation to women in Parliament and in State Assemblies on the pattern of 73rd and 74th Constitution Amendment Acts. It is a known fact that their representation in National and State Legislatures is abysmally low, ranging from 4 per cent to 10 per cent of the membership. The Bill for giving reservation to women is pending in the National Parliament. Hopefully political consensus would emerge and it would be through in near future. This will be a historic occasion and a revolutionary change in the process of political empowerment of women in the country.

The programmes are no longer gender blind or biased especially in the light of the fact that Karnataka Government is planning to amend the PR Act to fix the rotation in the reservation of seats in Zilla, Taluk and Gram Panchayats for two terms. They are empowering women, giving them wider choices and building the capabilities of women. Today, women are moving away from the traditional roles prescribed for them. They are learning the art of balancing domestic responsibility with professional ambition. No doubt, women are still entering unfamiliar arenas with many odds mostly social and cultural, against them. The institutional mechanisms, engendering public policies and a positive attitude will provide the necessary motivation to further reduce gender gaps, enhance the status of women and facilitate the movement from critical mass to critical action.

REFERENCES

'*Satellite based communication and training programme for Gram Panchayat Members—Stage 1*' and website of ANSSIRD, Mysore.

Subha, K. and Bhargava, B.S., '*Women in Panchayati Raj Institutions: Some Facts and Observations*', in '*Panchayati Raj and Empowering People: New Agenda for Rural India*', edited by D. Sudaram, Kanishka Publishers, New Delhi, 2007.

12

Empowerment of Women Elected Members of Kerala: What Next?

M. Retna Raj

Introduction

Women's political participation is a key component of democracy. The 73rd and 74th Amendments to the Indian Constitution provide clear space for localizing and engendering governance. The state of Kerala implemented the new provisions of the democratic process by enacting Kerala Panchayati Raj Act, 1994 and the Kerala Municipality Act, 1994. These Acts guaranteed decentralization and devolution of powers in terms of fund, functions and functionaries. Moreover, the Government of Kerala earmarked 35-40 per cent of its budgetary allotment for the local governments. The political entry of women as part of the one-third reservation in local governments has brought about a remarkable change in women themselves, their families, their immediate community and the political system as such. Since 1995 local government election, the mandatory allocation of 33 per cent of seats is in operation in Kerala and the 4th generation women elected members will be in power by October 2010. The introduction of systems and structures like women component plan, separate working group for women development, jagratha samitis, women status studies etc. have given an ultimate mandate for the women elected members of Kerala to intervene in gender mainstreaming activities.

Women in Leadership

The role of women in leadership positions has been a focused debate in the last two decades. At the international level, the United Nations Conferences on women have, in particular, advocated the need to increase the number of women in decision making positions, not only to ensure that women's interests are represented but also because of growing evidence that women's involvement improves the way in which leadership and decision making is practised.

The past few years have witnessed a growing interest in increasing the representation of women in politics at national, sub-national and local level. The reason for this is the obvious democratic deficit with regard to the participation of women. Women make up half the world's population but they are just 18 per cent of world's Parliamentarians. Even in advanced democracies the representation of women in National Legislatures has increased only marginally from 9 per cent in 1995 to 16 per cent in 2004 which is much lower than the critical mass of 30 per cent envisaged at Beijing (Jayal: 2005).

Several arguments are made justifying the desirability of women's participation in democratic institutions in general and in institutions of governance in particular. An leading argument in this regard reads like this, "unless historically excluded groups like women, racial minorities and disadvantaged groups are represented in Legislatures and decision making bodies their interests will not be articulated". The 'politics of presence' as mentioned by Anne Phillips (1995) is quite important for providing disadvantaged groups with guaranteed representation in public institutions, such as quotas in law making bodies, so that they may effectively represent their own needs and interests. A more balanced and effective representation in governance would lead to better decision making and policy priorities that reflect people's concerns and take into account the needs and interests of women. Although representation does not always translate into participation and much less into positive outcomes for women's development, enhancing women's representation is imperative to promote women's progress and to facilitate access to economic, professional and political opportunities. While women are underrepresented in positions of political power worldwide they have clearly had more success at gaining access to local level decision making positions than to those at Central Government level. Since local government, being much closer to enable the participation of women, is often a first step into a political decision making arena in which real differences can be made. Participation in local government is easier for women to fit into their lives, along with family, household responsibilities and employment. Local government is also seen as more accessible as there are more positions available. Local government can also be less intimidating as it is an extension of the great deal of involvement that women already have within their communities.

Impediments to Women's Entry into Public Life

The impediments to women's entry into public life were identified by many authors. Women's entry and productive role in governance are constrained by a number of factors like lack of gender sensitivity of those concerned, poor access to basic social services like education, unfriendly legal structures and absence of mechanisms which can ensure women's active participation in developmental and political processes for advancement.

There are several other impediments to women's entry into public life. The significant ones being noted by important authors is reviewed herewith:

(a) *Fundamental Inequality*: While women have constitutional rights they are not seen as equal, their roles are closely tied to their reproductive and household activities. As a result politics and community involvement are largely seen as unsuitable for them. Highly patriarchal societies enforce rules, responsibilities and behaviour for women, enforcing these norms in ways that affect their self-confidence, limiting their access to information and skills and reinforcing their lower status.

(b) *Discrimination*: Women face discrimination when standing for office and when elected or appointed to local government positions. Attitudes that put politics and decision making into the male preserve see women as incapable of management and governance roles.

(c) *Male environment within political institutions*: While there are few women on decision making bodies the styles and modes of working are those that are acceptable to men. This can limit the extent to which women can raise women's issues and issues of social justice. It is widely recognized that women comprise only a small percentage of the membership of parties. Women are also invisible in the decision-making bodies and rarely influence significant policy decisions. The terrain of electoral and party politics for women is clearly a difficult one. Political parties have generally functioned as the gatekeepers of male-dominated systems of power.

(d) *Costs*: Campaign expenses are prohibitive for women, particularly while they continue to earn less than men in the labour market. Once elected the rate of remuneration can be insufficient for what is almost a full time job. The lack of childcare arrangements and the timing of meetings can also be a barrier.

The focused Group Discussion held among a group of women elected leaders from Kerala indicates the following impediments as the reason for being ineffective in leadership positions:

1. Lack of knowledge and education on Panchayat system.
2. Difficulties in office management.
3. Lack of ability in managing different stakeholders and their opinion.
4. Double burden of work.
5. Male dominance.
6. Financial difficulties.
7. Constraints in travelling alone in night.
8. Mental stress and absence of self-confidence.
9. Lack of technical know-how in the implementation of projects.
10. Difficulty in responding at emergency situations.
11. Non-co-operation of employees, elected representatives and opposition party members.
12. Tendency of the family members and political parties to intervene in governance.
13. Difference of opinion with the local leadership of the political party.

Reservation and Women Empowerment

The Panchayati Raj system has provided a common platform for social, economic, political and legal advancement of women. This trend is promising for women in the sense that (i) Women became more visible in governance today than they were in the past. (ii) Women's issues are widely discussed.

Reservation of quota for women in local councils is considered as an important step towards gendering Local Governments of India. It is seen as an initial strategy for women's political empowerment. This is also based on the evidence that, in the absence of statutory provisions, women are unable to assume leadership positions through competitive electoral politics. Prior to 73rd and 74th Constitutional Amendments, the state of Karnataka went for mandating 25 per cent seat reservation for women in PRIs during the election held in 1987, as a result of which 14,000 women were elected to power.

As a result of women reservation in local governments, the percentage of women at various levels of political activity has shifted dramatically from 4-5 per cent pre-73rd and 74th Amendment to 32.8 to 50 per cent during post-73rd and 74th Amendments. As a result, the presence of 1.05 million elected women representatives are felt in the PRIs of India. The difference is also qualitative, because these women are bringing their experience in governance of civic society into governance of the State. In this way, they are making the State sensitive to issues of poverty, inequality and gender injustice.

The Global Gender Gap Report 2007 ranks India 114 out of 128 countries using a composite index of economic participation, educational attainment, political empowerment and health and survival. On economic participation and opportunity for women, India's ranking is 122, on educational attainment the ranking is 116, and on health and survival the ranking is 126. But in contrast to these, India's ranking on the political empowerment of women is 21 out of 128 countries, better positioned than that of Australia, Canada and the United States. This indicates the supreme influence that the women's reservation system of India has in the global development debate.

It is argued that increasing the representation of women in local governments has not automatically led to a more gendered analysis of the development issues like economic participation, educational attainment and health and survival. Nor has it necessarily raised the profile of women's needs and interests in the policy agenda. But there are now a large number of women who are in local leadership as well as in local politics because of their leadership qualities or visible changes in the articulation of ideas. This women in local leadership position shall have definite spiralling effects in improving the living conditions of the women of India with specific reference to economic participation, educational attainment and health and survival. This, in general, is challenging tasks ahead for the women elected members of India.

Policy Level Interventions to Mainstream Gender into Local Governance of Kerala

In Kerala, several attempts were made to integrate the gender and development approach in decentralized planning process. The important ones are listed below:

- Participatory study of the status of women in each area was made mandatory as a step to understand local specific issues of women and forming projects based on that.
- At least 10 per cent of funds need to be earmarked for women as Women's Component Plan (WCP).
- Working group on women was initiated to formulate projects for women. This working group is headed by a women elected member.
- Direction was given that women shall be represented in all subject-wise working groups.
- Attempts were made to improve women's participation in gram sabha and discuss issues of women. There shall be separate discussion group in gram sabha to discuss the development issues faced by women.
- Out of the two who get selected from each subject group in gram sabha, it was decided that one would be a woman. It was also directed that there should be a separate group in the development seminar to discuss issues of women and also that women's representation be there in all subject groups.
- A separate chapter on women and development was mandatory in the development report to be prepared by each local government.
- Special consideration has to be given in the fund allocation for women in general projects.
- Special subject committees are to be ensured in the Technical

Advisory Committees (TACs) which scrutinizes the projects to ensure that women are given due consideration in general projects and Women Component Plan.

- One-third women representation is to be ensured in beneficiary committees.
- Neighbourhood groups, Areas Development Societies and Community Development Societies were initiated as the new organizational forums for women. At the state level a coordinating body called *Kudumbasree* mission was formed to give overall guidance.
- *Anganwadis* were transferred to local governments. They became centre for women development.
- It was suggested to form vigilance cells (*Jagratha samithis)* at the level of each local government in the model of state women's commission to address issues of atrocities against women and to work towards preventing them.
- Gender awareness classes are organized for elected representatives and officials at regular interval.
- In the cost benefit assessment of the projects, a gender impact statement was made mandatory.

Due to these proactive policy interventions the women elected members do have resounding role to play to make the local governments gender-sensitive. This also provides a classical case for governance changing and shaping status of women.

Women Leadership in the Local Governments of Kerala

The introduction of quotas at the local government level was a natural response to the question of political justice for women. India has the largest number of women in governance. The states like Bihar, Rajasthan and Kerala have already allocated 50 per cent quota for women in local governments. The uniqueness in the women's quota of Kerala is that 50 per cent reservation in all the elected posts positions of local governments like President, Vice-President and Standing Committees.

As the Table 12.1 indicates the per cent of women members of PRIs to the total members is 35.24 per cent. This representation is just higher than the mandated quota. The high rate of women literacy (86.69%) has not acted as an enabling environment for smooth and

Table 12.1: Number of Women Elected Members in PRIs of Kerala

Panchayat Raj Institutions	*Number of women members*
Grama Panchayat	5701
Block Panchayat	695
District Panchayat	119
Total	6515
% of women members to the total elected members of PRIs	35.24

Source: Computed.

improved presence of women in local governance. Available data for 2007 indicates that Manipur has the highest women representation in PRIs (50.75%) followed by Bihar (46.68%) and Karnataka (43.19%). The states like Chandigarh (32.8%), Maharastra (33.33%) and Gujarat (33.34%) have lowest women representation.

Table 12.2: Women Elected Members of Kerala and India: Analysis based on selected indicators

S. No.	*Selected Variables*	*Kerala*	*India*
1.	Medium age of women elected heads	39.5	40
2.	Medium age of women ward members	39	38
3.	Women elected heads: educated middle school and above	93.8	52.4
4.	Women elected members: educated middle school and above	93	37.1
5.	% of women heads who said Panchayat work as primary occupation	90.6	26.5
6.	% of women members who said Panchayat work as primary occupation	87.4	12.5
7.	Elected heads who had not faced any constrains	68.8	77.8
8.	Percentage of members receiving training	100	57.1
9.	Proportion of women usually attending grama sabha (more than 50%)	87.5	13.9
10.	Interaction of women heads with local bureaucracy	100	63.5
11.	Affiliation and support from political parties	96.9	38.7
12.	Percentage of women heads often had instances of being ignored being a women	9.4	6.8
13.	Percentage of elected heads making efforts towards mitigating domestic violence	93.3	78.5

Source: Compiled from the "Study on elected women representatives in Panchayati Raj Institutions" Ministry of Panchayati Raj, Government of India, 2008.

Women Elected Members of Kerala: From Strengths to Opportunities

Based on Table 12.2 the following points could be highlighted as the special opportunities of elected women of Kerala:

1. High level of education leading to greater presence in governance.
2. Higher opportunity for women involvement in local governance in several capacities like Convener of Gram Sabhas, Chairperson of working groups, Member of Kudumbasree assessment committee, Chairperson of ward level jagratha samiti etc.
3. All the women members have attended training programmes. This is specifically due the presence of an exclusively mandated training Institute like Kerala Institute of Local Administration (KILA).
4. High level of involvement by the women elected heads for mitigating domestic violence.
5. Affiliation of women elected members with political parties. In fact near hundred percentage of seats are contested based on party politics. As a result, normally support is extended by the political parties to the women elected members.
6. Near hundred per cent of women elected heads and majority of the women elected members are involved in Panchayat activities as primary occupation. This is because, all the elected members including the women members have clear mandated space for involvement in local governance. This is further facilitated by the monthly honorarium given to the elected members. For example, in the case of Gram Panchayats, the Presidents are given Rs. 4,600, the Vice-Presidents Rs. 3,300, the standing Committee chairpersons Rs. 2,100 and the members Rs. 1,500 as monthly honorarium.
7. Interaction of women heads and women members with local bureaucracy is intense as majority of the cutting edge level officials are with the local governments.
8. Proportion of women usually attending gram sabha is very high. Usually it is more than 50 per cent.
9. About one-third of the elected women have previous membership and leadership association with the

Kudumbasree movement. This has contributed to the qualitative women leadership at the local level. This has enabled them to work on par with men leaders and has also given many women a greater understanding of the workings of politics, in particular the importance of political parties.

The above-mentioned indicators point out that elected women of Kerala are better positioned than their counterparts in other parts of the country. Hence it is natural to expect that these elected women have more opportunities to make their leadership presence more deep and intense.

Women in Local Government: Outcome

Despite numerous institutional, cultural and social constraints, the participation of women in local councils has had an empowering effect. The developmental impact of such participation has been clearly seen in the issues prioritized by women. In the Indian context women have worked towards getting drinking water, sanitation, housing, schools, primary health centres, and day care facilities for children etc. The outcome could be grouped as below:

1. *Pro-active Policy Decision*: The decision to upgrade the women's quota in local council from 33 per cent to 50 per cent during 2009 was unanimous in the Kerala Legislature. This is a notable recognition to the women leadership of Kerala.
2. *Transformative Leadership*: There is a growing recognition of the impact that women leadership has on political institutions and political agenda.
3. *Mainstreaming Political Leadership*: At least a minority section of women leaders who have excelled in local governance have been mainstreamed into local political leadership.
4. *Mainstreaming Gender as a Core Development Issue*: There have been several attempts to mainstream gender as a core issue in development planning at the local level. Due to the enlightened women leadership, gender issues are elaborately discussed in committee meetings and in every other planning forums of local governance. The women elected members

play an important role in pushing the women's issues forward for public discussion and decision making.

Sustaining the Transformation: What Next?

Women still face considerable handicaps to their involvement in politics; for example, inadequate capacity, the burden of reproductive and productive roles, a lack of self-confidence and the opposition of entrenched cultural and religious views. There has been changes in the processes and priorities of local governments in favour of women leadership. However, sustaining this transformation is a significant challenge. This is specifically because a good percentage of women heads have said that they often had instances of being ignored, being a woman.

1. There is a need for more enabling environment, which would allow local governments to become a process for the empowerment of women. Such an environment would include legal frameworks and services as well as packages of technical support.
2. There is a need to provide women with specific kinds of support which go beyond technical training. They need support to build solidarity amongst women, through strengthening links between women's organisations and elected bodies.
3. There is a need to initiate gender budgeting at local government level. "Gender Budgeting" is now recognized as a tool for empowering women. Gender Responsive Budgeting (GRB) is government planning, programming and budgeting that contributes to the advancement of gender equality and the fulfilment of women's rights. It entails identifying and reflecting needed interventions to address gender gaps in sector and local government policies, plans and budgets.
4. In Kerala, it is not possible for women to emerge as a politically significant group without the support of established political parties. It is therefore appropriate that the struggle to bring about a more inclusive polity and deliberative democracy is to be waged by ensuring real visibility for them in forums of the political parties.
5. Women should be given opportunities for working with institutions outside of the local self-government structures,

such as the governing bodies of Universities, Co-operatives, educational institutions, sector specific associations, trade unions, mahila mandals, registered societies etc. This will enable them to formulate their 'presence' to be felt by a wider society. Women reservation in local councils can only be a strategic necessity for women's empowerment rather than a corridor towards it. Higher representation of women in elected bodies alone, without sustaining measures such as greater presence and integration in political parties and other decision making bodies, cannot ensure their effectual participation in these bodies.

6. There shall be systems for making use of the former women elected members as support groups and mentors of present generation of women leaders. They can be effectively used as resource persons, working group members, members of vigilance committees etc. This will help for sustaining the interest created among them on decentralization. The get-together of former women members at block and district level will also be an added value at this level.
7. Continuous capacity building for encouraging women to effective participation in local councils and local development issues is necessary. This shall be taken care of jointly by specific mandated Institutions, NGOs and political parties.
8. There shall be steps towards formation of associations and federations of elected women members. These should function as platforms for coming together for articulating their problems as women Panchayat leaders, discuss issues regarding the institutional mechanisms for their empowerment, come up with a charter of issues to be mainstreamed into policy and advocacy support.

Engendering the local governments shall be the tasks ahead of women elected leaders of Kerala. Every decision taken and policy made at local government should have an orientation towards removing the existing discrimination faced by women of that locality. Increased representation of women in local council shall lead to increased decisions in favour of women.

REFERENCES

Chathukalam, Jos and John, M.S. 2000. 'Empowerment of Women Panchayat Members: Lessons from Kerala', *Asian Journal of Women's Studies,* Vol. 6, No. 4, 2000.

Drage, Jean 2001. 'Women in Local Government in Asia and the Pacific: A comparative analysis of thirteen countries', United Nations Economic and Social Commission for Asia and the Pacific.

Institute of Social Sciences (ISS). 1994. 'The New Panchayati Raj in Karnataka: An Evaluation'. New Delhi.

IRMA. 2008. 'The State of Panchayats: 2007-08: An introductory Assessment, vol. 1: Thematic Report'. Anand, Gujarat.

Jain, Devaki. 1992. 'Women: New visions of leadership'. A presentation at the Global Forum of Women. Dublin, July 9-12.

Ministry of Panchayati Raj, Govt. of India. 2008. 'Study on elected women representatives in Panchayat Raj Institutions', New Delhi.

Palanithurai. 'Elected Women Representatives and Emerging Alternative Governance'. Gandhigram, Tamil Nadu.

Radha, Bulu Roy Chowdhury. 2002. 'Women in Local Bodies', Discussion Paper No. 40, Kerala Research Programme on Local Level Development, Centre for Development Studies, Trivandrum.

Retna, Raj. 2004. 'Decentralisation and poverty reduction: Lessons from Kerala'. KILA Publications.

Sujaya, Devaki Jain. 2000. 'Role of Women in Decentralization', State Planning Board, Kerala.

Vijayan, Aleyamma, Bhaskaran, Seema and Jayasree, 2007. 'Gender and Panchayati Raj: 'Status of Women in Kerala', Sakhi Women's Resource Centre, Trivandrum.

13

Impact of Reservation and Participation in Terms of Empowerment of Women and Dalits in Panchayati Raj Institutions in India

Nupur Tiwari

Introduction

The Constitution (73rd and 74th Amendments) Act, 1992 sets out in detail in Article 243D, the manner in which reservations are to be provided to women and persons belonging to the Scheduled Castes and Scheduled Tribes. The clause is reproduced in full below:

243D. Reservation of seats.—(1) Seats shall be reserved for—

(a) the Scheduled Castes; and
(b) the Scheduled Tribes,

in every Panchayat and the number of seats so reserved shall bear, as nearly as may be, the same proportion to the total number of seats to be filled by direct election in that Panchayat as the population of the Scheduled Castes in that Panchayat area or of the Scheduled Tribes in that Panchayat area bears to the total population of that area and such seats may be allotted by rotation to different constituencies in a Panchayat.

(2) Not less than one-third of the total number of seats reserved under clause (1) shall be reserved for women belonging to the Scheduled Castes or, as the case may be, the Scheduled Tribes.

(3) Not less than one-third (including the number of seats reserved for women belonging to the Scheduled Castes and the Scheduled

Tribes) of the total number of seats to be filled by direct election in every Panchayat shall be reserved for women and such seats may be allotted by rotation to different constituencies in a Panchayat.

(4) The offices of the Chairpersons in the Panchayats at the village or any other level shall be reserved for the Scheduled Castes, the Scheduled Tribes and women in such manner as the Legislature of a State may, by law, provide:

Provided that the number of offices of Chairpersons reserved for the Scheduled Castes and the Scheduled Tribes in the Panchayats at each level in any State shall bear, as nearly as may be, the same proportion to the total number of such offices in the Panchayats at each level as the population of the Scheduled Castes in the State or of the Scheduled Tribes in the State bears to the total population of the State:

Provided further that not less than one-third of the total number of offices of Chairpersons in the Panchayats at each level shall be reserved for women:

Provided also that the number of offices reserved under this clause shall be allotted by rotation to different Panchayats at each level.

(5) The reservation of seats under clauses (1) and (2) and the reservation of offices of Chairpersons (other than the reservation for women) under clause (4) shall cease to have effect on the expiration of the period specified in Article 334.

(6) Nothing in this Part shall prevent the Legislature of a State from making any provision for reservation of seats in any Panchayat or offices of Chairpersons in the Panchayats at any level in favour of backward class of citizens.

The gist of these clauses are as follows:

(a) There are three kinds of reservations provided for in the Constitution as follows:

Kind of Reservation	*Roles of State and Centre*	*Clause*
To seats to be filled by direct election in each Panchayat for women, SCs and STs	Mandatorily prescribed by the Constitution itself, up to a minimum of 33 per cent for women and in proportion to the population of SCs and STs, in each Panchayat	Articles 243D(1), (2) and (3)
To posts of chairpersons in each panchayat	Mandatory according to the Constitution, but the detailed modalities of which are to be determined through state legislation.	Article 243D(4)
For backward classes of citizens	At the discretion of the State	Article 243D(6)

(b) Reservations to elected seats are mandated directly by the Constitution, in accordance with the following pattern:
   (i) One-third of the total number of seats to be filled by direct election in every Panchayat are to be reserved for women. This is inclusive of the reservation provided for women belonging to the SCs and STs (See (iii) below). [*See* Article 243D(3)]
   (ii) For persons belonging to the Scheduled Castes and Scheduled Tribes, reservations in each Panchayat are to be provided, based on the proportion of the population of SCs and STs respectively in each Panchayat concerned. [*See* Article 243D(1)]
   (iii) Within the reservation provided for persons belonging to the SCs and STs as detailed at (ii) above, not less than one-third of the total number of seats that are reserved for the respective categories in each Panchayat concerned are to be reserved for women belonging to the SCs and STs. [*See* Article 243D(2)]

(c) These seats may be allotted by rotation to different constituencies within a Panchayat. [Articles 243D(1) and 243D(3)].

(d) The provisions for reservations to the offices of Chairpersons are nearly identical to the above provisions regarding reservations to elected seats. The additional features of reservations to the offices of Chairpersons are as follows:
   (i) While providing for reservations up to a minimum level of one-third in respect of women and in proportion to the population in each Panchayat for SCs and STs, the manner in which this is done is left to the Legislature of a State to provide by law. [*See* Article 243D(4)].
   (ii) Unlike in the case of rotation of reservations to elected seats, which is discretionary, the rotation of reservations to offices of Chairpersons of different Panchayats is mandatory. [*See* the Second Proviso to Article 243D(4)].

Since the Constitution prescribes only a minimum level of reservation of one-third for women in Panchayats, States have the leeway to mandate more than that level. About one million women entered Panchayats after 73rd Constitutional Amendment Act. About 40 per cent of the elected women represented the marginalized sections. However, about 70 per cent women representatives were illiterate and most of them had no previous political experience. Therefore, it was but natural that there was a widespread apprehension that women will be manipulated by men. However, in spite of several instances of such manipulation and capitulation by women, the presence of such a large number of women in Panchayats has indeed had a deep impact on gender equity.

Though under Panchayati Raj system only 33 per cent reservation is made to women but Bihar took the bold step of reserving 50 per cent of the Panchayat seats for women. Currently, elected women representatives are in place in 54 per cent of seats in Bihar's Panchayats. Bihar's example was followed by Sikkim, which increased their reservations for women to 40 per cent and held their elections under the new arrangement in January 2008. Chhattisgarh, Madhya Pradesh, Rajasthan and Uttarakhand have passed laws increasing the reservations for women in Panchayats to 50 per cent. These changes will apply to the next elections to Panchayats in these States. Bihar, Rajasthan, Madhya Pradesh, Chhattisgarh, Himachal Pradesh and Uttarakhand have made 50 per cent seats available for women. This has given political and social exposures to backward, dalit, poor and illiterate.

A recent survey, commissioned by the Ministry of Panchayati Raj and executed by the Nielsen Company—ORG Marg under the guidance of an academic advisory committee, provides many new insights into Social and Political empowerment of women in the new Panchayati Raj Institutions(PRIs). This is the largest-ever survey on any aspect of Panchayat functioning, covering Gram Panchayats in 23 States, with a total sample size of over 20,000, including Elected Women Representatives (EWRs), Elected Male Representatives (EMRs), ex-EWRs, official functionaries and members of the community. Nearly three-fourths of the EWRs in the sample belonged to the Scheduled Castes, Scheduled Tribes and OBC categories, and were evenly divided above and below the poverty line.

Reservation has played a significant role as four-fifths of all the representatives got elected from reserved seats. The role of reservation was also evident from the fact that it emerged as an important motivator (43%) for contesting the first election as much as its withdrawal was an important reason for not contesting the election among former women representatives (39%).

The majority of the elected representatives had contested only one election (87%) and hence the proportion of first timers in politics was also high (86%). Around 14 per cent were re-elected more than once at the Gram Panchayat level. Further analysis showed that the majority of ex-women representatives could not get re-elected because the seat frorn where they were elected was de-reserved in the next round.

While no gender discrimination in the Panchayat is reported by 60 per cent of elected women representatives, acceptability in Panchayat meetings and enabling them to raise issues freely was mentioned by 94 per cent.

A supportive professional environment evidently motivates elected women representatives to perform better, as 60-64 per cent reported an increase in their interaction with line departments and parallel bodies.

Even the participation of common women citizens in various activities such as attending Gram Sabha meeting, etc. has reportedly increased (68-78%). However, issues related to the planning for rural development works and identification of BPL families were discussed mainly by the Male Pradhans and Ward Members.

While 21 per cent claimed to be self-motivated, about 22 per cent said that their spouse had inspired them, which was higher in the case of women representatives (30%). Interestingly, members of community groups (such as Mahila Mandals, Self-Help Groups, Youth Clubs, Cooperatives, etc.) seem to have played an important role, as 22 per cent of elected representatives reported how they were motivated to take the plunge in electoral politics.

However, 8 per cent of the elected representatives—mainly from West Bengal, Sikkim, Tripura and Kerala—also disclosed the role of political parties in motivating them. Husbands (30%) and other family members (12%) were reported as playing an important role in motivating women representatives to contest elections for the first time.

The economic status of more than half (54 %) of the elected representatives was Above the Poverty Line (APL) as per the village list reported by the respondents. There were a higher proportion of APL individuals in the case of Pradhans (72%), as compared to ward members (50%). Almost two-fifths (38%) of all EWRs were reportedly, below the poverty line, the majority of this category being ward members (41%) rather than Pradhans (24%). This indicates, overall, that the Pradhans are better off than other Panchayat Members.

However, not much difference was observed between the economic status of male and female elected representatives.

One-third of elected representatives report interactions with the police, local bureaucracy and officials in the line departments to discuss scheme and participation in election campaigns. Taking proactive initiatives in signing petitions, participating in protests, alerting media or notifying police/court about local problems was mentioned by 24-35 per cent of elected representatives.

That reservation has been critical to the representation of disadvantaged groups is confirmed by the fact that 88 per cent of them were elected on reserved seats. Approximately 85.8 per cent of all representatives surveyed were first-timers in the Panchayats, while 14.3 per cent had been elected for a second or third term. While 15 per cent of women Pradhans had been re-elected twice or more, 37 per cent of the male Pradhans had been similarly re-elected. Of the ex-EWRs interviewed, 11 per cent said they had contested but lost the election, while 39 per cent indicated that they did not contest a re-election because the seat had been de-reserved.

Now majority of women representatives are no more proxy of their male relative patrons. 58 per cent of women representatives are now taking their own decisions to contest elections. This is a big achievement. 15 per cent of women Pradhans are able to win elections second time. Women belonging to younger age groups of 21-35 years have shown better performance as compared to the women belonging to the age group of 35 years and above. Women members of active committees at village level were found to be more successful at Panchayat level. Again quoting the Report, Dalits were also benefited by the whole process. Reservation has inspired and prompted them to contest elections.

There can be no greater evidence for the fact that not only has Panchayati Raj attracted women to politics in large numbers, but also that this wish to contest for elections seems to be most keenly felt among the women belonging to the SCs and STs.

There is, however, big difference between representation and participation. It is easier to legislate representation, but it is rather a complex and difficult task to create conditions for participations. The proper representation does not automatically lead to proper participation. It is important that they are in a position to influence decision making and prepare and implement the schemes for economic development and social justice.

There are many instances of EWR of the Panchayat taking a keen interest and playing a significant role in the workings of grassroots politics. EWRs have initiated work on plans of bringing in piped water in the village and also to build schools as against infrastructural development favoured by men. Results from a nationwide survey of women's participation in Panchayats suggest that a majority of the EWRs report an enhancement in their personal effectiveness and image after being elected. They also report a reduction in household responsibilities. It has often been observed that women prioritise those developmental needs that seem to be more pressing from their perspective. Women are also seen to be more involved in monitoring the presence of teachers and medical staff in the school or health centre, and inspecting nutrition centres under the Integrated Child Development Scheme.

There are number of success stories in Bihar where EWR of the Panchayats have taken the lead in making efforts for smokeless stoves, creches, community halls, and have taken the initiative in family and matrimonial matters, counselling abusive and/or alcoholic husbands. Sometimes, women-headed Panchayats have even experienced a dramatic increase in their revenues, sponsoring the auction of village ponds, community forests and village markets for the larger welfare of the community.

A Cluster Group of Women SHGs from Block—Basopatti, Madhubani in Bihar where the total number of members are 45, used to conduct regular monthly meeting at block level on different issues. Kiran Devi got elected as *Sarpanch* from reserved seat in Raghai Panchayat, Bihar. The successful EWR, now act as kind of role models for the others. The increased proportion of the EWR has ensured the principles of justice between the sexes and this has certainly led to the fulfilment of certain interests of women, which may otherwise be neglected. It is for sure that without the system of reservation women would have had no role to play in grassroots politics in India. As statistics show, 95 per cent of women claimed they would never come to acquire positions in Panchayats, if there were no provision of reserving seats for them (Centre for Women's Development Studies 1999). Reservation has at least succeeded in bringing the womenfolk in rural India into the political forum and elected women could now imagine standing against a man in future.

In several instances, the Gram Sabha has persuaded women with leadership potential to stand for elections and this has far-reaching impact on the empowerment of women.

By all accounts, particularly with each election round, it is clear that women have certainly made their presence in the power struggles once dominated by men. Yet, the issue of surrogate participation of women is again one of those popular notions that just refuse to fade away. Yes, in some circumstances, where cultural and the social system is highly patriarchal, proxy participation by men continues. However, the situation is more complex than just that. There are positive and negative trends. For instance, even in States where women have traditionally been in the background of political participation, there has been a remarkable degree of acceptance of the participation of women in Panchayats as members and leaders. On the other hand, it would be naive to say that even in States where women have a much better status, surrogate representation has ceased to exist—it is perhaps more sophisticated and concealed, but its ill effects are equal. Third, even in circumstances where surrogate participation is seen the actual situation might be that the man is helping for some time—in fact, he might be playing a nurturing and consulting role, assisting the new woman entrant into the Panchayats. Fourth, while surrogate participation might exist for the first elected term of the woman, quite often we come across situations where women have increasingly asserted themselves, once they have gained confidence—even winning the next election on their own worth, rather than as symbols of their male backers. There are many instances where women have been self-motivated to fight an election. In several instances, the Gram Sabha has persuaded women with leadership potential to stand for elections. The self-help movement has also had a far-reaching impact on the empowerment of women and several of them who have gained confidence, economic visibility and the strength of numbers through SHGs have stepped into the Panchayats. Patriarchy is not reversed, or even significantly eroded, overnight. Thus, a change in political status may bring about a larger transformation in socio-economic processes.

The occupation of the poor and downtrodden of elected seats and chairperson's pots in grassroots democratic governments is a huge social and political revolution, the significance of which would take at least a generation to fully unfold. Surely, an endeavour to broad base democracy on this scale is bound to have shortcomings and setbacks, and would need course correction. However, there is no taking away from the fact that there have been huge benefits, which have not been fully understood or studied, to empowerment and development through Panchayati Raj.

There are a huge number of Panchayats working in different circumstances, the extent of empowerment of dalits and women vary from region to region and Panchayats work under different legal frameworks—as States have the discretion to define the scope and ambit of Panchayati Raj—every spectrum of political behaviour, ranging from abject subordination of women and dalits to remarkable instances of social and political assertiveness can be seen in the functioning of Panchayats. Therefore, examples are merely anecdotes—true only in respect of the instance quoted—and have very little value in terms of deriving conclusions about Panchayati Raj.

Heroic tales of women and dalits battling the odds abound in media reports and research studies. It is no accident that many of these accounts are from those States where the Panchayat system is weak and neglected. Very often these individuals are heroes because of defective Panchayati Raj. On the other hand, in States where the framework of Panchayati Raj provides a nurturing environment for grassroots empowerment and does not inhibit it, one finds a larger scope for people to function effectively, without having to resort to heroism. In fact, there are fewer odds to battle, in these States. In such States, since Panchayati Raj itself is a winner, those within it are all winners, in some measure or the other. Unfortunately, research in the functioning of Panchayati Raj often falls prey to anecdotes. Most studies have very low value as they often have poor sample sizes and biases of researchers, both positive and negative, creep into the conclusions. Finally, constitutionally mandated Panchayati Raj is too young to throw up time series analyses of any great value.

Cynics are fond of pooh-poohing decentralisation in India on the ground that all that is decentralised is corruption, and therefore, one needs to analyse why such a widespread negative impression about PRIs has taken root. Much of it, is a matter of selective memory and auto-suggestion—ignore the good stories and highlight the bad. However, the functioning of Panchayats is quite distinct from that of higher level governments. First, being closer to the people, a lot more corruption gets exposed to public view and compared to corruption at higher levels. Second, while grassroot level institutions have distinct advantages in localising government, they also face proximate political and social pressures that make traditional virtues of public administration such as impartiality, neutrality and anonymity difficult to realise locally. Third, regardless of whether PRIs are elected on a party basis or otherwise, they are political institutions. Elected members have constituencies both in the geographical and socio-political sense. One cannot avoid legitimate aspirations to nurse constituencies in today's context of highly competitive electoral politics and one must accept that there is bound to be a tendency to favour a region, a group of people or even individuals in developmental decision making. Fourth, unlike legislators, PRI elected representatives are vested with executive authority and are empowered to take decisions having financial implications and authorise expenditure from public funds, decide levels of taxation, exercise power of collecting taxes and regulatory powers which are of a quasi-judicial character.

Two things need to be done to make Panchayats more inclusive and effective as local governments. First inclusiveness has meaning only if Panchayats are given responsibilities in the letter and spirit of the Constitution. Unfortunately, Panchayati Raj is often a charade in several States and political rhetoric hides their marginalization. Both the Centre and the States need to bring in real devolution, which can be differentiated from the charade that Panchayati Raj has often become, as follows:

Real Devolution	*Not-so-real devolution*
Clear role assignment	Somebody else (above or below) for Panchayat performance responsible
Power to spend money	
Power to tax	Limited power to collect resources
Discretion in spending money	Scheme bound expenditure
Power to hire fire and control staff	Staff owned and assigned by higher level governments
Direct Accountability	Somebody else (above or below) acting for the Panchayat

Second, decision making processes in Panchayats need to be better defined, to diminish the possibility of elite capture, proxy participation, single point decision making and corruption. The formula for improving PRI functioning would follow a four-fold path; simplify, inform, review and hold accountable for non-performance or mal-administration. Some key steps in this regard are as follows:

(a) Well functioning Gram Sabhas are essential.

(b) Just as in the case of most government offices, a thick veil of secrecy hides inefficiencies, arbitrariness, corruption and nepotism from public gaze in PRIs too. An example of the secrecy that surrounds executive action in PRIs is seen in the selection of beneficiaries for various schemes. The logical transparent sequence ought to be the laying down of the selection criteria, publicising them, calling for applications through the Gram Sabha, processing them with reference to the criteria, making selections and ending with publicly explaining the rationale of the selection made. When there is a great deal of arbitrariness in decision making at the local level, records will not show how the choice was arrived at or whether various options and possibilities were analysed and on which criteria the final decision was made. Fairness at the cutting edge will need to be seen and corroborated by full disclosure, whatever may be the inconvenience and cost involved for the administration. Therefore, systems that ensure easy access for the citizen to information must be put into place. If the right to information is to have any meaning, information will have to be systematised and packaged in a manner that makes sense to those who seek it.

(c) We need to sytematise the process of recording decisions, to ensure the democratic functioning of Panchayats. There are seven linked aspects of ensuring that PRIs work more democratically as described below:

   (i) The emphasis on consensus in decision making should be approached with caution, while true consensus is appreciable, an unnecessary emphasis on consensus could stunt the growth of democracy. Consensus undermines democracy in two ways. First, in a consensus, the strongest voices prevail automatically. Thus it is easier for a situation of elite capture to prevail if business rules of representative bodies expressly prefer consensus in decision making. Reservations in favour of women and the socially disadvantaged do not make much sense in a consensus situation because one can just as easily silence the poor. The second disadvantage of a consensus situation is that elected representatives can hide behind a consensus decision to avoid responsibility and accountability to their voters.

Therefore, votes have always to be recorded. This is an important aspect of democratic PRI functioning. If there is a consensus or unanimity, even this should be recorded. The record of voting by individual members in PRI meetings could become the most important mechanism of opening up the proceedings to the public, particularly if there is express provision in the law for disclosing the voting pattern to the public. Mandatory public display of resolutions of the PRIs along with the record of members voting for or against them will enable the public to know what their members are doing for them. They will know how their member has articulated their concerns in meetings. More than anything else, this alone will be an effective mechanism of downward accountability.

(ii) Procedures for conduct of meetings will have to be laid may be necessary, in order to ensure that those who do not feel up to articulating their concerns in an open meeting can still make their presence felt in decision-making.

(iii) A strict quorum requirement will diminish the scope of marginalization in decision making.

(iv) Ensure that the body is collectively responsible for its actions. The requirement of collective responsibility is another method of increasing accountability of the body to the people. Once a member knows that his position is also in jeopardy as he is also vicariously responsible for wrong acts of his colleague-members in the body, there is a greater price to be paid for being a passive spectator to the proceedings. Members will be induced to participate meaningfully and there will be peer pressure on each other not to take wrong decisions.

(v) Make decision making committee based. Most Panchayat legislations provide for Standing Committees in Panchayats, but these provisions are neglected and hardly operatonalised. Committee based decision making diminishes the scope for elite capture and allows for the articulation of all voices.

(vi) Put in place mechanisms to open up the process of decision making is opened up to public gaze. Ordinarily, meetings shall be opened to the public. There must be full disclosure of facts in meetings, so that reasoned decisions can be taken. One method of doing this is to ensure a prior circulation of the agenda for a meeting and if necessary, allow one meeting to intervene before a decision is made. Thus a resolution can be introduced in a particular meeting and discussed, but voting could be held in the next meeting of the body.

(vii) Intervals between the rotation of reservations for women and SC and ST representatives need to be extended. If reservations are rotated after every 5 years term, it leaves very little incentive for the member elected on a reserved seat to perform, because he or she knows that next time around, there will only be a remote chance of being elected as she will not have the benefit of reservation in the same seat.

(d) Provide a right to recourse to an independent institutional mechanism that gives speedy relief to the aggrieved effectively bolsters empowerment through Panchayats. With greater devolution and decentralisation there will be a need to investigate independently complaints made by individuals, groups and even the Government relating to defective administration by local bodies. An Ombudsman system could provide a convenient and relatively low-cost mechanism to deal with complaints of mal-administration.

Experience over a decade and a half shows that the decision to devolve and the trigger to do so has always been driven politically. However, since in different states, the impetus has come from different political parties, it is difficult to say that one or the other party has been more Panchayat friendly than the other. It would be more accurate to say that within each political party, there are divided views on Panchayati Raj. However, no party today can openly question Panchayati Raj, that would be political suicide.

The other lesson that can be drawn from States that have devolved or are currently devolving with reasonable success, is that in all of them, the bureaucracy has played its part in proper design of systems, when backed by the political signal to devolve. Most such States, brought out a road map on devolution, which was widely discussed in public, before going ahead with a devolution plan. Behind successful devolution, there have always been a cabal of champions, from politics, the bureaucracy and civil society, who have contributed collectively to its success. Politically driven decisions to devolve, without sufficient backing in terms of changes in administrative and executive design have tended to flounder, with adverse consequences on those who motivated such changes.

As with most matters of empowerment, mere political will and articulation of policies will alone not translate into benefits for Women and Dalits. The translation into sensitive implementation would require changes in administrative and social structures. Moreover, a collaborative approach between the household, the community, the State, voluntary organizations and the media needs to be developed. The approach must also be multi-pronged, taking into account policies, laws, judicial processes, attitudes and social imaging of women.

REFERENCES

A Study in Grey by Niraja Gopal Jayal—Tuesday, April 29, 2008 at 2320 hrs IST posted online.

Alsop, Ruth, *et al.*, "Inclusion and Local Elected Governments: The Panchayati Raj System in India", Social Development Paper 37, *World Bank, South Asia Region, Social Development Unit,* Washington DC., 2001.

Buch, Nirmala, "Women and Panchayats: Opportunities, Challenges and Support" in L.C. Jain (ed.), *Decentralization and Local Governance,* New Delhi: Orient Longman, 2005.

Centre for Women's Development Studies, "From Oppression to Assertion: A Study of Panchayats and Women in M.P., Rajasthan, and UP.", *CWDS,* New Delhi, 1999.

Study on Elected Women Representatives in Panchayati Raj Institutions based on a Nationwide Survey by A.C. Nielson ORG-MARG, Ministry of Panchayati Raj, Government of India, New Delhi.

The State of Panchayats: 2007-08 (An Independent Assessment) Volume-One (Thematic Report) by Institute of Rural Management Anand (IRMA) with the Ministry of Panchayati Raj, Government of India, New Delhi.

14

A Critique on the Political Reservation and its Utilization by the Elected Women Representatives

K. Sathiabama

Introduction

The system of governance in India has undergone a radical change in the last fifteen years with the implementation of quota system for the women in the Panchayati Raj Institutions (PRIs). When comparing to all other countries in the world, India has more number of women politicians than the rest of the world. This could be considered as a social capital for development. In the recent years it has been noticed that women's participation in public sphere of panchayats has enhanced their status in their families, castes and villages. It also improved the self-image of women, confidence, self-esteem and experiences in the public sphere. But due to our patriarchal practices, traditional norms and cultural practices, the Elected Women Representatives (EWRs) are not able to perform their function properly. Moreover, the knowledge base of the elected women representatives on their roles and responsibilities in the local body institutions is under examination along with their performance. But at present, many research reports brought to light that the women elected representatives are performing their functions by breaking their barriers in the process of governance and development at grassroots. Against this background this article focuses its attention on reservation of seats for women in PRIs, gender issues and local governance and development, and tries to analyse whether the space created by the Constitution for EWRs is fully utilized by them.

By keeping the perceptions of elected women representatives in local governance from different research studies in the backdrop, the present study makes an attempt to develop a more nuanced theoretical view on the possibilities and obstacles for effective use of power by the elected women representatives in the context of low economic development.

Women's Reservation in PRIs

Prior to the 73rd Amendment, there was no significant presence of women in the local Government in India. Only a few women from elite family with political background were able to enter into politics. They were all supported by their families. For years, the federal government has tried to introduce a bill prescribing reservation for women in Parliament and Legislative Assemblies. It failed to get it passed in Parliament. How then did the two Houses of Parliament pass the provision for reservation of one-third of seats in PRIs for women without a single dissenting vote? Many arguments are projected about the acceptance of reservation to women in local governance. Some of the arguments are as follows:

It has been argued that the easy consent by politicians in Parliament to women's reservation in PRIs reflects their low valuation or indifference towards these institutions. Since these politicians do not consider PRIs as centres of power and authority, they do not care if women occupy one-third of the seats in these bodies. Even though some men would lose their positions in the PRIs as a consequence of such reservation, the politicians did not consider it a great loss or sacrifice.

It has also been suggested that the politicians looked upon the women's reservation as an opportunity for women in their families and kin groups. Once their own women were elected to these seats, they could control the local councils from behind the curtain. In effect, the politicians did not see much of a loss in the election of women to these reserved seats. Some politicians, argued, that women's reservation in the PRIs is a welcome sign to reduce bitter factional conflicts at the local level. They assumed that a contest among women would not be as fierce and expensive as among male candidates. Thus they could save their political capital for other, more serious, contests. Another argument is that the politicians were also influenced by continuous discussions and debates, for over three decades in various fora, about gender equality and justice. They did not mind about making a concession to a widely accepted principle, and thus deriving the satisfaction of seeming liberal and progressive as regards gender issues.

The final outcome of unopposed approval to the reservation of seats for women in PRIs seems to be due to a combination of all these factors.

Background of the Study

A leading Feminist economist Devki Jain said, "*Political empowerment through affirmative action is essential for women to break this hard rock of patriarchy.*"

The 73rd Constitutional Amendment Act prescribed not less than 33.3 per cent of seats for the women in the PRIs. However the effective power of women in the PRIs of India is often described as being surrounded by a range of hindering factors. The theoretical response by scholars has often been to use the concept of "proxy women" as a description of elected women only with formal power (Dahlerup, 2006: 13-14). Empirical studies also have made attempts to develop the knowledge of obstacles for effective use of power of the elected women in Indian PRIs, such as opposition from family of elected women, interference of husbands in political work, discrimination during political meetings, lack of support from local community, few economic incentives, illiteracy, and dependence on support from men (Baviskar, 2003:7-8; Hust, 2004:248-251; Rai *et al.*, 2006:236-237). All studies bundle together the different obstacles and ignore the scope of possibilities for elected women. Thus there is a need for a more nuanced theoretical view on the possibilities and obstacles for elected women. Moreover, there is a discrepancy between formal and effective power of elected women. With this purpose the study focuses on how elected women in the local governance have experienced their presence in the elected bodies in terms of effective use of power. The guiding questions for research will be the following:

1. What has been experienced as obstacles in their abilities to function as elected women representatives?
2. What has been experienced as opportunities in their abilities to function as elected women representatives?

The answers for the above questions are drawn from different reports and studies. Analysis and explanations are based on the secondary data.

Theoretical Background

Theoretically speaking by creating space for women in a representative body one cannot expect that the elected women representatives will perform the duties and responsibilities effectively and efficiently as they are in patriarchal society with all disabilities. Because of the space they come to power. But it does not mean they can function effectively. Many scholars noted that there is a difference between formal power and effective power among the elected women representatives, due to gender related issues. In an attempt to analyze these constraints Shvedova has created a framework where she identifies the obstacles that are faced by the elected women in Parliament.

Socio-economic Obstacles

- Lack of adequate financial resources.
- Limited access to education and choice of professions.
- The dual burden of domestic tasks and professional obligations.

Psychological/Ideological Obstacles

- Women's low self-esteem and self-confidence, endorsed by certain cultural patterns which do not facilitate women's access to political careers.
- Lack of media attention to women's contributions and potential.

Political/Institutional Obstacles

- Lack of party support, including financial and other resources to fund women's campaigns and boost their political, social and economic credibility.
- The type of electoral system as well as the type of provision of quota and the degree to which they are enforced.

- The tailoring of many of these institutions according to male standards and political attitudes.
- Lack of coordination with and support from women's organizations.

Shvedova focused on the importance of the degree of empowerment among the elected women. However, she does not discuss the aspect of the obstacles identified and how it can be valid in a context of low economic development. This highlights that, in a context with low economic development, the formal representation of women is even less synonymous with effective power. Mere women representation in politics doesn't mean that the women were empowered. Thus there is a difference between the formal and effective power among the women representatives.

Matland argues that one of the most important characteristics of society is that there is a correlation between the level of women's representation and the country's development. Accordingly development leads to a weakening of traditional values, decreases fertility rates, increases urbanization, greater education and labour force participation for women, and attitudinal changes. Matland's assumption is that when women are different from men in all levels of literacy, workforce participation, and university education—and thus not equal to men in the social spheres—they are less likely to be seen as much as equals to men in the political sphere.

Gender and Local Governance

The gender patterns in India are highly patriarchal with lower sex-ratio, patrilineal inheritance, patrilocal marriages, and gender discrimination in accessing public sphere (Mishra, 1998:48). In Omvedt's words, "*Girls are socialized to be mothers, wives and domestic workers under other's authority*" (Omvedt 2005:2). In the last fifteen years a system of quotas has been a part of a process to ensure the presence of women in the PRIs. However, it has been expressed in the literature that these elected women, will not automatically get the ability to participate in the elected bodies due to gender specified obstacles.

As noted in the literature on women in political bodies it is argued that representation of women is itself not sufficient (Hust, 2004: 27). A formal seat is not the same thing as the possibilities for an active participation. In a context of poverty this situation is even more obvious. As Hust discusses, in India most women undeniably lag behind men; women are less educated, less exposed, more dependent, and command lesser capabilities than the men (Hust, 2004: 31). However, the theoretical response to the question of the possibilities for women's effective power is quite scarce. The term "proxy women" is often used in the same way as "token", of elected women with only formal power (for example in Omvedt, 2005; Chattopadhyay and Duflo, 2003; Mishra, 1999). The concept Proxy women have been defined as "*figurehead elected women representatives who are supposed to do the bidding of male members of the family rather than take their own decisions*" (SAP Network, 2003).

Dahlerup rightly argued that women are dependent on their husbands and families and/or their parties (Dahlerup, 2006: 14; Dahlerup, 2005: 149). The term "proxy woman" might need to be elaborated further.

The concept is seldom nuanced or further discussed. Also, in using the concept of "proxy women", only bundling together the different obstacles of elected women and ignored the large scope for actual possibilities of elected women. In earlier researches the discussion of possibilities for participation has been neglected. Often the picture has been given that, on the way towards empowerment there are certain obstacles for elected women. An analysis of which factors that creates possibilities has been absent. Moreover, when researchers do unfold the different obstacles for elected women the picture is more diverse but still many factors seem to be absent. Some attempts to go beyond the concept of "proxy women" and make a more nuanced description of obstacles to elected women in a context of low economic development have been made in previous studies. An overview was made from different studies and the following obstacles for women participation in PRIs has been identified; opposition from family in the involvement of the woman in political work, influence of husbands, imposed institutional constraints (as the strategic use of 'vote of no confidence' for women Panchayat leaders), discrimination in the Panchayat meetings through seating arrangements, unwillingness from parties to nominate women on an "open" mandate, caste-based discrimination, lack of education and illiteracy among elected women (Baviskar, 2003: 7-8), low or not existing salary to Panchayat members gives members from a more resourceful background a relative advantage (Rai *et al.*, 2006: 236-237), frustration among elected women due to lack of control over financial resources, dependence on support from males (Hust, 2004: 248-251), a risk for a high rate of drop out of elected women during their term in office (Sivakumar and Maduresh, 2006: 6), and attitudes that women are not supposed to participate in the public sphere (Mahanta, 2007: 14), discrimination by the government officials, usual shyness and hesitation, lack of communication, administrative and managerial skills, lack of knowledge about the roles and responsibilities (Palanithurai, G., Uma, G., Vanishree, J., 2009: 59-78). These obstacles create a problematic situation for elected women in the PRIs. However, these results appear to present a shattered picture and are not easy to compare with research on obstacles for elected women in general. Furthermore, to focus on describing the obstacles of the elected women this research reproduces the problem inherent in the concept of "proxy women" that the scope towards the possibilities of elected women are forgotten. Though there are numerous obstacles presents, the possibilities for effective use of power must have arisen during the tenure of the elected women. Thus the focuses are to identify a need for a more diverse and nuanced view on both the obstacles and the possibilities for participation of elected women in a context of low economic development. Hence, this article focuses on how the elected women perceive the obstacles and possibilities for effective use of power and how these obstacles and possibilities relate with each other.

Analysis and Explanations

Many previous studies have focused on the obstacles faced by the elected women representatives and neglected the possibility factors. This study highlight the fact that the obstacles and possibilities as being close to each other. Much of the studies were concentrated on the obstacles faced by elected women representatives. Firstly, the obstacle and possibility factors were derived from secondary data source. Then the factors were divided into three broad categories based on Shvedova study on the obstacles faced by women representatives in Parliament. The three categories were, namely, socio-economic factors, psychological/ideological factors, and political/institutional factors. This three-fold division have developed in a diagram listed both perceived possibilities and obstacles under each broad category. The diagram should be interpreted as emphasizing the fact that possibilities and obstacles in many ways are derived from the different context (Fig. 14.1).

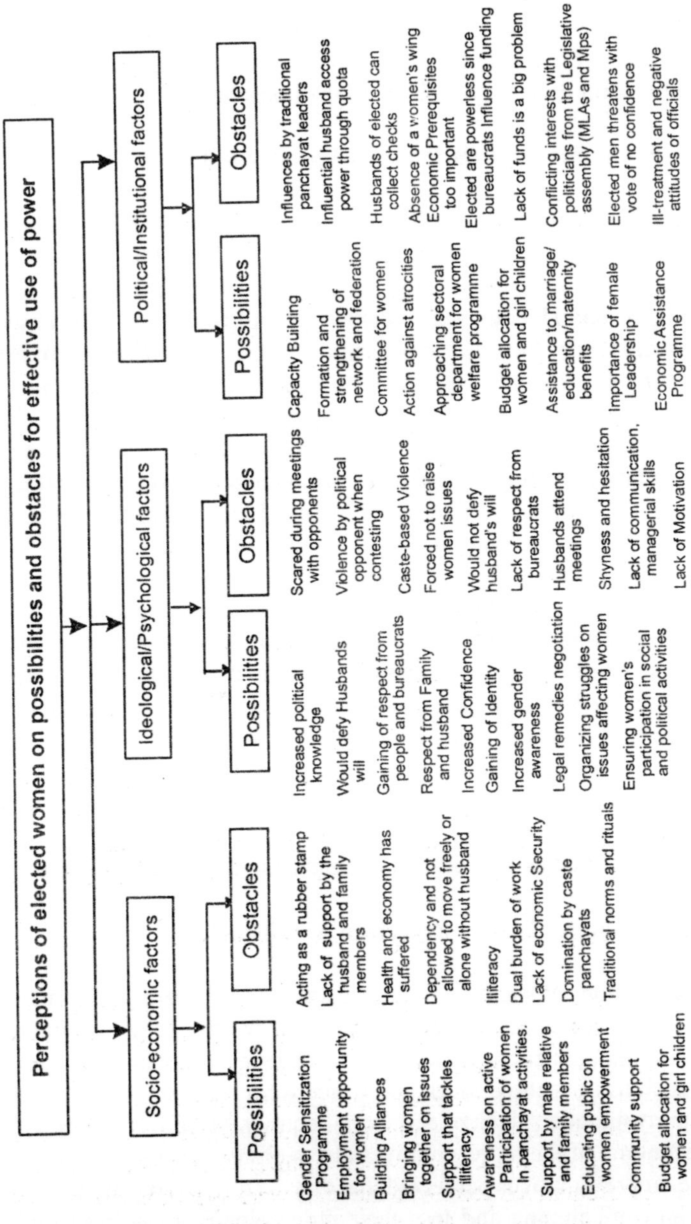

Fig. 14.1: Possibilities and Obstacles of Elected Women Representatives.

Socio-Economic Factors

The dimension of "Socio-economic factors" represents the perceptions connected to the elected women's situation on income, livelihood, education and division of labour in the household.

Socio-Economic Factors Perceived as Possibilities

Poverty plays an important role among the rural poor especially among the elected women representatives which leads to the problem of illiteracy, unemployment, large size family, female foeticide and infanticide, child labour, sexual harassment, ill-treatment, caste based violence. Hence, they are in a position to tackle their problem and the peoples' problem. This leads to dual burden to them. This is reduced by the support of male members in their family through gender sensitization and awareness programmes. The elected women representatives were getting support from husbands, sons and father-in-laws. The elected women will often need the help of the husband by sharing time consuming chores within the household. In a few places, the husbands have adjusted and taken up household chores. Hence, the workload of the women members has been reduced. Thus, an understanding is given that the individual strategies to cope with obstacles can become a possibility. In some places the community and castes also support the women members to tackle gender and caste related issues such as abolition of dowry, female infanticide, alcoholism, domestic violence against women, illiteracy, and abolition of child labour. By seeing the works done by the EWRs, the family members and the villagers started to support them. In many places they were re-elected and performing their functions very effectively.

Socio-Economic Factors Perceived as Obstacles

The perceptions of socio-economic obstacles factors are such as male domination, acting as a rubber stamp in the hands of their husbands or the traditional Panchayat leaders, dependency, illiteracy, dual work load such as household work and office work, lack of support from the family members, lack of economic security. Moreover, the Health and economy of the representatives also suffered. In some places the women representatives perceived that they were spending much more time on campaigning and loss their little belonging, asserts to win the election. Further due to heavy workload in house and office, they are not in a position to take care of their health and hence they were losing their health status. Many of the women representatives were from below poverty line and they were not getting any remuneration from the government for occupying a position in Panchayat. Due to lack of economic security they have to go for work to earn for their livelihood and for their family as well. Thus it become a major problem where the women leaders prefer to go for work rather than going to Panchayat office. Further they were dominated by their husbands and acting according to their husband's wish. So the EWRs have nominal power and the real powers were vested in the hands of their husbands or dominant caste members.

Psychological/Ideological Factors

The dimension of "Psychological/Ideological factors" represents perceptions related to the self-esteem of elected women, the norms and attitudes of their surroundings.

Psychological/Ideological Factors Perceived as Possibilities

The perceived psychological and ideological possibilities factors are such as increased political knowledge which enabled the elected women to acquire the necessary expertise that are historically denied to them. The elected women representatives started to fulfil their roles and responsibilities by the capacity building trainings. By knowing their rights there is a significant change in the increase of their self-confidence, self-esteem. There are elected women representatives who were re-elected by the people because of their effective and active performances.

Another aspect is that there is a change in power relations between the elected women and their husbands in the male dominated households. In many places the husband wanted to interfere in the roles and responsibilities of the EWRs. They gave instructions to the women representatives to perform their functions. If they refused to obey the order they have to leave the politics behind or to sacrifice their family life. But things changed through capacity building trainings, sensitization programmes, network meetings, workshops and seminars. After realizing their roles and responsibilities, the women started to work on their own. They were defying their husband's will or negotiating their husbands not to interfere on their roles and responsibilities. This is apparently an important aspect for the elected women to perform their functions. Further, they gained respect from people, political leaders and bureaucrats. By seeing the status of the elected women representatives, the family members and their husbands also started to give respect to them. In many places the women members were treated equally by the bureaucrats and politicians during meetings after gender sensitization programmes. They were trained towards legal measures and other supportive measures for their problems. Now they have started to redress their problems on their own through EWRs networks.

Psychological/Ideological Factors Perceived as Obstacles

Regarding the obstacles related to psychological and ideological factors are scared during meetings with opponents, usual shyness and hesitation, violence by traditional Panchayat leaders, husbands while attending meeting, caste-based violence, and voicelessness to raise gender issues. More number of elected women representatives were coming from the lower castes. So they were facing caste-based antagonism such as not to speak and sit in front of dominant caste people, physical violence, not to raise their voice in the meetings.

There are cultural patterns which do not facilitate women's access to political careers. In the first category there is an idea that woman belong to the home. So the family members and the males do not allow them to go outside from the home. The second one is that the women would not defy husbands' wish as husbands are top in hierarchical by nature, acting against the wish of the husband will lead an end to their family life. This shows a clear picture for non-participation of women in politics. Another widespread perception among the representatives is negative treatment and lack of respect from Bureaucrats and Politicians. The Representatives articulate that they feel treated disrespectfully by the clerks and government officers. In the meantime, the politicians also interfere in doing their functions. When they refused to obey the orders of dominant caste people; politician and government officers they were removed from the office by using vote of no confidence or their name will be spoiled by others. Another group of perceptions is related to the presence of husbands during meetings as an obstacle for participation. There is a norm related to the mindset connected to psychology and ideology among the males and females that the men are higher than women and having the right to attend the meetings and do all the outside activities.

Political/Institutional Factors

The dimension of "Political/Institutional factors" represents perceptions related to views on the political system and the institutional aspect of the PRIs in general.

Political/Institutional Factors Perceived as Possibilities

The perceptions referring to the political and institutional aspects on the possibilities factors for participation have not been studied in earlier studies. It is viewed that increasing knowledge on the importance of women leadership among the EWRs help them to perform their function in an effective way. In many places the women members feel free to share their problems with other women members and finding solution for their problems. One of the most important possibility factors to reduce the hindrances/obstacles of EWRs is capacity building training to the elected women representatives and formation and strengthening of elected women representatives networks. Experience of capacity building exercise programmes conducted by various agencies showed that the EWRs demand alternative arrangements for the continuous flow of information and consultancy to stabilize their activities for development. The existing local governance agencies do not provide space for grievance redressal for women leaders. Moreover, the requirements of the women leaders are not adequately fulfilled by these agencies. This has created a demand for a full-fledged professional agency to assist the women leaders. Hence, there is a need to focus on formation and strengthening of EWRs network. This network helps the women representatives to share their problems and solving it. Through this network they were meeting political party leaders, government officials, media, NGOs, activists regularly and presented their demands. The network facilitated women members in the following areas:

- Creation and dissemination of best practices.
- Improved interventions and approaches.
- Stronger partnerships, collaborations and institutional linkages.

- Improved networking.
- Creation of new ways of learning and working together. creation of an environment for learning and experiments.
- Recognition of possibilities for collaborative action.

Political/Institutional Factors Perceived as Obstacles

The perceived political/institutional obstacles are "the political institutions tailored according to the needs of men". Many empirical studies on elected women in the PRIs noted that influential husband access power through quota. A group of perceptions describe how the reform of reservation has been used by influential husbands to get even more influence. The quota is described to have been "invisibly captured". The Husbands of elected women representatives are collecting checks. In many cases the representatives also explain that husbands of elected women can issue checks for public funding. This system is perceived as being an obstacle to the independence of elected women. They get the signature on a check because anybody can cash it out. This should be changed. The women are like dolls/puppets in the hands of husbands. The funds allotted to the elected women panchayats were mostly collected by their husbands. Another group of perceptions are based on the thought that the challenges for women are so big in the current system that the only solution is female separatism. Experience from many research studies shows that there is absence of women's wing and elected women representatives federation and network. There should be a special wing for women. They are feeling that this is an arrangement especially made for them and they would not feel hesitant to bring out their problems. Since this is a male dominated society there should be a separation between men and women. This support structure will help the women to raise their voice against the discrimination and violence against women.

Women leaders thus provide a field for leadership development in terms of knowledge, skills, attitudes, networks, systems, institutions and values. Higher the possibility for building the capacity and establishing support structures for the elected leader, higher will be the possibility for performance.

Facilitating Factors Responsible for the Performances of Elected Women Representatives

The overall analysis from the secondary data source shows that the performance of elected women representatives was determined by a set of factors. These factors help the elected women representatives to actively participate in the activities of the Panchayats. Thus the performance of the elected women representatives is determined by a set of factors as explained in Fig. 14.2.

Conclusion

The perceptions of elected women representatives in local governance have developed a more nuanced view on the possibilities and obstacles for the effective use of power. The main result was presented into three broad categories in a mapping technique. It narrates that there is a discrepancy between the formal and effective use of power among elected women. A number of gender-based obstacles are perceived by the elected women representatives. Many researchers have noted the points to the fact that presence of women in politics is in itself not enough to ensure their possibility on effective use of power. Furthermore, that the reservation is not a guarantee for participation of the elected women. Hence, there is a need to support the elected women representatives to perform their functions effectively.

There is coexistence of possibilities and obstacles for participation of the respondents. Earlier studies show that the picture is often given that on the way towards empowerment of elected women certain obstacles can be present, but seldom there is a discussion of the actual possibilities. On the contrary, the possibilities were identified indeed are absolute factors working as a support for the elected women, such as capacity building programmes, formation and strengthening of women networks, support from the civil society, government officials, media. The perceived possibilities and obstacles in the same mapping contribute to an underdeveloped theoretical discussion. In analyzing the identified perceptions it becomes clear that the elected women's situation is more multifaceted than often described. This coexistence of possibilities and obstacles can be seen as an argument against the view in earlier research where the elected women are pictured either as "proxy women" or full feathered politicians. It indicates that the hindering and supporting factors are derived from the same context and often interconnect with each other; the earlier dualistic description is probably not very useful. An aim in this study after answering the questions of research was to discuss the room for

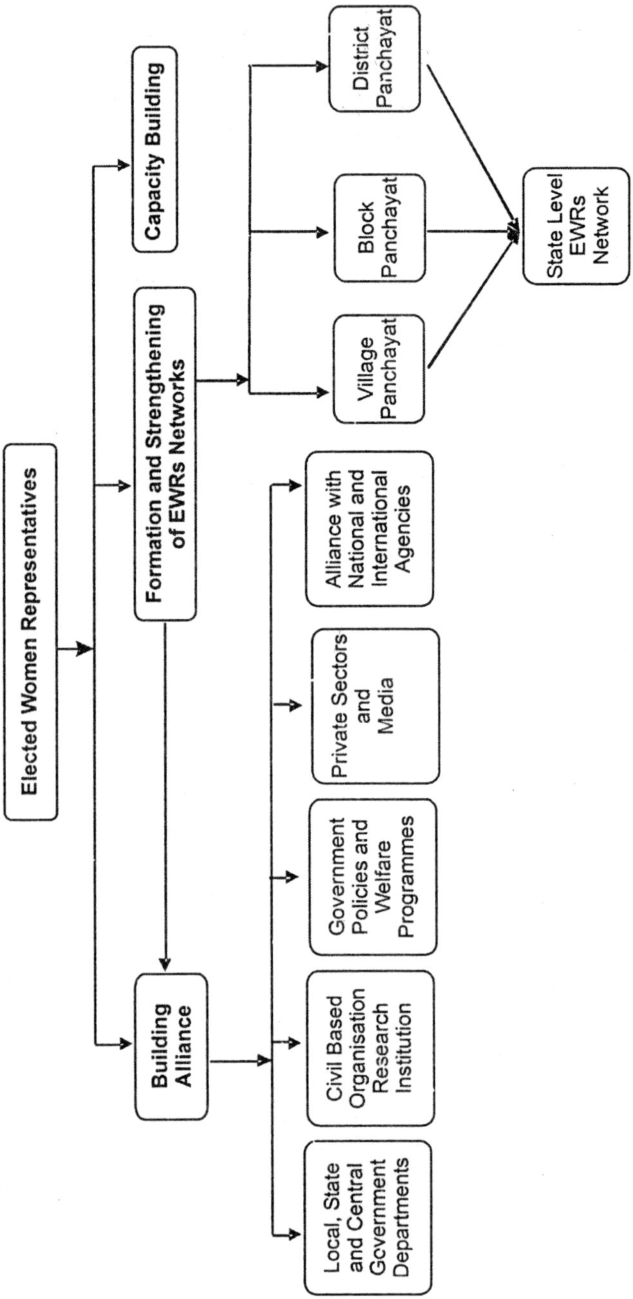

Fig 14.2: Facilitating factors responsible for the performance of Elected Women Representatives

participation of women in a wider perspective. From the findings on the possibilities for elected women narrates that the women have come to positions in the local bodies due to provisions made in the Constitution. The attitude of society towards women has started changing. But, in the process of empowering women, hurdles are still remaining. Steps are being taken by women, of their own accord, to overcome those hurdles. To fight against the obstacle/hindrance an organized movement of the masses is essential. In order to make the women to achieve results in their positions an array of interventions is necessary. It is also proved by the possibility factors such as Gender Sensitization Programmes, building alliances with civil society, NGOs, Government Department, Gender budgeting, capacity building programme, women welfare programmes and the formation and strengthening of EWRs networks organized by different research Institutions, government departments and other support structures the women representatives were performing their functions effectively.

The women representatives need orientation, sensitization, capacity building, information and counselling continuously through organization and other support structures. This will help the women leaders to perform their assigned role in a better and effective way. When women leaders respond to socio-political challenges, they were supported by organizations and institutions which work for their empowerment. Wherever such interventions are available, the achievements of women leaders are substantial and impressive. The government has to respond to the needs of these women leaders only when they are supported by organizations well-known for their credentials and are too reckoned with as a force.

Can these results be understood in a wider perspective? What does it mean that elected women in a context of low economic development face a diverse range of obstacles as well as possibilities in their effective use of power? It brings a more complicated and diverse view of the discrepancy between formal power and effective power of elected women. Obstacles and possibilities exist at the same time and derive from the same context. This indicates that there is no 'magical fix' to ensure the political participation of elected women. In the Indian debate over reforms of quotas for women there is a tendency among scholars to argue that elected women either becomes "proxy women", or empowered politicians. This study indicates that possibilities and obstacles exist at the same time and that a dualistic view is not very useful. Hence the elected women representatives are utilizing the possibility factors and supporting structures to overcome the struggles in their way for empowerment.

REFERENCES

Baviskar, B.S., 2003: *Impact of women's participation in local governance in rural India*, paper presented at the Rural Network Conference, Inverness, June 2003. Accessed from *http://action.web.ca/home/sap/.../SAP%20W%26E%20Workshop,%20Baviskar.doc*

Chattopadhyay, Raghabendra and Duflo, Ester, 2003: *The impact of reservation in the panchayati raj: Evidence from a nationwide randomized experiment*, IIM Calcutta and MIT, November 2003. Accessed from *http://ideas.repec.org/p/feb/natura/0027.html*

Dahlerup, Drude, 2005: *Increasing Women's Political Representation: New Trends in Gender Quotas*, in Ballington, Julie and Karam, Azza (ed.): Women in Parliament: Beyond numbers, revised edition, Stockholm: International IDEA, Publications Office, 2005. Accessed from *www.parlamento.gub.uy/parlamenta/descargas/.../Ballington_2005_IDEA.pdf*

——*The Story of the Theory of Critical Mass, Politics and Gender 2(4)*, Cambridge Press, 2006. Accessed from *http://www.allacademic.com/meta/p_mla_apa_research_citation/0/3/9/8/0/p39807_index.html*

Hust, Evelin: *Women's political representation and empowerment in India: A million Indiras now?*, New Delhi: Manohar Publications, 2004. Accessed from *https://editorialexpress.com/cgi-bin/conference/download.cgi?db...id...*

Mahanta, Upasana: *The political empowerment of minority women through PRI: A critical asessment of India's experiment with affirmative action*, 2007 Accessed from *http://www.dcrcdu.org/apisa%20website/PAPERSThird%20APISA%20Congress,%202007/Upasana%20Mahanta%20and%20Samrat.pdf*

Matland, Richard E.: 'Women's Representation in National Legislatures: Developed and Developing Countries'. *Legislative Studies Quarterly*. Vol. 23, no. 1, 1998. pp. 109-125. Accessed from *http://orion.luc.edu/~rmatlan/pdf/1998WomensRepresentationin NationalLegislatures.pdf*

Omvedt, Gail: Women in governance in South Asia, *Economic and Political Weekly*, Vol. 40, no. 44-45, October 29-4 November, pp. 4746-4753, 2005. Accessed from *www.sacw.net/Wmov/index.html*

Palanithurai, G., Uma, G. Vanishree, J., "*Networking of Elected Women Representatives*", Concept Publishing Company Pvt. Ltd., New Delhi, 2009.

Rai, M. Shirin; Bari, Farzana; Mahtab, Nazmunessa and Mohanty, Biduyt: *South Asia: Gender quotas and the politics of empowerment—a comparative study,* in Dahlerup, Drude (ed.): *Women, quotas and politics*, London: Routledge, 2006. Accessed from *http://www.quotaproject.org/other/Aksel_Sundstroem_Thesis.pdf*

SAP Network, 2003: Summary of workshop in "*Women's Empowerment in the Context of Local Government in India*", New Delhi on October 20-21, 2003. Accessed from http://action.web.ca/home/sap/india_resources.shtml?x=48752&AA_EX_Session=88d7f8d350980bba1d32cf3d6f0fcf35

Shvedova, Nadezhda: *Obstacles to Women's Participation in Parliament*, in Ballington, Julie and Karam, Azza (eds): *Women in Parliament: Beyond numbers*, revised edition, Stockholm: International IDEA, Publications Office, 2005. Accessed from *http://www.idea.int/publications/wip2/upload/2.%20Obstacles_to_Women's_participation_in_Parliament.pdf*

Sivakumar, Sowmya Kerbert and Madhuresh: *Study of 97 women elected chairpersons in Bihar's Panchayati Raj*: *Summary of findings*, for The Hunger Project, March 2006. Accessed from *http://www.quotaproject.org/other/Aksel_Sundstroem_Thesis.pdf*

Sundstrom, Aksel, *Leaving the 'proxy women or politician dichotomy: A qualitative study of the possibilities and obstacles for elected women's participation in Indian local governance*", Minor field study, Department of Political Science, University of Gothenburg, 2008. Accessed from *http://www.quotaproject.org/other/Aksel_Sundstrom_Thesis.pdf*

Bibliography

A.C. Nielson ORG-MARG, *Study on Elected Women Representatives in Panchayati Raj Institutions*, New Delhi: Ministry of Panchayati Raj, Government of India, 2008.

Anand, Inbanathan, *The New Panchayati Raj in Karnataka: An Evaluation.* Institute of Social Sciences: New Delhi, 1992.

Alsop, Ruth, *et al.*, *Inclusion and Local Elected Governments: The Panchayati Raj System in India*, Social Development Paper 37, Washington DC.: World Bank, 2001.

Amitabh Behar, Yamini Aiyar: "Networks of Panchayat Women: Civil society space for political action" from *Economic and Political Weekly*, (November 22, 2003), Vol. 40, No. 2.

Antrobus, Peggy J., *Global Women's Movement*: *Origin, Issues and Strategies*, Bangalore: Books for Change, 2004.

Ashok Kumar Jha, *Women in Panchayati Raj Institutions,* New Delhi: Anmol Publications, 2004.

Bandopadhyaya, D., "Panchayats in Karnataka", *Economic and Political Weekly,* Vol. XXXVII, No. 35, (August 31-September 6, 2002).

Bandyopadhyaya, S. *Non-farm Employment and Role of Panchayat*: *Some Experiences,* Midnapur: Vidyasagar University, 2002.

Basu, D.D.: *Introduction to the Constitution of India*, New Delhi: Prentice Hall: 1994.

Buch, Nirmala, "Women and Panchayats: Opportunities, Challenges and Support" in L.C. Jain (ed.), *Decentralization and Local Governance,* New Delhi: Orient Longman, 2005.

Burke, E., "Speech to the Electors of Bristol", *The Works of the Right Honourable Edmund Burke,* Vol. 2, Boston: Little Brown, 1774.

Bharat, Dograo: "Women make a remarkable Contribution", *Mainstream*, (June 21, 2003).

Carr, M., Chen, M., Jhabwala, R. (ed.), *Speaking Out, Women's Economic Empowerment in South Asia,* New Delhi: Vistaar Publications, 1998.

Centre for Social Medicine and Community Health, *Reproductive Health:India's Primary Health Care,* New Delhi: Jawaharlal Nehru University, 1998.

Centre for Women's Development Studies, *From Oppression to Assertion: A Study of Panchayats and Women in M.P., Rajasthan, and UP*, New Delhi: *CWDS,* 1999.

Chathukalam, Jos and John, M.S. 2000, "Empowerment of Women Panchayat Members: Lessons from Kerala", *Asian Journal of Women's Studies,* Vol. 6, No. 4, 2000.

Childs Sarah, and Krook Mona Lena, *The Substantive Representation of Women: Rethinking the Critical Mass 'Debate'*, paper presented at the annual meeting of the American Political Science Association, Washington: American Political Science Association, 1-4 September 2005.

Childs and Krook, "*The Substantive Representation of Women: Rethinking the Critical Mass 'Debate'*." Washington, DC: American Political Science Association, September 1-4, 2005.

Das, P., Bandyopadhyay, S. and Majumdar, T., *Panchayat Finance: A Study of Some Gram Panchayats with special focus on own source Fund*, Midnapur: Vidyasagar University, 2002.

Das, P., Bandyopadhyay, S. and Majumdar, T., *Panchayat Raj System and Rural Development in West Bengal: A Study Based on Household Survey of Some Villages of the district of Midnapur*, Midnapur: Vidyasagar University, 2002.

Desai, N. and Thakkar, U., *Women in Indian Society,* New Delhi: National Book Trust, 2001.

Dahlerup, Drude, "From a Small to a Large Minority: Women in Scandinavian Politics", *Scandinavian Political Studies*, 1988.

Devi, Lakshmi, *Women in Politics Management and Decision Making Process,* New Delhi: Anmol Publications, 1998.

Drage, Jean, 'Women *in Local Government in Asia and the Pacific: A comparative analysis of thirteen countries'*, Phitsanulok: Asia-Pacific Summit of Women Mayors and Councillors, 18-22 June, 2001.

Dhanda, M. (ed.)., *Reservations for Women,* New Delhi: Women Unlimited, 2008.

Dywer, Peter, *Understanding Social Citizenship: Themes and Perspectives for Policy and Practice*, London: The Policy Press, 2004.

Foucault, M., "Power/Knowledge". *Selected Interviews and Other Writings 1972-1977*. (ed.) New York: Pantheon Books, 1981.

Foucault, M., "The Ethic of Care for the Self as a Practice of Freedom", in J. Bernauer and D. Rasmussen (eds.), *The Final Foucault*, Boston, Mass: MIT Press, 1988.

Foucault, M., 'Governmentality' in Graham Burchell, Colin Gordon and Peter Miller (eds.) in *The Foucault Effect: Studies in Governmentality*. Chicago, IL: University of Chicago Press, 1991.

Foucault, M., 'About the Beginning of the Hermeneutics of the Self' (transcription of two lectures in Dartmouth on November 17 and 24, 1980), (ed.) Mark Blasius in *Political Theory*. Vol. 21, No. 2. (May 1993).

Fraser, Nancy, "Rethinking the Public Sphere: A Contribution to the Critique of Actually Existing Democracy". *Social Text*. No. 25/26: 1990.

Fraser, Nancy, "Social Justice in the Age of Identity Politics: Redistribution, Recognition and Participation". *The Tanner Lectures on Human Values*. (ed.) Grethe B. Peterson. Salt Lake City: University of Utah Press, 1998.

Fraser, Nancy, "Rethinking Recognition". *New Left Review*. May-June, 2000.

Gender Equality Striving for Justice in an Unequal World, Paris: United Nations Research Institute for Social Development, 2005.

Gariyali, C.K., *Inching Forward: Political Empowerment of Women in Commonwealth Countries*, Chennai: Vetri Publishers: 2000.

Gopalan, S. and Shiva, M., *National Profile on Women, Health and Development: Country Profile-India*, Chennai: Voluntary Health Association of India and World Health Organisation, 2000.

Gloppen, S., Ranker, L. and Tostensen, A., "Responsiveness to the Concerns of the poor and Accountability to the Commitment to Poverty Reduction", *Working Paper* 2003; 9, Norway: chr michelsen institute., 2003

Grazia, Ade, "Representation: Theory", in *International Encyclopedia of Social Science,* New York: Macmillan, 1968.

Grey, Sandra, *Women and Parliamemary Politics: Does Size Matter? Critical Mass and Women MPs in the New Zealand House of Representatives,* 51st Political Studies Association Conference, Manchester: 10-12 April 2001.

Gupte, M. and Shatrughana, V., *Shrama Shakti Report,* GOL, 1988.

Habermas, Jurgen, *The Theory of Communicative Action.* Vols. 1 and 2. London: Heinemann, 1981.

Habermas, Jurgen, *The Structural Transformation of the Public Sphere: An Inquiry into a Category of Bourgeois Society*. Cambridge MA: The M.I.T. Press, 1989.

Habermas, Jurgen, "Struggles for Recognition in the Democratic Constitutional State" in *Multiculturalism*. (ed.) Amy Gutman. Princeton: Princeton University Press, 1994.

Hindess, Barry, *Discourses of Power: From Hobbes to Foucault*. Oxford: Blackwell, 1996.

Hunold, C., "Corporatism, Pluralism and Democracy: Towards a Deliberative Theory of Bureaucratic Accountability Governance", London: Blackwell Publishers, *Governance: International Journal of Policy and Administration,* Vol. 14, No. 2, November 2001.

Interview with Jagraani Devi, Gram Pradhan from U.P., *from Seminar.*

Jayal, Niraja Gopal, *A Study in Grey*—Tuesday, April 29, 2008 *at 2320 hrs IST* posted online.

Jain, D., "Valuing Women's Work: Time as a Measure", *Economic and Political Weekly,* vol. XXXI, no. 43, (October 26, 1996).

Jain, Devaki, *Women: New visions of leadership.* A presentation at the Global Forum of Women. Dublin, (July 9-12, 1992).

Jain, Shilpa, *Redefining the Politics of Presence: Women in Panchayati Raj Institutions in Rajasthan and Kerala,* presented in B.A. thesis in Departments of Political Science and Women's Studies at Harvard University, 1998.

Jill, M. Bystdzienski, *Women Transfc..ning Politics: World wide Strategies for Empowerment,* Indiapolis: Vintage, Indiana University Press, 1992.

Joshi, R.P. and Narwani, G.S., *Panchayati Raj in India: Emerging Trends Across the States,* New Delhi: Rawat Publications, 2002.

Theory and Society, Springer Netherlands, Volume 28, number 1 (February 1999).

Kapur Mehta, A., "Recasting Indices for Developing Countries: A Gender Empowerment Measure", *Economic and Political Weekly,* October 26, Vol. XXX1, No. 43, 1996.

Kramarae, C. and Spender, D., *Routledge International Encyclopedia of Women: Global Women's Issues and Knowledge,* Vols. I, II, New York: Routledge, 2000.

Krishnaraj, M. (ed), *Women in the Data Systems,* Mumbai Research Centre for Women's Studies, SNDT Women's University, (2002).

Kishwar, Madhu, "Women and Politics: Beyond Quotas", *Economic and Political Weekly,* Vol. 31, No. 43, (26 October, 1996).

Kumud Sharma, "Transformative Politics: Dimensions of Women's Participation in Panchayati Raj", *Indian Jo:.rnal of Gender Studies,* 5: 1, 1998.

Lahiri, A., Chakraborty, L. and Bhattacharya, P.N., *Gender Budgeting in India.,* New Delhi: The National Institute of Public Finance and Policy, 2002.

Lederman, D., Loayza, N. and Soares, R.R., "Accountability and Corruption: Political Institutions Matter", *World Bank Working Paper no. 2708,* Washington, DC: World Bank, 2001.

Leela Kasturi, 'Pernicious or necessary?' Discussion on Women's Reservation Bill, from *Indian Journal of Gender Studies,* 6:1, New Delhi: Sage Publications,1999.

Mahajan, R., *Maharashtra Human Development Report,* Maharashtra: State Planning Board, 2002.

Mazumdar, Vina, Historical Soundings, *Seminar,* 1997.

Menon, N., "Reservations and Representation", *Seminar*, Special Issue on 'Empowering Women', No. 457, September: 15-16, 1997.

Menon, N., "Elusive 'Woman': Feminism and Women's Reservation Bill". *Economic and Political Weekly*. Vol. 35. No. 43, (28 October, 2000).

Mehta, H.S., "The Constitutional Legal Perspective on Panchayati Raj", in R.P. Joshi (ed.,) *Constitutionalization of Panchayati Raj: A Reassessment*, Rawat Publications, New Delhi: 1998.

Mehta, G.S., *Participation of Women in Panchayati Raj System,* Kaniska Publishers, New Delhi, 2002.

Ministry of Panchayati Raj, Govt. of India. *Study on elected women representatives in Panchayati Raj Institutions*, New Delhi, 2008.

Mishra, Debiprasad, "The State of Panchayats: 2007-08: An Introductory Assessment", *Quarterly Publication of Institute of Rural Management: Gujarat*, vol. 12. Nos. 1 and 2 (January to June, 2008).

Mishra, N., *Poverty in South Asia,* Authors Press, Delhi, 2001.

Moser, C., *Gender Planning and Development,* London: Routledge, 1993.

Moncrieffe, J.M., "Accountability: Idea, Ideals, Constraints, Democratization", *International Political Science Review*, Vol. 8 (3), 2001.

Mujumdar, N., "Rural Development: New Perceptions", *Economic and Political Weekly,* Vol. XXXVII, No. 39 (September 28, 2002).

Mukherjee, M., "Towards Gender-Aware Data Systems: Indian Experience", *Economic and Political Weekly,* Vol. XXXI, No. 43 (October 26, 1996).

Murthy, R.K., *Building Women's Capacities, Intervention in Gender Transformation,* Sage Publications, New Delhi, 2003.

Nerulkar, A. and Patel, V., *Women and Development,* SNDT Women's University, Mumbai, 1995.

Nussbaum, M., *Women and Human Development: The Capability Approach,* Kali For Women, Delhi, 2000.

Palanithurai, G., "The Empowerment Process: Women Representatives in Grassroots Institutions in Tamil Nadu", *Indian Social Science Review*, Vol. 6, No. 1 (January-June, 2004).

Palanithurai, G., *Report of the Project on Associating Elected Women Representatives in Local Governance*, Gandhigram: Rajiv Gandhi Chair for Panchayati Raj Studies, 2005.

Palanithurai, G., *Women in Governance at Grassroots*, Gandhigram: Rajiv Gandhi Chair for Panchayati Raj Studies, 2004.

Palanithurai, G., "Women in Governance for Development at Grassroots", *The Indian Journal of Public Administration*, Vol. 10, No. 1 (January-March, 2004).

Palanithurai, G., *Are they Withdrawing from Public Space*, Gandhigram: Rajiv Gandhi Chair for Panchayati Raj Studies, 2005.

Palanithurai, G., *Capacity Building for Local Body Leaders*, Concept Publishing Company, New Delhi, 2003.

Palanithurai, G., *Elected Women Representatives and Emerging Alternative Governance*. Gandhigram, Rajiv Gandhi Chair for Panchayati Raj Studies, Monograph, 2005.

Palanithurai, G., *Leadership Matters in Grassroots Governance*, Concept Publishing Company, New Delhi, 2006.

Palanithurai, G., *Process and Performance of Gram Panchayat Women and Dalit Presidents,* Concept Publishing Company, New Delhi, 2005.

Palanithurai, G., *Empowerment of Women, Experience of the Elected Women Representatives in Grassroots Institutions,* Gandhigram, Rajiv Gandhi Chair for Panchayati Raj Studies, 2002.

Palanithurai, G., Uma, G., Vanishree, J., *Networking of Elected Women Representatives,* Concept Publishing Company, New Delhi, 2009.

Pal, M., "Empowerment at Grassroots", *Economic and Political Weekly,* Vol. XXXVII, No. 38, September 21, 2002.

Pandey, Sumana, *Women in Politics*, Rawat Publications, New Delhi, 1990.

Pankajam, G., *et al.* (Edited). *Women in India Today Their Status and Justice,* Peace Publication, Kanyakumari, 2008.

Pateman, Carole: "Democracy, freedom and special rights", from David Boucher and Paul Kelly (ed.): *Social Justice: From Hume to Walzer,* Routledge Publications, London, 1998.

Pitam, Singh, *Women Legislators in Indian Politics,* Concept Publishing Company, New Delhi, 2003.

Philips, A. *The Politics of Presence: The Political Representation of Gender, Ethnicity and Race*. Oxford: Clarendon Press, 1995.

Phillips Anne, *Engendering Democracy.* University Park, USA: Pennsylvania State University Press: 1991.

Phillips Anne, "Must Feminists give up on Liberal Democracy", from *Democracy and Difference*, Polity Press: 1993.

Pitkin Hanna Fenichel, *The Concept of Representation*, Los Angeles: University of California Press, 1972.

Poornima and Vinod Vyasulu, *Women in Panchayati Raj: Grassroots Democracy in India,* paper presented in the meeting on women and political participation: 21st Century Challenges, UNDP, New Delhi, 24-26 March, 1999.

Prasad, R.N., *Governance of India: Issues and Perspectives*, Concept Publishing Company, New Delhi, 2002.

Radha, Bulu Roy Chowdhury, *"Women in Local Bodies"*, Discussion Paper No. 40, Trivandrum, Centre for Development Studies, 2002.

Rajalakshmi, V., *The Political Behaviour of Women in Tamil Nadu,* Inter-India Publications, New Delhi, 1985.

Retna Raj, *Decentralisation and Poverty Reduction: Lessons from Kerala,* Trissur: KILA Publications, 2004.

Satellite based communication and training programme for Gram Panchayat Members—Stage 1 and website of ANSSIRD, Mysore.

Sartori, G., "Representational System", in *International Encyclopedia of Social Sciences,* Macmillan, New York, 1968.

Sahbhagi Shikshan Kendra, Interview with Jagraani Devi, Gram Pradhan from U.P., *from Seminar*, 514, June 2002.

Saksena, Kiran (ed.), *Women and Politics,* Gyan Publishing House, New Delhi, 2000.

Schutz, Alfred, *The Phenomenology of the Social World.* Evanston: Northwestern University Press, 1967.

Schutz, Alfred (with Luckmann T.), *The Structures of the Life-World.* Stanford Encyclopedia of Philosophy, First published Tue Oct 29, 2002, substantive revision Tue Mar 16, 2010.

Sen Arnartya, *The Argumentative Indian: Writings on Indian History, Culture and Identity*, London: Allen Lane an imprint of Penguin Books, 2005.

Senior Fellow, Institute of Social Sciences, Southern Regional Centre, No. 9, 8th Main, 8th Cross, Malleswaram, Bangalore-560003.

Sharma, Kumud, "Transformative Politics: Dimensions of Women's Participation in Panchayati Raj" from *Indian Journal of Gender Studies.*

Sharnin, Ishrat, Kumari Ranjani, *Gender and Local Governance: A New Discourse in Development*, SANEI, 2001.

Sridharan, Damyanty and Rodic, Vesna (ed), *Breaking the Political Glass Ceiling: Women and Local Governance in South Asia*, Friedrich Ebert Stiffung, New Delhi, 2004.

Sujaya, and Devaki Jain. *Role of women in decentralization*, Trivandrum: Kerala: State Planning Board, 2000.

Subha, K. and Bhargava B.S., "Women in Panchayati Raj Institutions: Some Facts and Observations", in *Panchayati Raj and Empowering People: New Agenda for Rural India* (ed.), D. Sudaram, Kanishka Publishers, New Delhi, 2007.

Sugana. B, "Strategies for Empowerment of Rural Women", *Social Welfare,* Vol. 49, August 2002.

Squires, J., "Rethinking the Boundaries of Political Representation" in Sylvia Walby (ed.,) *New Agendas for Women,* London: Macmillan, 1999.

Tambiah, Yasmin (ed.), *Women in Governance in South Asia: Reimagining the State*, Colombo: International, Centre for Ethnic Studies, 2002.

Times of Madurai, Published by Projects Abroad, Madurai, March issue no. 4.

The Hunger Project, *Thus Spoke the Press: Select Articles on Elected Women Leaders in Village Panchayats,* The Hunger Project, New Delhi, 2006.

The Republic of India: *Tamil Nadu Women's Development Project Completion Evaluation,* Report 340, April 2000.

Ul Haq Mahabub, "The Human Development Paradigm", in Fukuda Parr and Shivakumar (eds), *Readings in Human Development,*Oxford University Press, New Delhi, 2004.

UNDP, *Essays on Gender and Governance*, New Delhi: Human Development Resource Centre, UNDP, 2003.

Vanishree, J., "Women in Power: Critical Mass to Critical Action", *Women's Link*, Vol. 12: No. 3, July-September 2006.

Vijayan, Aleyamma, Bhaskaran, Seema and Jayasree; *Gender and Panchayati Raj; Status of Women in Kerala* Trivandrum: Sakhi Women's Resource Centre, 2007.

Vincent, Louise, "Quotas: Changing the Way Things Look without Changing the Way Things Are". *The Journal of Legislative Studies*, Vol. 10, No. 1, Spring: 71-96, 2004.

Young, Iris Marion, "Representation and Social Perspective", *Inclusion and Democracy*, (chapter 4), London: Oxford University Press, 2000.

Websites

Baviskar, B.S. 2003: *Impact of women's participation in local governance in rural India*, paper presented at the Rural Network Conference, Inverness, June 2003. Accessed from *http://action.web.ca/home/sap/.../SAP%20W%26E%20Workshop,%20Baviskar.doc*

Chattopadhyay, Raghabendra and Duflo, Ester 2003: *The impact of reservation in the panchayati raj: Evidence from a nationwide randomized experiment*, IIM Calcutta and MIT, November 2003. Accessed from *http://ideas.repec.org/p/feb/natura/0027.html*

Dahlerup, Drude: *The Story of the Theory of Critical Mass, Politics and Gender 2(4),* Cambridge Press, 2006. Accessed from *http://www.allacademic.com/meta/p_mla_apa_research_citation/0/3/9/8/0/p39807_index.html*

Dahlerup, Drude, 2005: *Increasing Women's Political Representation: New Trends in Gender Quotas*, in Ballington, Julie and Karam, Azza (eds.): Women in Parliament: Beyond numbers, revised edition, Stockholm: International IDEA, Publications office, 2005. Accessed from *www.parlamento.gub.uy/parlamenta/descargas/.../Ballington_2005_IDEA.pdf*

Devaki Jain: *Panchayati Raj: Women changing Governance*, Monograph Series from UNDP/BDP/SDG—Gender and Development Programme. *Accessed from http://www.undp.org/gender/resources/mono_05.htm*

Hust, Evelin: *Women's political representation and empowerment in India: A million Indiras now?*, Manohar Publications, New Delhi, 2004. Accessed from *https://editorialexpress.com/cgi-bin/conference/download.cgi?db...id...*

http://pmindia.nic.in/cmp.pdf

http://www.indiatimes.com/The-Womens-Reservation-Bill/The-origin/photostory/5661781.cms

http://www.editorialjunction.com/?p=4670

http://www.un.org/democracyfund/Docs/UNSG%20Guidance%20Note%20on%20Democracy.pdf

http://panchayat.nic.in/data/1227156093695~Study% 20on%20EWRs%20in%20Panchayati%20Raj%20In stitutions.pdf

http://offerings.nic.in/directory/

http://www.solutionexchange-un.net.in/decn/cr/res06030901.pdf

http://pa.oxfordjournals.org/cgi/content/abstract/61/2/237

http://www.southasianmedia.net/index_opinion.cfm?category=women&country=India

http://www.frontlineonnet.com/fl2704/stories/20100226270400400.htm

Matland, Richard E.: 'Women's Representation in National Legislatures: Developed and Developing Countries'. *Legislative Studies Quarterly.* Vol. 23, no. 1, 1998. pp. 109-125. Accessed from *http://orion.luc.edu/~rmatlan/pdf/1998WomensRepresentationinNational Legislatures.pdf*

Mahanta, Upasana: *The political empowerment of minority women through PRI: A critical assessment of India's experiment with affirmative action,* 2007. Accessed from *http://www.dcrcdu.org/apisa%20website/PAPERSThird%20APISA%20Congress,%202007/Upasana%20Mahanta%20and%20Samrat.pdf*

Mrinal Pande: *India's nurseries of politics: Political rise of women in India,* UNESCO Courier, June, 2000 Accessed from *http://www.findarticles.com/p/articles/mi_m1310/is_2000_June/ai_63692788*

Omvedt, Gail: *Women in governance in South Asia, Economic and Political Weekly,* Vol. 40, nos. 44-45, October 29-4 November, pp. 4746-4753, 2005. Accessed from *www.sacw.net/Wmov/index.html*

Pearls of Wisdom. Empowering Women Quotes.*www.s.appyr.net*

Parpart Jane *et al.*, *www.idrc.ca/en.en/ev-27444-20\-\-Do-Topic.htm*

Poornima and Vinod Vyasulu: *Women in Panchayati Raj: Grassroots Democracy in India*, Paper presented in 'Meeting on Women and Political Participation: 21st Century Challenges org. by United Nations Development Programme, 24-26 March, 1999, New Delhi. Accessed from *http://magnet.undp.org/events/gender/india/VYASULU3.htm*

Rai, M. Shirin; Bari, Farzana; Mahtab, Nazmunessa and Mohanty, Biduyt: *South Asia: Gender quotas and the politics of empowerment—a comparative study,* in Dahlerup, Drude (ed.): *Women, quotas and politics*, London: Routledge, 2006. Accessed from *http://www.quotaproject.org/other/Aksel_Sundstroem_Thesis.pdf*

SAP Network 2003: summary of workshop in "*Women's Empowerment in the Context of Local Government in India*", New Delhi on October 20-21, 2003. Accessed from http://action.web.ca/home/sap india_resources. shtml?x=48752&AA_EX_*Session=88d7f8d350980bba1d32cf3d6f0fcf35*

Shvedova, Nadezhda: *Obstacles to Women's Participation in Parliament*, in Ballington, Julie and Karam, Azza (eds.): *Women in Parliament: Beyond numbers*, revised edition, Stockholm: International IDEA, Publications Office, 2005. Accessed from *http://www.idea.int/publications/wip2/upload/2.%20Obstacles_to_Women's_participation_in_Parliament.pdf*

Sivakumar, Sowmya Kerbert and Madhuresh: *Study of 97 women elected chairpersons in Bihar's Panchayati Raj: Summary of findings*, for *The Hunger Project*, March 2006. Accessed from *http://www.quotaproject.org/other/Aksel_Sundstroem_Thesis.pdf*

Sundstroem, Aksel, "Leaving the 'proxy women or politician dichotomy: A qualitative study of the possibilities and obstacles for elected women's participation in Indian local governance", Minor field study, Department of Political Science, University of Gothenburg, 2008. Accessed from *http://www.quotaproject.org/other/Aksel_Sundstroem_Thesis.pdf*

Shilpa Jain: *Redefining the Politics of Presence: Women in Panchayati Raj Institutions in Rajasthan and Kerala*, Online Article Accessed from *http://www.swaraj.org/shikshantar/papers_politics_presence.html*

www.ipu.org

Index

5-point programme, 17
73rd Constitutional Amendment Act, 36, 45, 59-60, 69, 77, 103, 165, 182, 196

Abdul Nazeer Sab State Institute of Rural Development (ANSSIRD), 158-159, 161-164, 166
Above the Poverty Line (APL), 184
Absolute factors, 207
Academic institutions, 1
Adult education scheme, 125
African National Congress (ANC), 30-31, 82
Alcoholism, 93, 202
Anti-arrack movement, 50
Atrocity Act, 87
Authoritarian rule, 108
Authoritarian systems, 42

Backward Castes (BCs), 53
Bahujan Samajwadi Party (BSP), 91
Bargaining power, 93
Belief systems, 118
Budgetary associations, 143
Budgetary funds, 146
Budlender, Debbie, 143

Capacity building programmes, 159, 161-162, 207, 209
Case analysis, 1
Cash-earning projects, 54
Caste
    backwardness, 53
    balance, 53
    -based antagonism, 204
    -based discrimination, 85, 199
    -class-ethnic lines, 82
    discrimination, 94
    groups, 65
    hierarchies, 85, 154
    identity, 84
    inequities, 104
    lines, 53
    -oppressed women, 86
    positions, 95
    representation, 46
    shift, 46
    structures, 82, 86
    system, 127
Census method, 62
Cervical cancer awareness, 135
Charitable trusts, 147
Civil society, 102, 150, 164, 193, 207, 209
Civil society organizations, 36, 141
Committee on the Status of Women in India (CSWI), 31, 43, 81, 156
Communalism, 42
Communication technology, 159
Community Agency for Social Enquiry, 143
Community development, 24, 42
Community forests, 186
Composite index, 171
Constituency development fund, 13

Continuous sensitization programme, 6
Core Development Issue, 176
Corporate sector, 149
Council of Europe Informal Group of Experts, 141

Critical Action Theory, 32
Cursory analysis, 18

Dalit women, 16, 85, 130
Day care facilities, 176
Decentralization of power, 24, 77, 161
Decentralized local power system, 73
Decision-making power, 89
Democratic development, 108
Democratic institutions, 168
Department of Rehabilitation and Aftercare Services, 156
Department of Women and Child Development, 142-143
Department of Women and Child Welfare, 156
Development radars, 145
Devolution of power, 10, 14, 42, 167
Digital transmission studio, 160
Directive Principles of State Policy, 154
Directorate of Rural Development, 67
Disadvantaged groups, 127, 160-161, 168, 185
Discursive contestation, 88
Disempowerment, 153
District Presidents Association (DPA), 134, 136
Dominant caste, 48
Domination of party politics, 32

Economic models, 103
Economic Survey, 149
Egalitarian Political System, 34
Elected Male Representatives (EMRs), 183
Elected Women Representatives (EWRs), 1-12, 14-22, 43, 59-60, 62-63, 65-75, 83, 85-88, 92-96, 124-125, 127-128, 183-184, 186, 194-197, 199-209
  accountability of, 70
Election camp-posters, 129
Electoral systems, 107, 197
Employment guarantee scheme, 134, 136, 142
Empowerment of women, 10, 93, 100, 105, 108, 111-112, 115-116, 122, 144, 146-147, 170, 177, 180, 186-187
Empowerment
  bolsters, 192
  economic, 142
  grassroots, 188
  political, 88, 115, 171, 196
  women's, 41, 44, 115, 139, 150, 153, 158, 178
Ethnic groups, 102
Europe Informal Group, 141
EWR Federation, 19-20
EWRs report, 186

Face-to-face training programmes, 159
Facilitation programmes, 157
Federations of Elected Women Representatives, 128
Female separatism, 206
Feminism, 40
Focus Group Discussions (FGDs), 84-85
Formal institutions, 40
Fuel
  technology, 150
  allocation, 172
  raising, 131
Fundamental Inequality, 169
Fundamental Rights Resolution, 42

Gandhi, Rajiv, 31
Gandhigram Rural Institute, 10-11, 17, 19
Gandhigram Rural University, 3
Gender and Development, 26, 105, 153, 172
Gender awareness class, 173
Gender budgeting policy, 141, 143
Gender Development Index, 144
Gender Development Indicators, 147
Gender empowerment measure, 34
Gender Equity Index (GEI), 144
Gender identities, empowered, 88
Gender Responsive Budgeting (GRB), 143, 177
Gender sensitization programmes, 128, 204, 209
Gendered Political Institutions, 35
Global Gender Gap Report, 171
Governance reforms, 117
Gram Panchayat Women Leaders Federation, 20

Gram Panchayats (GPs), 13, 19-21, 86-87, 94, 160-163, 165, 183
Gram-swarajya, 42
Grassroots institutions, 24, 96
Grey, Sandra, 33

Health camps, 135
Health Department, 9
Hegemonic power centre, 82
Himachal Pradesh, 45, 50, 183
Housing tax, 72
Human Development Index, 145
Human Development Report (HDR), 108, 144-145, 149
Human rights movements, 25
Hunger Project, 6, 11, 19, 116

IAY scheme, 73
Inclusive elements, 153
Independence movement, 43
Indirect taxes, 146
Industrial pollution, 8
Infant Mortality Rate (IMR), 145
Information technology, 148
Infrastructural development, 186
Institute of Social Science, 45
Institutional
  constraints, 199
  credit, 148
  designs, 99
  linkages, 205
  loopholes, 45
Institutionalized arrangements, 61
Institutions of governance, 13, 168
Integrated Child Development Scheme, 186
International Institute for Democracy and Electoral Assistance, 25
International Training and Research Centre for Women, 25
International women movement, 25
International women's day, 103
International Women's Year, 25, 156

Jagratha samiti, 175
Janata Dal party, 43
John, Mary, 91

Kalelkar Commission for Backward Classes, 31
Kerala Institute of Local Administration (KILA), 137, 175
Kerala Municipality Act, 167
Kudumbasree mission, 173, 176

Land reform, 1
Leadership
  association, 175
  development, 206
Liberal feminism, 25
Linear regression analysis, 73, 75
Linear regression method, 63
Lord Ripon's Resolution, 41

Macro analysis, 96
Mahatma Gandhi, 19, 116
Mahila Samakhya Programme, 49
Male dominated society, 170, 206
Male power, 52
Maternal Mortality Rates (MMR), 145
McAllister, Ian, 34
Medical camp, 135
Millennium Development Goal (MDG), 7
Minor forest, 148

Nairobi International NGO forum, 26
Namadhu Gramam scheme, 73
National Common Minimum Programme, 100
National Council for Women in India, 31
National Human Development Report, 149
National Institute of Rural Development, 45
National Plan of Action for Women, 156
National Policy for Empowerment of Women, 116
National political systems, 159
Negative treatment, 204
Nehru, Jawaharlal, 42, 103
Nehru, Kamla, 104
Nielsen Company, 183
Nirmal Gram Puraskar Award, 135
Nodal advocacy departments, 143
Non-cooperative attitudes, 8
Nutritious noon meal schemes, 36

Ombudsman system, 192

Oppressed caste, 88
Other Backward Castes (OBCs), 53, 87, 91

Panchayat Area Development Fund, 13
Panchayati Raj Act, 158, 164
Panchayati Raj Amendment Bill, 165
Panchayati Raj Institutions system (PRIs), 41-42, 44-47, 49, 51-52, 55, 79, 82-83, 88, 92, 163, 173-174, 188-191, 194-196, 198-200, 205-206
Parent Teachers Association (PTA), 38
Parliamentary Union Council, 27
Participatory development, 150
Participatory training methodology, 159
Party politics, 32, 52, 170, 175
Passive non-cooperation, 48
Patriarchal society, 17, 92, 95, 169, 197
People's Organizations, 128, 131
Peoples' Planning Campaign (PPC), 95
Perspective budget analysis, 18
Phillips, Anne, 40, 82, 168
Pitkin's Theory, 60, 75
Planning Commission, 144, 146
Policy advocacy, 19
Political empowerment of women, 55, 60, 165, 171, 183
Political revolution, 187
Positive campaign, 164
Poverty alleviation programmes, 148-149
Power struggles, 187
Powerlessness, 53, 103, 108
Preferential treatment, 81
Pre-independence days, 31
Prevention of Atrocity Act, 87
Primary Health Centre (PHCs), 131
Proactive policy interventions, 173
Professional taxes, 72
Public Works Department (PWD), 9

Quota system, 120, 165, 194, 198

Rationalist movement, 31
Rayawaram Gram Panchayat, 9
Religious ceremony, 87
Representation
    descriptive, 60
    formal, 60, 198
    political, 61, 117
    substantive, 60-61, 68, 75
    symbolic, 60-61, 63, 65, 75
Reservation
    groups, 61
    policy, 41, 54, 125
    politics of, 92-93
    rotation of, 182, 192
    and Women Empowerment, 170
Resource allocation, 141, 150
Resource centre, 11
Role conflicts, 124
Role models, 11, 20, 109, 186
Roosevelt, Eleanor, 25
Rotation System, 164
Rural Development and Panchayati Raj Department, 159-160
Rural development schemes, 5, 22
Rural development sectors, 148

Samajwadi Party (SP), 91
Sanger, Margaret, 111
Sarva Shiksha Abhiyan Scheme, 132
Satellite based Training and Communication (SATCOM), 160, 162
Scheduled Castes and Scheduled Tribes, 45-46, 62, 104, 121, 180-183, 185
Sectoral departments, 13
Sectors, 114, 142-143, 177-178
    core, 147
    empowered, 108
    formal political, 43
    general developmental, 142
    social, 149
    strategic, 148
    women-related, 114
Self-Help Groups (SHGs), 6, 8, 13, 37-38, 49, 73, 86, 94, 149, 157, 184, 187
Self-help movement, 187
Self-sacrificial altruism, 92
Sensitization programmes, 157, 203
SGRY-II scheme, 72
Sharp, Rhonda, 140
Shram Shakti Report, 149
Skepticism, 52
Skewed Groups, 32
Social reforms, 79
Social revolution, 156
Social Studied Trust, 45

Social welfare schemes, 157
Socio-economic development, 42, 142
Socio-economic factors, 200, 202
Socio-political awareness, 55
State Finance Commission, 132
Status of Women in India, 43
Steinem, Gloria, 114
Structural Adjustment Programme (SAP), 25-26, 146
Sukhdeve, Rita, 94

Tamil Nadu Panchayati Raj Act, 11, 22, 136
Tamil Nadu Women's Development Project, 116
Taxation policies, 150
TB awareness, 135
Teli caste, 87
Theni District President's Association, 136
Third World, 26
Tutsi tribe, 105

United Nations (UN), 24-25, 27, 103, 154
United Nations Convention on Elimination, 27
United Nations Development Fund for Women, 25, 143
United Nations Development Programme, 29
United Nations Voluntary Fund for Women, 25
Universal Declaration of Human Rights, 157
Upper caste women, 84
Upper-caste persons, 87
Urbanization, 198
USAID policy, 25
Uttarakhand, 183

Village Development Fund, 67
Village Panchayat Fund, 72
Vincent, Louise, 82
Violence, caste-based, 204

Women
  activism, 80
  adequate representation of, 27, 31, 114
  advancement of, 102, 115, 154
  component plan, 114, 146-147, 172
  day, 111
  destitute, 156-157
  development corporation, 156
  development, 17, 25-26, 167, 173
  empowered, 88, 113
  empowerment policy, 149
  empowerment, indicators of, 112
  entrepreneurship development, 113
  federation, 11, 129
  invisibility of, 95-96
  legislators, 108, 155, 165
  literacy, 173
  oppressed, 88
  in panchayati raj, 103, 166
  parliamentarians, 28
  patriarchal families, 146
  persuaded, 186-187
  politicians, 33-34, 52, 194
  pradhans, 185
  proxy, 196, 199-200, 207, 209
  reformers, 79
  reservation, 92, 171, 178
  role of, 100
  transforming, 41, 51
  underrepresentation of, 25, 28, 30
  upliftment, 141
  welfare programmes, 209
Women's movement, 26, 36, 42-43, 55, 79, 91, 155
  autonomous, 126
  sustained, 156
Women Panchayat
  leaders, 178, 199
  members, 157, 165
Women representatives, 2, 11-12, 18, 41, 46, 50, 54-55, 72, 81, 93-94, 105, 157, 183-185, 202-203, 209
  house-arrested elected, 4
  perceptions of elected, 195, 207
  performance of elected, 207-208
Women's Reservation Bill, 91, 99, 103, 106, 108
Women's solidarity, 52
World Conference on Women, 27, 115